THE CHANGING RURAL VILLAGE IN AMERICA

THE CHANGING RURAL VILLAGE IN AMERICA
Demographic and Economic Trends Since 1950

Harley E. Johansen
Professor of Geography
University of Idaho

Glenn V. Fuguitt
Professor of Rural Sociology
University of Wisconsin-Madison

BALLINGER PUBLISHING COMPANY
Cambridge, Massachusetts
A Subsidiary of Harper & Row, Publishers, Inc.

International Standard Book Number: 0-88410-692-6

Library of Congress Catalog Card Number: 82-22693

Printed in the United States of America

Library of Congress Cataloging in Publication Data

Johansen, Harley E.
  The changing rural village in America.

  Includes bibliographical references and index.
  1. United States—Rural conditions. 2. Villages—
United States. I. Fuguitt, Glenn Victor, 1928– II.
Title.
HN57.J63 1983   307.7′62′0973   82-22693
ISBN 0-88410-692-6

To Nancy and Martha

CONTENTS

List of Figures   xi

List of Tables   xiii

Preface   xvii

1. **THE AMERICAN RURAL VILLAGE**   1
   - The Settlement System   4
   - Scope of This Study   6
   - Description of Sample   9
   - Data Sources   12
   - Research Themes   12
   - Chapters to Come   18
   - Notes   19

2. **GROWING AND DECLINING VILLAGES**   22
   - Introduction   22
   - Objectives and Procedures   23

Trends in Village Growth   25
Factors Associated with Village Growth   26
Village Growth Patterns   37
Multivariate Analysis   41
County Growth Factor Elaborated   44
Growth of Villages Compared to Other
    Population Units   50
Another View: Responses of Village
    Mayors   51
Summary and Conclusions   53
Notes   57

3. THE SOCIAL CHARACTERISTICS OF
    VILLAGES   59
    Introduction   59
    Data and Procedures   61
    Villages in the Settlement Hierarchy   62
    Village Characteristics by Accessibility
        and Growth   71
    Village Characteristics and the
        Turnaround   77
    Summary and Discussion   81
    Notes   83

4. ECONOMIC ACTIVITIES IN VILLAGES   85
    Business Activities Since 1950   88
    Distribution of Villages by Business
        Activity   96
    Patterns of Economic Change   98
    Post–1970 Business Activities   102
    Conclusion   105
    Note   106

5. VILLAGE RETAIL AND SERVICE ACTIVITIES   107
    The Village as a Shopping Center   111
    The Structure of Retail Activities   120
    Post–1970 Trends   130
    Summary and Conclusions   134

6. **VILLAGES AS RESIDENTIAL AND
   TRADE CENTERS**   137
   **Trends in the Population-Trade
      Relationship**   139
   Models of the Change in Retail Activities   148
   Discussion   158

7. **LOCAL PROMOTION, EXPANSION OF
   COMMUNITY FACILITIES, AND VILLAGE
   GROWTH**   161
   Village Promotion Activities   163
   Expansion of Community Facilities   166
   **Factors Associated with Promotion and
      Facilities Expansion**   168
   **Promotion, Facilities Expansion, and
      Village Growth**   172
   Discussion   178
   Notes   181

8. **NEWCOMERS AND OLDTIMERS**   183
   Newcomer-Oldtimer Differences   187
   **Differences and Level of Population
      Growth**   189
   Discussion   193
   Notes   195

9. **THE AMERICAN VILLAGE AND ITS FUTURE**   197
   Village Trends and the Settlement System   200
   The Dying Village   203
   **Rural Settlement Efficiency, Public Policy,
      and the Village**   205
   The Future of the Village   209

Appendixes
   Appendix A.   Sample Design   219
   Accessibility Measure   221

**Appendix B.   Evaluation of Dun and
Bradstreet Reference Book Listings as a Source
of Economic Data for Small Communities**   **223**
    Dun and Bradstreet Listing Procedure   **224**
    Comparison with Yellow Page Directories   **225**
    Field Check of Current Listing   **227**
    Summary   **227**

References   **231**

Index   **249**

About the Authors   **259**

LIST OF FIGURES

1-1   Map of Sampled Villages   10

2-1   Village Distribution by Percentage of Change in Pop-
       ulation   26
2-2   Village Distribution by Population Change for U.S.
       Regions   30
2-3   Village Distribution by Population Change for County
       Growth Quartiles   33
2-4   Village Distribution by Population Change for Urban
       Accessibility Quartiles   36
2-5   Village Distribution by Population Change for Initial
       Size Groups   39

3-1   Distribution by Age for Residence Groups, United
       States, 1970   63
3-2   Distribution by Age for Nonmetropolitan Residence
       Groups, United States, 1970   64
3-3   Net Migration Rates by Age for Village Categories of
       Population Change, 1960-70   65

4-1   Percentage of Villages by Number of Establishments
       of Each Economic Activity Each Year   97

4–2   Percentage of Villages in Initial Size Categories That Lost, Remained Stable, or Gained Establishments of Various Activities Each Decade   99

5–1   Frequency of Villages by Number of Business Units   115
5–2   Ranking Procedure Used to Group Activities   121
5–3   Frequency of Growth and Decline of Selected Functions by Total Number of Functions in Village   128

6–1   Relationship between Village Population and Business Activities at Each Time   139
6–2   Path Diagram for Model I   151
6–3   Path Diagram for Model II   154
6–4   Path Diagram for Model III   157

LIST OF TABLES

1-1   Number and Total Population in Nonmetropolitan Places Having Less Than 2,500 People, United States, 1900–80   3

1-2   Sample Distribution   11

2-1   Percentage of Villages Growing, by 1980 Metropolitan Status, 1950–60, 1960–70, 1970–80   27

2-2   Mean Annualized Change and Percentage of Places Growing, Villages by Four Regions, 1950–60, 1960–70, 1970–80   28

2-3   Mean Annualized Change and Percentage of Places Growing, Villages by Quartiles of County Growth, 1950–60, 1960–70, 1970–80   32

2-4   Mean Annualized Change and Percentage of Places Growing, Villages by Quartiles of Accessibility Score, 1950–60, 1960–70, 1970–80   35

2-5   Mean Annualized Change and Percentage of Places Growing, Villages by Four Size Groups, 1950–60, 1960–70, 1970–80   38

2-6   Percentage Distribution by 1950–80 Growth Patterns for Villages Grouped by Region, County Growth, Accessibility, and Initial Size   40

2–7   Analysis of Variance for Independent Variables and Regional Interactions, 1950–60, 1960–70, 1970–80   42

2–8   Regressions of Annualized Population Change for All Villages, 1950–60, 1960–70, 1970–80   43

2–9   Regressions of Annualized Village Population Change and County Population Change with County Independent Variables, 1950–60, 1960–70, 1970–80   48

2–10   Percentage Change in Metropolitan and Nonmetropolitan Incorporated Place and Nonplace Segments, United States, 1950–80   51

3–1   Demographic Variables by Residence Group, United States, 1970   66

3–2   Socioeconomic Variables by Residence Group, United States, 1970   67

3–3   Economic Activity by Residence Group, United States, 1970   69

3–4   Number of Villages, Total Populations, and Mean Village Size, Sample Villages by Growth and Location   72

3–5   Village Population Characteristics by Growth Patterns and Accessibility   74

3–6   Patterns of Differences for Population Characteristics, Turnaround Growth and Turnaround Decline Villages   78

4–1   Inventory of Economic Activity in Sampled Villages   90
4–2   Number of Manufacturing Firms in Sampled Villages   94
4–3   Economic Activities in Villages, 1975–80   104
4–4   Professional Services in Villages   105

5–1   Retail and Service Establishments and Functions by Region   113

5–2   Individual Business Activities in Sampled Villages   118

5–3   Mean Number of the Five Functions in Each Group Present by Total Number of Functions in Village   122

5–4   Coefficients of Reproducibility from Guttman Scaling of Selected Functions   127

5–5   Retail/Service Activities in Villages, 1975–80   131

5–6   Percentage Distribution of Villages by Pattern of Change for Individual Activities, 1975–80   132

5-7   Responses to Question, "Where do most people in
        your community go to obtain . . . ?"   133

6-1   Population and Retail Establishments and Functions
        by Region   141
6-2   Population Associated with Specific Functions   144
6-3   Regression Analysis of Retail and Service Units by
        Population and Accessibility   146
6-4   Regression Analysis of Retail and Service Units by
        Population and Other Economic Activities   147
6-5   Path Coefficients for Model of Change in Trade and
        Population with Urban Accessibility   151
6-6   Path Coefficients for Model of Change in Trade,
        Population, and Industry   155
6-7   Path Coefficients for Model of Change in Population
        and Industry with Accessibility   157

7-1   Promotional Activities of Villages, 1975-80   165
7-2   Expansion of Facilities, 1975-80   167
7-3   Bivariate Correlations and Standardized Regression
        Coefficients (Betas) for the Association between the
        Promotion Scale and the Facilities Scale and the
        Independent Variables   171
7-4   Bivariate Correlations and Standardized Regression
        Coefficients for Change Variables with Independent
        Variables   175

8-1   Questions on Newcomer-Oldtimer Relations in Grow-
        ing Villages   186
8-2   Bivariate Correlations and Standardized Regression
        Coefficients for Newcomer-Oldtimer Differences with
        Selected Independent Variables   191
8-3   Bivariate Correlations and Standardized Regression
        Coefficients (Betas) for the Association between the
        Facilities Scale and Old-New Differences with Other
        Independent Variables   192

A-1   Balance Sheet of Number of Nonmetropolitan Incor-
        porated Places under 2,500 Population, United States,
        1900-80   220

PREFACE

At a time when nearly three-fourths of our population resides in urban places, a book on rural villages may initially appear to be of limited interest. While most Americans live in cities, however, villages (places with less than 2,500 population) are considerably more numerous than cities, and, as governmental units and residential communities, many play an important part in our settlement system.

In the relatively short history of American settlement, villages have moved through societal and technological changes unmatched in most countries of the world. Although some villages are recent additions, most emerged during earlier times of settlement expansion, and many became cities or larger towns through continued growth. Villages have shared in the recent increase in rural population growth, with some beginning to expand after years of stagnation or decline. This unanticipated trend has created on the part of many Americans a renewed interest in rural areas, including small towns and villages. Similarly, structural changes in the economy of rural areas have led to revised functional roles for village communities.

This work began several years ago as an attempt to understand the changes that were specifically related to the village communities' dual role as centers of residential and economic activity. Drawing on numerous studies of villages over the years and from selected parts of the country, we soon realized that several interpretations were emerging on the patterns and causes of change. We also noted that, while population trends had been analyzed on a national basis, the last nationwide study of village economic characteristics and trends was that of Brunner and his associates, which ended in 1936. We therefore set out to conduct a comprehensive study of villages on a national scale to reveal the consistency of patterns and processes among places throughout the country and to observe the structural changes that have occurred during the post–1950 period, a time of major changes in rural society. Our work, therefore, encompassed the recent turnaround in population growth toward nonmetropolitan areas, and we have observed this trend in the villages studied.

We have examined the village as a part of the larger settlement system, looking at its role as both a residential community and a center of trade and other economic activities in light of structural changes throughout the system. We present here our findings and interpretation of the data and welcome commentary from others interested in these issues.

The primary support for this research came through a cooperative agreement between the Economic Development Division, U.S. Department of Agriculture, and the College of Agricultural and Life Sciences, University of Wisconsin (Madison). Analysis was aided by a grant to the Center for Demography and Ecology, University of Wisconsin (Madison), from the Center for Population Research of the National Institute of Child Health and Human Development. Significant support and assistance also was received from the College of Mines and Earth Resources, and the Research Foundation of the University of Idaho, as well as from the Regional Research Institute and the University Foundation at West Virginia University.

Data collection, analysis, and writing have been shared equally by the authors as a joint effort throughout this work. We are grateful to the many people who contributed their efforts and ideas to the study during the various stages from data collection to preparation of the final draft. Our list is long and includes Mary Jacobs who, along with Mark Van Cleave, developed most of the programs necessary to build the many data files; Jane Pfund, Nancy Eaton, Carol Martin, Marvin Pippert and Mary Traeger, who compiled, coded, and edited data and interviewed village mayors; Philip Groth, Tim Heaton, Dan Lichter, and Pat Ballard, who helped with data analysis and offered many analytical suggestions; Michelle Lee and Chris Fox, who typed the manuscript and the many revisions during the writing stage, as well as Amy Glynn and Karen Weed who assisted with the references and proofreading.

We are especially grateful to our colleagues who reviewed the manuscript and gave us many helpful suggestions. These include Calvin Beale (whose encouragement, many good ideas, questions, and suggestions throughout the research project are also acknowledged), Kevin McCarthy, Curtis Roseman, David Brown, and Dan Lichter. Selected chapters were reviewed by Mark Baldassare, Tim Heaton, Craig Humphrey, and Richard Krannich. Finally, we owe our greatest debt to our wives, Nancy and Martha, for their continued support, considerable sacrifices, and unending patience throughout the long period of research, writing, and rewriting necessary to carry this project through. Without their help and encouragement, this work would likely have remained just a mass of data on our shelves.

Moscow, Idaho   Harley E. Johansen
Madison, Wisconsin   Glenn V. Fuguitt
July 1983

1 THE AMERICAN RURAL VILLAGE

> . . . Optimo City, then, is actually a very familiar feature of the
> American landscape. But since you have never stopped there except to
> buy gas, it might be well to know it a little better. What is there to see?
> Not a great deal, yet more than you would at first suspect.
>
> J. B. Jackson

Optimo City (pop. 10,783; see Jackson 1952) is larger than what
most Americans consider a village to be, but as a relatively small
urban place it typifies an image of small towns held by people
everywhere—that is, most people are superficially familiar with
villages but have little knowledge of their detailed complexity. To the
average urbanite, contact with small towns or villages has been
limited to the brief glimpse one gets while passing through on the way
to somewhere else. With the development of interstate highways, even
this brief contact is reduced to a blur of houses, trees, and a few tall
structures, such as a water tower or grain elevator, as people move
along these corridors, casually noticing the countryside.

Villages, as we will refer to places of less than 2,500 population, are
individually unimportant to a majority of people, yet as part of a
larger urban system they have played an important role in the
economic and social life of rural America. It is the purpose of this
work to examine what this role is today and how it has changed over

1

the period since 1950. Despite long-standing predictions that the village was dead or at least dying, this unit has prevailed as part of our settlement structure, though its bases for existence have undoubtedly been changing. Furthermore, there is evidence that something new is going on in rural America, including its villages, and within the limits of our data and research perspectives we want to find out what is happening and why.

Years of outmigration from villages, especially of younger people, and an appearance of decline or stagnation among the shops on main street have long given rise to predictions of village decline. Since as early as the 1890s, literature on the village or small town has reflected a common expectation that small towns were doomed to fail as the automobile and better roads and communications freed rural residents from their dependency on local merchants (Fletcher 1895; Gillette 1923; Carlyle 1931; Lively 1932a, 1932b; Olson 1952; Colladay 1952; Paulsen and Carlson 1961; Kendall 1963). Similar concern was expressed for the village future in Britain during this time as centralization of trade and service functions was experienced (Mess 1938; Wightman 1954; Chisholm 1962).

Numerous examples certainly exist that support the earlier predictions of decline, especially among retail trade centers in agricultural areas where today empty storefronts abound along once busy main streets. Yet, even in villages with the most deserted main streets, one often finds nearly complete occupancy of houses, albeit with fewer and perhaps older people in each. These conditions indicate that some villages have experienced rather severe adjustments to forces of change and, although most have not disappeared, that some may appear ready to toll the death knell, especially to the outside observer accustomed to more signs of life in larger cities.

What most prophets of doom failed to predict, however, was the persistence of villages as residential communities with a strong will to survive. Years of outmigration of younger people, repeated loss of local services, and numerous shifts in employment base have not offset the inmigration of people from urban and other rural areas, or natural population increase, along with local entrepreneurship and adaptability among local residents to a changing economic and social structure.

Table 1–1 shows the increase throughout this century in the number and total population in nonmetropolitan incorporated places under 2,500. (A constant 1960 nonmetropolitan area was employed.) Though increasing in numbers and population, villages nevertheless

Table 1-1. Number and Total Population in Nonmetropolitan Places Having Less Than 2,500 People, United States, 1900–80.[a]

	Number of Places	Population (Thousands)	Percentage of U.S. Population	Percentage Growth Since Previous Census		
				Village by		U.S. Total Population
				Class[b]	Place[c]	
1900	7,496	5,139	6.8	—	—	—
1910	9,792	6,561	7.1	27.7	22.5	21.0
1920	10,865	7,288	6.9	11.1	12.2	15.0
1930	11,382	7,478	6.1	2.6	5.9	16.2
1940	11,208	7,555	5.7	1.0	6.4	7.3
1950	11,174	7,606	5.0	.7	10.7	14.5
1960	11,334	7,652	4.3	.6	8.9	18.5
1970	11,233	7,787	3.8	1.7	7.0	13.3
1980	11,428	8,211	3.6	5.4	14.7	11.5

[a]Located in counties nonmetropolitan as of 1960.

[b]Percentage change in total population shown in column 2.

[c]Aggregate percentage of change of nonmetropolitan incorporated places less than 2,500 at beginning of period followed through the decade.

Source: Compiled by authors.

are a declining proportion of the total U.S. population, with the high point in this regard reached in 1910 as rural settlement was coming to a close.[1] The current population in such villages, however, is not insignificant, being larger than that of all but eight of the fifty states.

An upturn in population growth became apparent in nonmetro-politan America in the early 1970s. This unprecedented and largely unanticipated shift may be a significant development for village America. Note that there was a parallel upturn in overall village population growth according to Table 1-1. When the same places are followed across the decade (whether or not they grow out of the village class), 1970–80 growth was larger than growth of the United States as a whole. This has not occurred since the 1900–10 decade.

Although specific consideration of villages had to await the 1980 census, a considerable amount of research during the past ten years has shown that many rural areas, often remote and formerly declining, have experienced population gain in the post-1970 period and that other rural areas with a history of growth are increasing more rapidly than before. This cannot be explained by natural increase, which has generally declined, and the net balance of migration now favors nonmetropolitan over metropolitan areas (Beale 1975; Beale and

Fuguitt 1978; McCarthy and Morrison 1979 among others). These changes appear to be part of a wider range of shifts in the location of economic activities away from cities and of increased ability and/or inclination of people to choose to live in lower density amenity areas. This is exemplified by growth processes favoring the regions of the South and West and smaller metropolitan areas as well as the nonmetropolitan sector (Berry and Dahmann 1980; Sly et al. 1980; J. Long 1981; L. Long and Frey 1982). Research on residential preference among Americans has revealed a common desire among urban residents to live in smaller communities (Zuiches 1981). An important recent finding of Zuiches and Reiger (1978) in one rural area was that a higher proportion of younger people preferred not to migrate to larger cities than did their predecessors interviewed at two earlier times. This could indicate a potential for population growth through reduced outmigration where preferences can be realized.

The nonmetropolitan turnaround, as it is often called, has undoubtedly affected many villages through altered levels of population change, modifications of their economic bases, relations with other units, and internal social organization. In order to examine possible aspects of such changes, we must turn first to a consideration of the rural village as part of an overall settlement system.

THE SETTLEMENT SYSTEM

The traditional view of the settlement system as developed by sociologists (especially human ecologists), geographers, economists, and others is of a territorial division of labor with units of the system integrated through their social and economic functions (e.g., Hawley 1950; Duncan et al. 1960; Berry 1978; Bourne and Simmons 1978; Hansen 1978). For societies such as the United States, major elements of the system are cities and metropolitan areas, which are related in some sort of a functional hierarchy. An important theoretical perspective on this system is the central place model of Christaller (1966), but there are other less formal approaches, such as the metropolitan dominance perspective of the human ecologists or the size-function hierarchy exemplified by Duncan et al. (1960). In a dynamic sense, social and economic innovations and general growth impulses are thought to flow down the hierarchy (Berry 1973; Thompson 1975). Wider regions are considered to be organized around the urban system with metropolis-hinterland relationships, and, overall, the region with the oldest major metropolitan areas (the Northeast) tends to be preeminent in a heartland-hinterland relationship.

This picture of a spatial hierarchy of concentrated urban development appears to be particularly appropriate for the era when manufacturing and primary production was the basis of the economy, and rests in part on assumptions of advantages coming from agglomerative settlement in the organization of production, social services, and other institutions. There have been, however, countervailing trends throughout the century in deconcentration of people and activities around large cities, which were made possible by innovations in transportation and communication. This led to a recognition or delineation of specific influence regions primarily around large cities, giving rise to the Standard Metropolitan Statistical Area (SMSA) of the U.S. Government, the Urban Field (Friedmann and Miller 1965), Daily Urban Systems (Doxiadis 1968; Berry 1973), and similar concepts, generally based upon the area of actual or potential commuting. Whereas these were viewed as developing ecological units that could transform the older metropolis-hinterland relations with new functional interrelations (Martin 1957; Berry and Kasarda 1977), the sources of change and the very bases of the system were thought to continue to be urban. These processes describe both a downward transmission of economic development through "hierarchical diffusion" and a spatial process of transmission outward from metropolitan core to peripheral "urban fields," other metropolitan centers, and regional centers of lower level.

This general model of urban and regional development has been widely accepted and has formed the basis of the growth center strategy for intervention to promote economic development in lagging regions. Growth center strategy of regional planning is based on the assumption that lack of urban development prevents economic development (Hansen 1972; Berry 1973) and that concentrated investment to aid industrial growth can spur urban growth and, in turn, raise the level of living in the hinterland through "spread effects." The logic of this strategy is based in the theory that economic growth, and, correspondingly, population growth, is predominantly a function of city size and location relative to a city. The centralizing tendencies experienced during recent decades have supported these ideas empirically, yet something rather different seems to have happened during the 1970s. In a discussion of this turnabout, Berry (1978) describes it as a "counterurbanization conundrum" that population and economic trends perceived in the mid-1960s were in many cases directly reversed a decade later.

Prior to the last two decades, patterns of change in nonmetropolitan population and economic activities were consistent with traditional views. Since that time, however, a number of divergences have been noted including a less concentrated pattern of population growth and a similar deconcentration of employment in manufacturing and services (Menchik 1981; Till 1981; L. Long and DeAre 1982). This growth has extended well beyond any accessible "urban field" and is no longer concentrating in larger towns or more urbanized areas at the expense of smaller towns, the open country, or generally less urbanized areas.

Some researchers have looked upon this turnaround as evidence of a significant change in the American settlement system (Vining and Strauss 1976; Fisher and Mitchelson 1981). Furthermore, it is a phenomenon not unique to the United States but experienced recently in other advanced industrialized nations (Berry 1978; Vining and Kontuly 1978; Wardwell 1980). Others, however, have argued that it is simply an extension of old trends, from either methodological (Gordon 1979) or evolutionary perspectives (e.g., Borchert 1967; Wardwell 1977; Hawley 1978; Morrill 1979). From the latter view the post-1970 trends, though perhaps unexpected at this time, represent an equilibrium stage, a new form of diffuse urbanism, or a new level in the ongoing process of metropolitan concentration and spread. Whether ultimately viewed as new or part of an older process or both, we believe that there is no question that the new trend is different and that it constitutes a necessary backdrop for our study on contemporary villages in America.

SCOPE OF THIS STUDY

Villages have recently experienced a period of major adjustment in response to urban-centered innovations and pressures. The period since about 1950 may have been the most significant because urbanization reached its peak during this time. Dramatic changes in agriculture and other primary industries have transformed rural society. The farm population is now only a small proportion of the total, and there have undoubtedly been settlement effects from technological developments in transportation and communication, changes in lifestyle and social values, and a generally increased standard of living among rural residents, as well as from intended and unintended government policy and programs.

This study will provide an assessment of today's village community (defined here as an incorporated place with less than 2,500 population) and will attempt to demonstrate, on a national scale, the process of change in village demographic and economic characteristics during the recent period of adjustment. The time frame of the study is 1950–80, and data have been taken from various sources to analyze population and economic characteristics during that time.

Specific research problems will be developed in more detail in the individual chapters to follow. A general guiding hypothesis, however, is that with the coming of the new settlement trends of the population turnaround, we should find, over the past thirty years, an increasing divergence of village population and economic growth patterns from the patterns we would predict in terms of the traditional hierarchical settlement structure approach.

Fisher and Mitchelson (1981) discuss Hage's (1979) viewpoint that the urban hierarchy may be breaking down, replaced by greater nonmetropolitan growth and increased interdependence among smaller cities and towns. These "horizontal linkages" would resemble the "dispersed city" hypothesized in earlier writings on the urban system (Burton 1963) and parallel notions of the urban field around metropolitan centers, but they would not necessarily be limited to a near metropolitan location. It is increasingly recognized that inter-community linkages among large and small places need not follow a central place structure, particularly with the expansion and proliferation of multilocational organizations (Pappenfort 1959; Pred 1977).

Writers have been concerned about the possible place of the small town or village in this changing urban and metropolitan system. Numerous accounts of small town revival and of renewed interest in small town and other rural residential settings have been circulating recently, suggesting a quite different outlook for future population and perhaps economic trends in these places than they have previously experienced (Morrison and Wheeler 1976; McCarthy and Morrison 1979; Morganthau et al. 1981; Eberle 1982). Without a systematic study of these communities throughout this period of settlement transition, however, we cannot hope to understand their involvement in the process of structural and locational change in the urban pattern.

This is a macrolevel study with individual villages taken as units of analysis. We have utilized a few standard variables to indicate the place of villages in the settlement structure:

1. Size in population or number of economic activities or functions (as the most important simple index of position in the urban hierarchy);
2. Location with respect to larger centers (given the concern about competition and symbiotic relations among places in the hierarchy as influenced by their relative locations); and
3. Region of the country (to detect the consistency of village characteristics and trends in selected groups of states representing major regions).

Size and location are together basic dimensions in central place theory, which seems an appropriate part of the traditional approach to use in this study, particularly in considering the trade center function that has been important for many villages. Alonso (1973) notes, moreover, that in an urban field situation a smaller place may "borrow" some of the advantages of larger places nearby, so one should expect location with respect to larger places to have important implications for much of this work. Although our samples are small, we also take up regional differences in villages where possible and appropriate. Again, regional trends and differentials are an important aspect of the settlement structure, and new trends (e.g., resurgence of the South) have created considerable concern and attention. The basic scope of the study, however, is necessarily that of a national overview of village trends, although there are undoubtedly further regional and subregional differences that need to be better understood (Fuguitt and Beale 1978).

Change in population, and level and change in economic activities are treated either as independent or as dependent variables in various parts of the study. First we examine village population change as a dependent variable, in an effort to understand more about how the new population trends have been experienced by villages and whether this is accompanied by a change in factors associated with their growth and decline. Then we look at population characteristics of villages as related to their position in the settlement structure, so that size and growth patterns are treated as independent variables. Next, we consider trends in village economic activities, the structure of retail trade among places differentiated by size, and the interrelations of trade, population, and other economic changes, for villages differentiated by size and location.

Although in this study we often are concerned with structural variables such as size and location, it goes without saying that the settlement system, though necessarily having a physical dimension, is not a mechanical device but is basically brought about and transformed through patterned social relationships within and across its community elements. Though a detailed study of such relationships is beyond the scope of this work, through an interview survey of 100 mayors we are able to look at villages more explicitly as social and political communities, and assess their organized efforts to attract industry, expand service facilities, and grow in population. Further, as a possible consequence of growth, we consider the problems in social relations reported between the new and old residents of growing villages.

The literature on villages in the United States contains many examples of research based on a single community or state or substate grouping of villages or small towns. These studies have revealed some consistent patterns of population change and regularities in other characteristics. Most, however, do not examine both population and business characteristics and trends, nor do they cover the same time period so as to facilitate direct comparison. The last published study of both population and economic trends in American villages at a national scale was done in 1924 through 1936.[2] Another look is now overdue.

DESCRIPTION OF SAMPLE

The unit of study is the nonmetropolitan incorporated place of 2,500 or fewer residents for both population and economic analysis. Data were collected for a sample of villages in the conterminous United States drawn by Fuguitt (1968), which includes 572 or approximately 5 percent of the 11,334 incorporated places of less than 2,500 population in 1960 that were located outside of SMSA counties. (For details on sampling procedures, see Appendix A.)

Table 1-2 includes the distribution of villages in the sample by state and census division. Several regional breakdowns were used in this work, but all are combinations of the divisions shown in Figure 1-1.

Figure 1-1. Map of Sampled Villages.

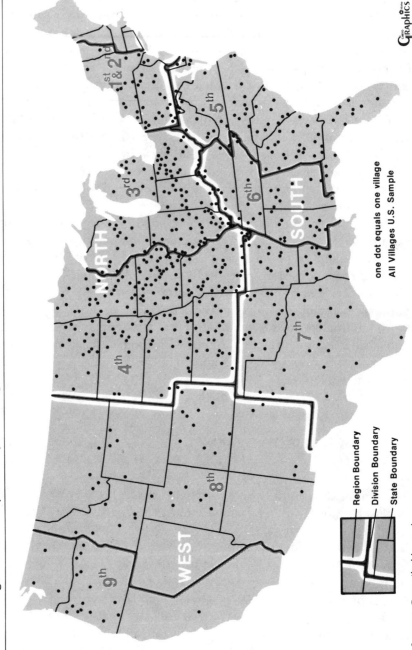

one dot equals one village
All Villages U.S. Sample

Region Boundary
Division Boundary
State Boundary

Source: Compiled by authors.

Table 1-2. Sample Distribution.

State	No. Villages	State	No. Villages
Division 1 and 2—Northeast		*Division 6—East South Central*	
Vermont	1	Kentucky	10
New York	12	Tennessee	9
New Jersey	2	Alabama	10
Pennsylvania	20	Mississippi	13
TOTAL	35	TOTAL	42
Division 3—East North Central		*Division 7—West South Central*	
Ohio	25	Arkansas	14
Indiana	18	Louisiana	11
Illinois	36	Oklahoma	19
Michigan	13	Texas	22
Wisconsin	17	TOTAL	66
TOTAL	109	*Division 8—Mountain*	
Division 4—West North Central		Montana	4
Minnesota	30	Idaho	6
Missouri	37	Wyoming	4
Iowa	42	Colorado	13
North Dakota	16	New Mexico	4
South Dakota	16	Utah	7
Nebraska	22	Arizona	1
Kansas	24	TOTAL	39
TOTAL	187	*Division 9—Pacific*	
Division 5—South Atlantic		Washington	3
Delaware	2	Oregon	15
Maryland	6	California	1
Virginia	5	TOTAL	19
West Virginia	6	TOTAL UNITED STATES	572
North Carolina	13		
South Carolina	10		
Georgia	21		
Florida	12		
TOTAL	75		

Source: Compiled by authors.

Villages are most numerous in the North region of which the West North Central division has the greatest number (Figure 1–1). The West has considerably fewer villages, probably as a result of the sparse settlement in much of this region along with a lesser tendency to incorporate small places in western states. A total of forty-two states are represented in the total sample.

We must deal only with incorporated places, since the U.S. census does not report unincorporated places under 1,000 in size and there is considerable turnover between decades in those over 1,000 (Fuguitt 1965a). Duncan and Reiss (1956) estimated that for 1950 perhaps 50 percent of the population in places under 1,000 in size lived in unincorporated centers. We know also that states vary in incorporation laws and in the extent to which small places are incorporated, as noted above. In short, the findings reported here may not be representative of all population nodes in that size range. Yet those studied do constitute a concrete, meaningful universe—that is, each is a center that has a separate political existence.

DATA SOURCES

Population data are from published and unpublished sources of the U.S. censuses for 1950 through 1980. Economic data are from Dun and Bradstreet Reference Books (1950, 1960, and 1970). An evaluation of the Dun and Bradstreet data is presented in Appendix B. Additional economic data and information on village developments in public services, infrastructure improvements, promotional activities, and relationships with newcomers were obtained early in 1981 from a telephone interview survey conducted with mayors in a subsample of 100 villages. These villages were drawn systematically with a random start from the original sample ordered by census division. The resulting subsample is equivalent to slightly less than 1 percent of the universe of villages and retains the regional and size distinctions of the larger sample.

RESEARCH THEMES

Several research themes have emerged from the various academic disciplines in prior work pertaining to the American village. These range from a focus on the inner workings of rural society to the outward appearance or form of rural settlements and the process by which they emerge (see Lewis 1979). We will briefly address a few of the most important themes here.

Community Structure and Organization

An important and familiar research theme has been the study of community social organization and process. This work has been diverse, representing a variety of approaches and research strategies, but most studies would come under the heading of sociology or cultural anthropology. (Recent reviews of rural community research include Ford and Sutton 1964; Saunders and Lewis 1976; Wilkinson 1978; Goudy and Ryan 1982.) The human ecological perspective on the community has already been noted above in the discussion of the settlement system. Social processes, including collective actions and community decisionmaking, have received considerable attention in recent years, and other research has considered community attachment, satisfaction with services, and quality of life.

Community case studies have provided an in-depth ethnographic examination of the culture, institutions, and social structure of a single community. Generally they have revealed a complex social structure and a system of informal customs and norms that are not evident to the outside observer. Complex linkages within and outside the community are operating even in the smallest places and are responsible for shaping the village into what we see at any point in time (Vidich and Bensman 1968; Stephenson 1968; Hatch 1979; Rowles 1983).

A theoretical issue and debate running through much of the community literature concerns the autonomy of the local community. Warren (1956, 1972) advanced the theoretical distinction between vertical and horizontal linkages, with the former representing the influences impinging on the community from outside and the latter, on elements making for coherence in the community. To the extent that social and institutional relationships are extralocal—or not based on locality considerations—the autonomy of the local community is eroded. Much work, including some of the community studies discussed above, has pointed to the declining autonomy of local units; perhaps the best known is Vidich and Bensman (1968). Shifts in this direction were indicated by several longitudinal community studies (Gallagher 1961; Smith 1974; Richardson and Larson

1976). The view of the disintegrating local community—helpless in the web of mass society—is criticized by Richards (1978) as over-drawn. He notes that most research on which the view is based is for a single point in time and argues that the vertical dimension of integration has been strong for small rural communities from the beginning of American settlement. Richards cites work that leads him to attach more importance to local leadership and attitudes in supporting a continuance of local autonomy, though he suggests perhaps a dual structure of decisionmaking may emerge relating to the horizontal and vertical dimensions. Both he and Warren (1972) have also criticized the "mass society" concept as being overly vague and not particularly helpful in formulating research or drawing conclusions about community structure and change. Clearly, the last word has not been said on the changing social organization of the local rural community, and we will give attention to this issue at various points in this work.

Population Characteristics and Trends

Another important theme in the research has been the study of popu-lation in small towns and villages and, particularly, how it has changed over time. Research in this area has been a central focus of rural sociologists since the early 1900s (see Smith 1970; Frankena 1980). Their work has emphasized differential rates of population change and the factors associated with growth and decline in rural communities. Each new census has resulted in a series of descriptive and analytical studies that include consideration of the rural popula-tion, such as detailed research monographs based on the 1950 and 1960 census results (Duncan and Reiss 1956; Hathaway et al. 1968). Due to a lack of published data on social and demographic character-istics in villages, most analytical work has ignored these issues and focused instead on population size and change. Notable exceptions include Duncan and Reiss (1956) and Fuguitt (1968), who analyzed social characteristics for villages based on U.S. census unpublished data for 1950 and 1960, respectively. Similarly, a lack of data and legal boundary definition for unincorporated rural communities has prevented work on these, aside from a few case studies (e.g., Trewartha 1943).

The issue of population distribution in rural areas has received much attention from rural sociologists and recently from geographers, especially as it affects provisions of service in rural communities and the spatial distribution of towns and cities and their growth patterns (Anderson 1950; Golledge et al. 1966). Differential patterns of population change in villages have consistently been attributed to several village characteristics, including location relative to larger urban centers, population and economic trends in the vicinity or hinterland of the village, transportation connections including access to interstate highways, initial size of population, and other local conditions or events that affect the distribution and natural change of populations (Hart and Salisbury 1965; Beale 1974; Fuguitt and Beale 1976). Recent migration trends favoring rural areas may offer villages an opportunity to remain viable, perhaps accompanied by some adjustment problems where growth is rapid (Frankena 1980).

Village Economy

One of the most important research themes concerning villages has been the issue of the village economy, especially the retail/service sector and its viability. Numerous studies, many published as Agricultural Experiment Station Bulletins, have documented the various activities found in the agricultural trade centers of selected states— beginning with Galpin's work in Wisconsin (1915) and continuing through the early 1960s (e.g., Landis 1932; Chittick 1955; Anderson 1961; Wakeley 1961; Barkley 1962). A major finding in these studies has been the loss of retail/service business coinciding with declining population and greater mobility among rural residents (Carlyle 1931; Paulsen and Carlson 1961; Hodge 1965; Folse and Riffe 1969; Johansen and Fuguitt 1973, 1979, 1981). Village communities appear to have been in a tenuous situation regarding their viability as centers of retail trade for the better part of this century, and many have attempted to survive by adapting to changing needs of their hinterland population. Some have been targets for revitalization, including historic preservation under programs administered through local and regional planning offices (Cohen 1977). The success of these relatively recent efforts remains to be tested systematically, but early results seem promising in some cases (Ziegler and Kidney 1980).

Additional research has been directed toward individual developments in small towns and villages, including both primary and secondary activities. Studies of mining towns, lumber towns, and other primary industry settlements have outlined the form and processes of change in these communities (e.g., Davis 1938; Holmes 1971). Recent developments in energy resource areas have resulted in a large number of studies concerning the effects of rapid growth on small communities (see Frankena 1980). Most of these report or predict major adjustment problems where a rapid influx of migrants occurs, especially in the smaller villages, although some forecasts of the more extreme social problems have been questioned regarding their basis for prediction (Gillard 1982).

Manufacturing activities in villages have also received attention by researchers interested in industrial location patterns. Lonsdale and Browning (1971) reported an increase in plant locations in rural southern communities that is indicative of industrial location trends throughout the country, as manufacturing industries recognize comparative economic benefits from rural locations and as transportation connections have improved for rural locations. Additional research has concerned the strategies for attracting industry to the small town as a means of improving the local economic base (Tweeten 1974; Wagner et al. 1979), while Summers et al. (1976) examined the impact and contribution of industrial development on nonmetropolitan communities using case studies from throughout the United States. Their research demonstrated generally positive results from new industrial developments in rural communities.

Central Place Studies

Theoretical explanations of village development and village characteristics have viewed the village, appropriately, as part of a larger system of urban places. The most elaborate of these has been Christaller's (1966) central place theory and its concept of a hierarchical spatial structure of places arranged by size and complexity. The idea of regularity in size and spacing of agricultural trade centers had been proposed earlier by Galpin (1915), a rural sociologist working with farming communities in southern Wisconsin, and was also developed by Losch (1954), a contemporary of Christaller.

Christaller (1966) developed a theoretical framework that explains the diversity and spatial arrangement of central places according to competition among sellers for consumers. The central places (trade centers) are assumed to be competing in space for customers according to their functional offerings, each of which has a maximum range in space or radius of drawing power determined by population density and nearness of competing centers, and a minimum threshold population necessary to support it. The resulting system of trade centers will have a hierarchical size distribution based on the centrality of the functional offerings of all places in that system, and will approach a spatial equilibrium with centers of similar size being approximately an equal distance from each other.

Empirical tests of central place theory were conducted in several parts of North America during the 1960s and revealed some close approximations to Christaller's ideal model in the areas that most closely met the uniform conditions assumed by the theory (see Berry 1967; Marshall 1969). Although Christaller allowed for change in the arrangement of centers with variations in the basic factors of population density, transport costs, and nearness to competition, most empirical applications of his theory have not considered temporal aspects of central place systems but have instead been directed toward the identification of a hierarchy and range and threshold values within a system at a given time.

Parr and Denike (1970) formulated a process of change within the functional composition of the hierarchy in response to shifts in population (and their effect on demand distribution), changes in technology (transportation and marketing methods), and regional economic growth. Arguing deductively, they predicted that functions will shift upward or downward within the hierarchy as entry conditions are modified for particular goods and services, resulting in a loss of functions from lower levels to intermediate range centers. The intermediate shopping centers also receive functions from higher levels where regional economic growth occurs. Villages fall at the lower end of the urban hierarchy posited in central place theory and consequently have the smallest range, the least central functions, and serve the most common needs of their hinterland populations. Furthermore, as the smallest places, villages should be the last to receive new functions introduced to the system of places and the first to lose them when they are not supported by sufficient demand (Christaller 1966).

As the smallest places in the hierarchy, villages are, therefore, at the "cutting edge" of the urban system where primary production meets the processing and consuming market, as described by Brunner et al. (1927) for agricultural villages in the United States. Their condition is thus affected by forces both from the primary production systems (as in agriculture, forestry, and mining but also including recreational developments) and also from the larger urban centers that affect lifestyles and economic viability. Villages depend largely on primary resource development for their supporting population and serve as a link between these industries and the larger urban system, yet at the same time they suffer competition from larger centers for the trade generated by the people engaged in the resource industries (Parr and Denike 1970).

Working in a settlement process framework, Hudson (1969a) developed a model along principles of plant ecology to explain settlement beginning on a frontier. His process involved three stages: (1) colonization—the process of inmigration on the frontier; (2) spread—the process of natural increase in the population; and (3) competition—where overpopulation results in a weeding out of the weaker members resulting in fewer settlers and eventually a condition of stability.

Although designed with individual farm families as the settlement unit, Hudson's model can be applied to trade centers in agricultural areas, which theoretically develop parallel to farm population growth and distribution and which, when met with declining hinterland population or declining demand must also face competition from nearby and distant centers. Consequent adjustments under such conditions could include specialization in certain activities, which would result in "outsized functions" in some villages and would disperse goods and services into a larger market area than the individual villages previously had served (Hart et al. 1968). Hudson's competition phase should result in a lower density of settlement as it continues. The density of village settlements has remained much the same in rural America during the recent past, although some settlements have disappeared completely or remain only as ghost towns and some new communities have emerged. Within the villages, however, there has been decline of trade center functions. The density of these functions among all villages has declined significantly, following periods of colonization and spread (Johansen and Fuguitt 1979, 1981).

CHAPTERS TO COME

An examination of the American village as a center of residential and economic activity follows, beginning in Chapter 2 with an analysis of recent and current population patterns. Population change in villages and associated factors are analyzed in an attempt to explain differential patterns of population growth and decline.

Chapter 3 presents a detailed account of social characteristics in villages, comparing villages with other urban and rural population segments on measures such as age distribution, educational attainment, income, and other social characteristics. Villages are differentiated by recent population growth trends to compare characteristics of villages in turnaround growth and decline counties.

Chapters 4, 5, and 6 focus on economic activities, beginning in Chapter 4 with a discussion of the variety of different economic activities found in villages and how these have changed since 1950. Chapter 5 presents an analysis of change in the retail and service sector and looks at the hierarchical structure of these and what adjustments have occurred since 1950. Chapter 6 contains an analysis of the relationship between village population and retail/service business and develops models of change in business incorporating urban accessibility and basic economic activities.

Current activities by village governments or community groups to improve the local infrastructure and promote industrial and other business development are examined in Chapter 7 and associated with measures of their possible consequences. The issues of community attitudes toward growth and relations between newcomers and old-timers are explored in Chapter 8, and in Chapter 9 we conclude with a summary statement and view of the village of the 1980s.

NOTES

1. A detailed balance sheet, showing the components of changes in the number of villages, is included in the Appendix as Table A-1. These components are additions due to new incorporations, or due to the decline of places into the village class, and subtractions due to the growth of places out of the class or due to disincorporations. In brief, it shows that once incorporated, villages seldom disappear. The major trend is the decline in the number of new places to a low level by 1930, as the rural settlement structure was established, with other elements of the balance sheet producing only a small amount of turnover in any given decade.

2. This is still the most comprehensive U.S. rural community study ever made. Initiated by Edmund Brunner under the sponsorship of the Institute of Social and Religious Research, it included 140 incorporated villages of 250–2,500 population purposively selected to represent

agricultural service centers throughout the nation. One or two research workers spent several weeks in each village collecting data in 1923–24, and restudies were made in 1930 and 1936. Other data were obtained from sources such as the U.S. census and Dun and Bradstreet. Reports on the first survey include Brunner et al. (1927), Brunner (1928), and also Fry (1926) for accompanying census analysis. The first resurvey was covered in Brunner and Kolb (1933) and the second in Brunner and Lorge (1937). More recently T. Lynn Smith and Olaf Larson, who were involved in earlier field work, restudied villages in Indiana, Minnesota, and North Dakota (Smith 1974) and New York (Richardson and Larson (1976).

2 GROWING AND DECLINING VILLAGES

INTRODUCTION

Recent changes in U.S. village population must be considered in the context of the remarkable shift in national growth patterns first noted in the early 1970s and often referred to as the "nonmetropolitan population turnaround." This trend has been well documented (see Zelinsky 1978 for a bibliography; see Brown and Wardwell 1980 and Briggs and Rees 1982 for more recent work). The level of nonmetropolitan population growth increased during recent decades so that by 1970 it generally exceeded that for metropolitan areas, in dramatic contrast to earlier times. The new trend is not just a spillover growth from adjacent metropolitan areas, and although there are specific subregions of particularly rapid growth, the trend is widespread throughout the country. Further work has led to generalizations about factors associated with the degree of net migration gain for counties, and interview surveys have thrown considerable light on reasons for migration to nonmetropolitan areas and the characteristics of the migrants.

This new development makes the examination of population trends an obvious starting point for our study of contemporary village

21

America. Despite the considerable amount of research on the turn-around, little has been done relating to cities (J. Long 1978, 1981; McCarthy 1980; Fuguitt, Lichter, and Beale 1981), and none has given separate attention to smaller places. In this chapter we will trace the population growth patterns of U.S. nonmetropolitan villages over the past thirty years (1950–80), the period immediately prior to and including the turnaround. Patterns for each decade are associated with several variables (selected on the basis of past research and theory) in order to better understand relationships involving village population growth and decline and how these relationships may be changing.

Prior to the turnaround, the dominant pattern of population change was concentration into metropolitan areas and decentral-ization within these areas consistent with the hierarchical view of urban and metropolitan structure discussed in Chapter 1. Growth was greatest in and around large cities: Larger metropolitan areas grew faster than smaller ones, and larger cities generally grew faster than smaller cities and villages outside metropolitan areas. Metro-politan influence was shown by the faster growth in nonmetropolitan counties adjacent to metropolitan centers, or by regular distance gradients of population growth diminishing into the countryside. Overall, this trend reflected a centralization of economic activities, especially trade and manufacturing, which was generally ascribed to economies of scale and externalities related to the greater accessibility of population and other economic units. At the same time, the decline in the relative importance of agriculture and other extractive indus-tries accentuated slow growth and population loss in more remote rural areas. Underlying these explanations is the assumption that overall there is a net flow of people in the direction of developing economic opportunities.

It is in this context that most villages were seen to have a bleak future. With centralization of trade and services, including govern-mental activities such as education and medical care, the major functions of the village were being transferred to other units, with this shift possibly exacerbated by a declining population in village service areas. Though some industries might locate or expand in villages or nearby areas, agglomerative economies were expected to keep this to a minimum, except possibly for some less than desirable low-wage establishments that might "trickle down" to remote areas in search of cheap labor. Thus the only bright spot would be for some larger villages, which could have advantages due to their size and the variety of activities they offer, and for villages near larger centers that could transform their major function to that of a bedroom community.

The pattern of growth among units of the settlement system has undergone a process of change to become decidedly different in 1970–80 than it was in 1950–60, when it was generally consistent with the trends discussed above. This change is not restricted to relative metropolitan and nonmetropolitan growth. The South increased its growth level to join the West as the two fastest growing regions of the country. Smaller SMSAs are now growing more rapidly than larger ones. In nonmetropolitan areas, although counties adjacent to SMSAs continue to grow faster than others, the nonadjacent counties had a greater increase in the rate of growth to a higher level by 1970–80 than metropolitan areas as a whole. Also, whereas larger cities in nonmetropolitan areas previously grew more rapidly than smaller ones, in many circumstances today the reverse is true, and for the first time the population outside cities is growing faster than the city population overall, even in remote locations (Fuguitt, Lichter, and Beale 1981; J. Long 1981). Together these shifts show a broad pattern of deconcentration that goes well beyond a simple extension of growth at the peripheries of metropolitan centers.

Economic shifts away from large-scale manufacturing production, the decentralization of manufacturing and other activities oriented to markets rather than resources, and the "bottoming out" of losses due to agriculture have been given attention in explaining these changes in population growth. Furthermore, there was an increase in the footloose population and presumed greater emphasis on amenities and low population density in making individual migration decisions as well as in the location of new economic activities (Dillman 1979; Zuiches 1981).

OBJECTIVES AND PROCEDURES

The purpose of this chapter is to examine, in the context of these unanticipated changes, levels and variations in nonmetropolitan village population change over the thirty-year period since 1950. The first question is whether levels of nonmetropolitan village growth have increased over this time as a part of the turnaround phenomenon. Next, several factors that help to define the village in the settlement structure are associated with village change, including: region of the country (in order to define the large-scale setting of the villages), population change in the county (given the presumed interdependence between villages and other nearby population units), accessibility to large centers, and initial size of place.

Previous research, consistent with the older trend of metropolitan concentration, has generally shown that villages have higher levels of growth if they are near cities and also that larger villages have higher levels of growth than smaller ones. We need to determine the extent to which these relations have been altered recently. Similarly, county population change has been associated positively with village change, indicating that the village shares to some degree in the growth of its local setting. In this connection also we will consider how county level variables used in other research to examine the turnaround are associated with the population growth of sample villages and their counties for each decade since 1950. Given the increasingly diffuse nature of settlement, we predict that the importance of the county growth variable should increase over time, even while there is a decrease in the effect of initial size and urban accessibility as indicators of the position of the village in the urban-metropolitan settlement hierarchy.

Because the available data are limited, it is impossible to associate other socioeconomic variables with population change, as has been considered in parallel work for cities (for example, Wheat 1976; Bradbury et al. 1982). Many such variables along with other population characteristics are considered for groups of villages in Chapter 3, however, and Dun and Bradstreet and the mayors' survey data on retail and industrial establishments are associated with population change in Chapter 6. The mayors also provided us with some useful insights on why their growing or declining villages were changing, and this information is summarized at the conclusion of the present chapter.

Most of the analysis to follow consists of comparisons of growth levels and factors associated with growth across the three decades 1950–60, 1960–70, 1970–80. As explained in Appendix A, the original sample was modified so that only villages under 2,500 in size at the beginning of each decade are considered, making the number of cases slightly different for each ten-year period. Growth patterns are examined in one section of the chapter, however, for places under 2,500 in 1950 followed over three decades.

Population figures are from publications of the U.S. Bureau of the Census. No data are available on annexation by places this small, although we recognize that a high proportion of the growth in nonmetropolitan places over 2,500 was associated with annexation in the 1950–60 and the 1960–70 period (Klaff and Fuguitt 1978). Of course, growth associated with annexation is real growth, but population increases at the periphery of places may not be captured by a village if annexation is not carried out. We must deal with population change in the village as a political unit, and although this has an intrinsic significance, it is not always the same as change in the number of people living in a population center if it coul' be delineated for each census simply on the basis of settlement dens. y.

TRENDS IN VILLAGE GROWTH

Villages have shared in the recent revival of nonmetropolitan growth. In Figure 2–1 percentage change was calculated for each place under 2,500 at the beginning of a decade, and the percentage distribution of places by percentage change is shown for each ten-year period. For both 1950–60 and 1960–70 about one-half of the villages were growing, but this was true for two-thirds of the villages over 1970–80. This shift is also seen in terms of the five different change categories of the figure, particularly for the growth and decline extremes. From the 1950s to the 1970s, the proportion of villages growing more than 20 percent in a decade increased from 16 to 26 percent whereas the proportion of villages losing more than 10 percent in a decade dropped from 27 to 15 percent of the total. Although earlier work with nonmetropolitan counties has shown a more or less regular gradation in increased levels of growth over the thirty-year period (Beale and Fuguitt 1978), here we see that in terms of percentage distributions the largest increase in level of growth for villages was between the last two decades.

An important question regarding this observed upturn in growth in the 1970s is the extent to which it might be due to the definition of nonmetropolitan that was used in the study. The universe here includes villages in all counties that were not designated as metropolitan in 1960. Although using an early definition might be considered more appropriate for looking at changes over time, an immediate issue raised by Figure 2–1 is whether the apparently increased growth

Figure 2-1.   Village Distribution by Percentage of Change in Population.

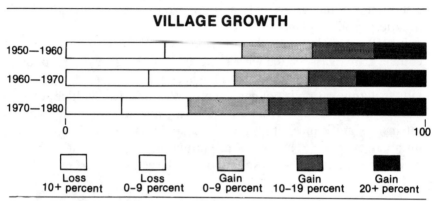

VILLAGE GROWTH

| | Loss 10+ percent | Loss 0-9 percent | Gain 0-9 percent | Gain 10-19 percent | Gain 20+ percent |

Source: Compiled by authors.

levels for nonmetropolitan villages are due simply to the spread of metropolitan areas since 1960. Table 2–1 gives the results of a trichotomous classification of places according to whether they were in 1980 metropolitan areas, in nonmetropolitan counties adjacent to such metropolitan areas, or in nonadjacent nonmetropolitan counties. For conciseness, the summary measure, percentage of places growing, is used although the pattern of results with the more detailed percentage change distributions is consistent with these findings.

Table 2–1 shows that the new village growth is not attributable to metropolitan expansion between 1960 and 1980. Villages in 1980 nonmetropolitan counties were about as likely to grow as those in the total sample and the level of growth increased in the 1970s in the same way. The small number of villages (approximately eighty, or 14 percent of the total for each decade) in counties that became metropolitan between 1960 and 1980 were considerably more likely to grow as would be expected.

Nor is the increased likelihood of growth in nonmetropolitan areas simply metropolitan spillover. The difference between adjacent and nonadjacent counties in growth levels is seen here to have been rather large in the 1950s but to have virtually disappeared by the 1970s. The greatest increase in the proportion growing over the last two decades, from 44 to 63 percent, was registered by villages in those counties that were not adjacent to a 1980 metropolitan county. This is consistent with previous research using counties as units. (For example, Beale and Fuguitt 1978.)

Table 2-1. Percentage of Villages Growing, by 1980 Metropolitan Status, 1950–60, 1960–70, 1970–80.

Metropolitan 1980 Status	Percentage of Villages Growing		
	1950–60	*1960–70*	*1970–80*
Metropolitan in 1980	70	70	74
Nonmetropolitan 1980	48	50	64
Adjacent county	57	56	65
Nonadjacent county	38	44	63
TOTAL SAMPLE	51	53	66
(Number of cases)	(559)	(570)	(564)

Source: Compiled by authors.

FACTORS ASSOCIATED WITH VILLAGE GROWTH

These initial results show a recent increase in growth levels of villages, although there is still considerable variation in growth from village to village. The increased levels of village growth also cannot simply be explained by the metropolitanization process. Consequently, we have undertaken a systematic consideration of some basic factors one would predict to be associated with village population change on the basis of theory and previous research. These variables are region of the country, level of county population change in which the village is found, accessibility to larger places and initial village size; they are indicators of the position of these places within the settlement structure of the nation. By examining the changes over time in the resulting associations, we can draw some tentative conclusions about whether the increased levels of village growth reflect changing relations between villages and other population units.[1]

In this section we present a tabular analysis showing mean annualized rates of population change (Tables 2–2 through 2–5) and variations in the rates (Figures 2–2 through 2–5) for different levels of each independent variable.[2] The percentage of places growing also is included in the tables, as well as Etas from analyses of variance. In a section to follow, the same variables are considered together in a regression analysis.

Region

Small cities and towns are not autonomous units, so we would predict that not all of this variation in growth is due to the unique experiences of individual centers. We would expect, for example, levels of small town growth to be different for different regions of the country and would want to look for possible systematic associations between changes in village growth and the overall interregional population shifts that have attracted so much attention recently.

Table 2-2. Mean Annualized Change and Percentage of Places Growing, Villages by Four Regions, 1950–60, 1960–70, 1970–80.

Region and Decade	Mean Annualized Change/1,000	Percentage of Places Growing	Number of Villages
1950–60			
North	5.5	65	145
Plains	–3.6	39	181
South	2.0	51	176
West	3.7	53	57
TOTAL	1.3	51	559
ETA	0.14[a]	0.19[a]	
1960–70			
North	3.8	54	145
Plains	–1.8	41	187
South	8.7	64	181
West	0.6	51	57
TOTAL	3.2	53	570
ETA	0.18[a]	0.19[a]	
1970–80			
North	6.5	61	148
Plains	6.7	61	180
South	12.8	71	184
West	23.3	79	52
TOTAL	10.2	66	564
ETA	0.18[a]	0.13[a]	

[a] Significant at the 0.05 level.

Source: Compiled by authors.

Regional growth differences for villages are given in Table 2–2. The four regions identified are: North, which includes the New England, Middle Atlantic, and East North Central census divisions; the South, which includes the South Atlantic, East South Central, and West South Central divisions; the West, which includes the Mountain and Pacific divisions; and the West North Central division. The latter division is considered separately because of the high concentration of villages there and because it includes the northern plains area, which has had a distinctive pattern of widespread nonmetropolitan population decline even into the 1970s. The West North Central division (hereafter referred to as "Plains," for convenience) is a subregion of relatively low density that remains highly dependent upon agriculture. (See map in Figure 1–1.)

Both the annualized change measure averaged over the villages and also the percentage of places growing show considerable differences by region for each decade (Table 2–2). Analyses of variance indicate that all comparisons are significant at least at the 0.05 level. All regions had higher mean annual population changes in 1970–80 than 1950–60, showing the turnaround for villages to be a national phenomenon. The mean for the North increased the least, however, and indeed the percentage of places growing for that region dropped from 65 to 61 over the period. In terms of relative position the North's shift was dramatic, as it dropped from the most rapid to the least rapidly growing region for villages. The Plains continued to be an area of slow village growth, although it exhibited considerable increase over time. Only four out of every ten places in the Plains were growing in 1950–60, though this was true of six out of every ten in the most recent decade. The overall growth rates of both the North and the West were somewhat lower in the 1960s than the 1950s, but the Plains had a small increase and the South a somewhat larger increase in mean rate. By 1970–80, however, the West had by far the highest mean rate, which was almost twice as large as that for the South and more than double that of the nation as a whole.

Reporting only mean values may conceal important differences in the distributions of villages by population change. Such distributions are shown by region in the bar graphs in Figure 2–2. The proportion of places annually losing 10 or more per 1,000, or gaining 10 or more per 1,000, is generally consistent with the mean values in Table 2–2. An exception is the comparison of the North and the Plains for 1970–80. Although the two regions have essentially the same mean and same percentage of places growing, the Plains has relatively more

Figure 2–2. Village Distribution by Population Change for U.S. Regions.

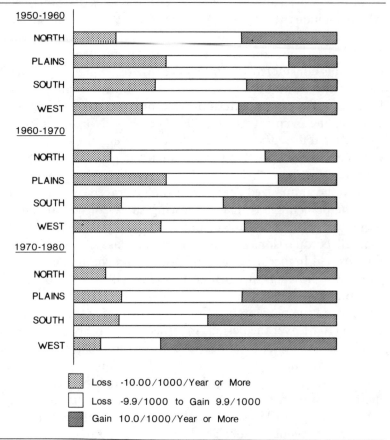

Loss	-10.00/1000/Year or More
Loss	-9.9/1000 to Gain 9.9/1000
Gain	10.0/1000/Year or More

Source: Compiled by authors.

places both in the rapid growth category, and in the rapid decline category.

The proportion gaining more than 10 per 1,000 per year correlates well with the total regional population growth for the regions in the 1970–80 period, with the West highest, followed by the South, the Plains, and the North, in that order. In earlier decades, the West also had a considerably higher rate of total population gain than the other regions but was behind one or more other regions in village growth. Earlier growth in the West was more concentrated in states on the Pacific coast, where there are relatively few nonmetropolitan villages, but more recently the Mountain states in that region have experienced very rapid growth in total and nonmetropolitan population. Unlike the West, the increase in village growth began in the South in the 1960–70 period. This may have been related to the deconcentration of manufacturing, which was particularly important in the South at that time, whereas the emergence of new energy developments and recreation, evidently were important factors in the 1970–80 growth of the nonmetropolitan West.

County Growth

Moving attention to the local setting, one would predict that villages should reflect the growth trends of their nearby areas as part of the interdependence that exists among units in the settlement structure. Specifically, the hypothesis considered here is that village growth is associated with growth of the county in which the village is located, excluding the population of that village (Thomas 1970; Fuguitt 1972). A practical dimension of this is the prescription sometimes given that efforts to stem decline or develop economically should be carried out on a county or regional basis rather than by individual centers.

This variable raises a question concerning the direction of causation. In some instances, the basis for growth could be primarily in the village, and this may spill over into the other population units of the area. A more likely situation, however, is that the larger area or regional circumstance leads to a prevailing growth or decline pattern that tends to be followed by villages as well as by other population units. In other words, the village may follow the growth of its county, or both the village and the balance of its county may grow in response to external factors. Simply because of its small proportional population it should be unusual for a village to be in a position to influence strongly the growth or decline of its county. For 87 percent of the cases in our sample, the village was less than 10 percent of the county population at each census since 1950, so it is more plausible that the village would follow in the general growth circumstances created within larger units rather than the other way around.

We calculated the annualized growth rates for each county that included a sample village, after removing the village's population. For villages in more than one county, we used the county in which the place had the most population in 1960. Villages were arranged in quartiles of county growth, and the average annualized village growth for each quartile, along with the percentage of places growing, is

Table 2–3. Mean Annualized Change and Percentage of Places Growing, Villages by Quartiles of County Growth, 1950–60, 1960–70, 1970–80.

County Growth Quartile and Decade	Mean Annualized Change/1,000	Percentage of Places Growing	Number of Villages
1950–60			
1st quartile	16.6	76	140
2nd quartile	2.2	55	140
3rd quartile	− 4.8	40	140
4th quartile	− 9.1	33	139
TOTAL	1.3	51	559
ETA	0.38[a]	0.25[a]	
1960–70			
1st quartile	12.3	69	142
2nd quartile	8.2	63	143
3rd quartile	− 0.3	48	142
4th quartile	− 7.5	32	143
TOTAL	3.2	53	570
ETA	0.31[a]	0.29[a]	
1970–80			
1st quartile	20.8	78	141
2nd quartile	12.8	71	141
3rd quartile	7.0	67	141
4th quartile	0.0	46	141
TOTAL	10.2	66	564
ETA	0.27[a]	0.25[a]	

[a] Significant at the 0.05 level.

Source: Compiled by authors.

given in Table 2–3. There is a rather strong association between village and county growth for each decade, with both village growth measures showing a consistent ranking over the quartiles of county growth, and Etas ranging from 0.25 to 0.38. Figure 2–3 reveals this consistency also for the proportion of places at the extremes of positive or negative population change.

Figure 2-3. Village Distribution by Population Change for County Growth Quartiles.

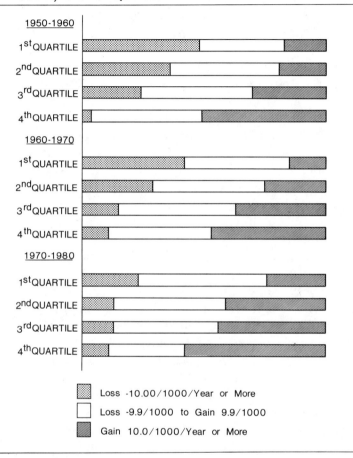

Source: Compiled by authors.

Accessibility to Cities

Given the general process of decentralization of residences, services, manufacturing, and retailing going on around most cities, a reasonable prediction is that villages near larger places would be more likely to grow than other villages. This is based on findings from several previous studies (Northam 1963; Hart and Salisbury 1965; Hodgson 1972; Fuguitt and Beale 1976; Roseman 1977). Many places appear to be changing their primary function from rural service centers to residential centers for families whose bread winners work elsewhere.

Other work locations, of course, may be in or near the village but in enterprises directly or indirectly stimulated by the proximity of cities.

An accessibility score was calculated for each of the villages for 1950, 1960, and 1970. (See Appendix A.) The three sets correlated almost perfectly, so villages were arranged in quartiles of accessibility as of 1960, and the mean annualized population change and percentage of places growing over each decade are given for each quartile in Table 2-4. There was a strong rank-order relation between quartiles of accessibility and population growth in the 1950s and the 1960s. In 1950-60, for example, the percentage of places growing ranged from 70 percent in the highest quartile of accessibility down to 37 percent in the lowest, and comparable figures for the 1960s were 66 and 34 percent. Over 1970-80, however, accessibility was much less important. Although the growth measures are in a consistent rank-order relationship, differences between quartiles are smaller and the Etas are nonsignificant.

The distributions of villages by annualized change shown in Figure 2-4 are consistent with patterns of the mean and percentage growing values in the corresponding table. The decline in importance of urban proximity for village growth parallels change in growth patterns for nonmetropolitan counties, as found in recent studies of the nonmetropolitan population turnaround. These studies have shown that the growth difference has declined between counties adjacent and not adjacent to metropolitan counties, and that growth was particularly rapid in the counties having only smaller incorporated centers rather than cities (Fuguitt, Lichter, and Beale 1981). Recall also that Table 2-1 shows essentially no difference between adjacent and nonadjacent counties in the percentage of villages growing in the 1970s.

Our accessibility measure does not reflect, however, possible changes in the significance of city population size and distance over the thirty-year period. The deconcentration of economic and trade activities from larger to smaller cities and into their peripheries, and the improvement of highways and possible increased tendency to travel long distances, has in all likelihood increased the accessibility of many villages to urban-like activities and services, even though population-distance relations in an index such as ours remain virtually unchanged. Consequently, although many remote areas have been growing recently because of qualities relating to activities such as recreation and energy developments (Heaton et al. 1981), a part of this attenuation of the accessibility-growth association may be due to

Table 2-4. Mean Annualized Change and Percentage of Places Growing, Villages by Quartiles of Accessibility Score, 1950–60, 1960–70, 1970–80.

Accessibility Quartile and Decade	Mean Annualized Change/1,000	Percentage of Places Growing	Number of Villages
1950–60			
1st quartile	12.2	70	140
2nd quartile	2.6	55	137
3rd quartile	− 3.3	41	140
4th quartile	− 6.3	37	142
TOTAL	1.3	51	559
ETA	0.38[a]	0.25[a]	
1960–70			
1st quartile	9.4	66	140
2nd quartile	8.3	65	144
3rd quartile	0.0	46	142
4th quartile	− 4.8	34	140
TOTAL	3.2	53	570
ETA	0.24[a]	0.27[a]	
1970–80			
1st quartile	13.0	69	140
2nd quartile	11.7	69	142
3rd quartile	8.7	66	140
4th quartile	7.3	58	142
TOTAL	10.2	66	564
ETA	0.08	0.10	

[a] Significant at the 0.05 level.

Source: Compiled by authors.

increased generalized accessibility across constant population/ distance relationships.

Size of Place

The fourth and last factor hypothesized to be associated with population change is the initial size of the village. Through the years a

Figure 2-4. Village Distribution by Population Change for Urban Accessibility Quartiles.

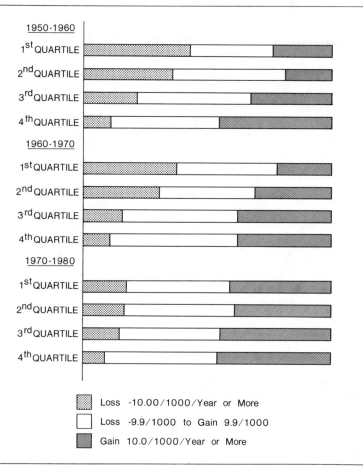

Source: Compiled by authors.

large number of studies has shown a positive relation between initial village size and its population change over a subsequent period (see, for example, Ratcliffe 1942; Brunner and Smith 1944; Hart and Salisbury 1965). The usual interpretation is that smaller places are not growing as rapidly because of a centralization of trade and services within the urban or central place hierarchy. With increasing availability of transportation, rural people have a wider range of choices of places to go, and at the same time demand for goods and services has become more specialized. Furthermore, larger villages, because they offer more services, are more likely to be attractive for other economic activities, such as manufacturing and as residential centers. In this process smaller villages may be bypassed in favor of larger villages, towns, and cities nearby.

In the early 1970s, however, research showed that this association had weakened in comparing 1960–70 with 1950–60, with an increase in levels of growth for smaller villages not equalled by those in the larger size classes (Fuguitt and Beale 1976). Subsequent investigation revealed the positive relationship continued to be strongest in the Plains area, where one might expect a predominance even today of the trade center function and classical central place relationships (Fuguitt and Beale 1978).

Results over the thirty-year period within our village sample indicate a continuation of the 1950–70 trend to a possible reversal of the size-growth association by 1970–80 (Table 2–5). In the latter period the highest mean annualized rate is found for places of less than 250 population as of 1970, although the percentage of places growing is positively associated with initial size as in previous decades and neither relationship is statistically significant. This unusual result, with two summary growth measures showing different directions of association, is matched by a very suggestive pattern in the annualized change distribution in Figure 2–5. The percentage of villages in the high decline group (declining 10/1,000/year or more) is negatively associated with initial size for each ten-year period, though differences among size groups are decreasing across the decades. (That is, the smaller the place, the greater the likelihood of a high rate of decline.) The proportion in the high growth group (growing 10/1,000/year or more), however, reverses its association with initial size during the thirty-year period, being clearly positive in the 1950s and negative in the 1970s. In the 1970s according to Figure 2–5, smaller places were more likely than larger ones to either be growing rapidly or to be declining rapidly. We will give attention to this unanticipated finding in the discussion to follow.

VILLAGE GROWTH PATTERNS

To further explore the variation in village population changes across decades, we classified places by their growth and decline pattern between 1950 and 1980. There are eight possible growth or decline combinations, ranging from unbroken growth to unbroken decline across the three ten-year periods. Each combination has been coded

Table 2-5. Mean Annualized Change and Percentage of Places Growing, Villages by Four Size Groups, 1950–60, 1960–70, 1970–80.

Initial Size and Decade	Mean Annualized Change/1,000	Percentage of Places Growing	Number of Villages
1950–60			
1,000–2,499	6.2	60	137
500–999	7.2	63	147
250–499	0.1	48	141
LT 250	− 9.2	33	134
TOTAL	1.3	51	559
ETA	0.25[a]	0.23[a]	
1960–70			
1,000–2,499	7.4	64	138
500–999	2.2	53	134
250–499	2.2	50	147
LT 250	1.2	45	151
TOTAL	3.2	53	570
ETA	0.10[a]	0.14[a]	
1970–80			
1,000–2,499	8.3	72	134
500–999	9.3	64	140
250–499	8.1	67	132
LT 250	14.1	59	158
TOTAL	10.2	65	564
ETA	0.09	0.10	

[a]Significant at the 0.05 level.

Source: Compiled by authors.

here. For example, the code GGG refers to a village that grew in the 1950s, the 1960s, and the 1970s. Similarly a GDD village grew in the 1950s, but declined in the 1960s and the 1970s. Places included in this analysis had less than 2,500 people in 1950 and a reported population in all subsequent censuses through 1980. The six mixed patterns are combined into two categories and the four groups resulting are: (1)

Figure 2–5. Village Distribution by Population Change for Initial Size Groups.

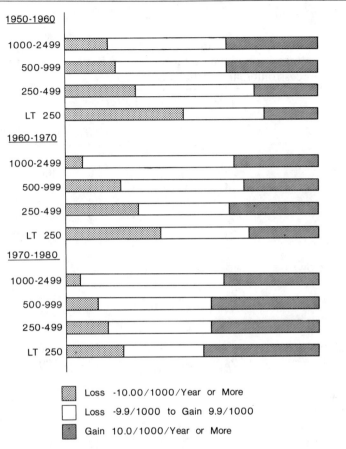

Source: Compiled by authors.

126 sustained growers (GGG), making up 23 percent of all villages; (2) 227 turnaround growers (——G) (the sum of 72 GDG, 79 DDG, and 76 DGG), which includes 42 percent of the villages; (3) 122 turnaround decliners (++D) (the sum of 36 GDD, 44 GGD, and 42 DGD), or 23 percent of villages; and (4) 65 sustained decliners (DDD), or 12 percent of all villages. The fact that one place in four is a turnaround decliner, and that another 12 percent has lost population each decade for thirty years, underscores the point that the recent population growth turnaround in nonmetropolitan areas has not reached every small village. (For a similar analysis of counties, see Brown and Beale 1981.)

Table 2–6 gives the distribution by growth patterns for each of the four population change factors previously considered; region, county growth 1950–80, accessibility, and size in 1950. The frequency tables

Table 2-6. Percentage Distribution by 1950–80 Growth Patterns for Villages Grouped by Region, County Growth, Accessibility, and Initial Size.[a]

| | 1950–80 Growth Patterns | | | | | Number of |
	GGG	--G	--D	DDD	Total	Villages
Region						
North	25	34	32	9	100	146
Plains	14	45	21	21	100	175
South	30	42	20	8	100	166
West	27	55	11	7	100	55
TOTAL	23	42	23	12	100	542
County growth 1950–80:						
1st quartile	69	26	5	0	100	137
2nd quartile	22	53	25	0	100	135
3rd quartile	1	59	39	1	100	135
4th quartile	0	31	21	48	100	135
TOTAL	23	42	23	12	100	542
Accessibility						
1st quartile	38	32	23	5	100	137
2nd quartile	29	38	27	6	100	133
3rd quartile	11	55	22	12	100	133
4th quartile	15	42	18	25	100	139
TOTAL	23	42	23	12	100	542
Size 1950						
1,000–2,500	28	39	25	8	100	137
500–999	35	36	20	9	100	147
250–499	16	50	21	13	100	135
LT 250	12	45	24	20	100	121
TOTAL	23	42	23	12	100	540
Number of villages	126	227	122	65	540	

[a]Includes villages under 2,500 in 1960 and reported in censuses of 1960 through 1980.

Source: Compiled by authors.

on which these four panels are based yielded separate chi square values that were each significant at the 0.01 level, indicating an association between the thirty-year village growth patterns and region, county growth, accessibility, and initial size.

Sustained growth was least likely to be found in the Plains, whereas sustained decline was most likely there. On the other hand, 45 percent of the Plains places are in the turnaround growth category, a percentage exceeded only by the West. The North has the highest proportion, about one-third, classed as turnaround decline.

Comparing quartiles of 1950–80 county growth, there is the expected association for the sustained growth and the sustained decline categories. In fact, the two high county growth quartiles have all but one of the sustained growth villages, and the lowest county growth quartile includes all but one of the sustained decline villages. A similar though less extreme pattern is found for accessibility and size of place. Turnaround growth, however, is highest for the middle quartiles of county growth followed by the lowest quartile and for the lowest quartiles of accessibility and size of place. In sum, sustained growers were more likely to be found in accessible locations and in locations of high 1950–80 county growth and to be initially larger in size. Sustained decliners were more likely to be in inaccessible locations of lower county growth and to have been initially small in size. Turnaround growers are more like sustained decliners in these ways, which is consistent with both the recent lower association of population growth with accessibility and also with change in the direction of this association with initial size that was found in comparing the most recent ten-year period with previous decades.

MULTIVARIATE ANALYSIS

Having shown in detail the separate associations of village growth with each of the four basic factors—region, county growth, urban accessibility, and initial size—for the three decades, the next step is to carry out a multivariate analysis. Table 2–7 provides the results of an analysis of variance to test for a regional effect, net of county growth, location, and size. As expected, size, location, and county growth are together significantly associated with village growth during each decade. The regional increment (determined by adding binaries for three of the four regions to the model) is significant only in the 1960s, though the F value approaches significance for the 1970–80 period as well. This indicates that differences across regions in village population change, shown in the preceding section, prevail only for the 1960s when differences in the other independent variables are taken into account.

Going beyond this, we tested for interaction between region and the other three variables. Here we are interested in seeing whether the net effects of size, location, and county growth are different across regions. The interaction terms add a significant increment to R squared for the 1950–60 period only, when the regional increment is smallest and nonsignificant. Since region appears to be relatively unimportant with these data in a multivariate context, it will not be considered further. This does not nullify the real differences between regions found earlier but suggests they may be explained in part by regional variations in other factors, such as village size, location, and the growth experience of nonmetropolitan counties. One should keep

Table 2–7. Analysis of Variance for Independent Variables and Regional Interactions, 1950–60, 1960–70, 1970–80.

Components and Decade	R squared	df	
1950–60			
Size, location, county growth	0.27546	3	$F(3,555) = 70.33^a$
Plus regional binaries	0.28128	6	
Regional increment	0.00582	3	$F(3,552) = 1.48$
Plus regional interaction	0.32110	15	
Interaction increment	0.03982	9	$F(9,543) = 3.54^a$
1960–70			
Size, location, county growth	0.13299	3	$F(3,566) = 28.94^a$
Plus regional binaries	0.15163	6	
Regional increment	0.01864	3	$F(3,563) = 4.12^a$
Plus regional interaction	0.1603	15	
Interaction increment	0.02440	9	$F(9,554) = 1.82$
1970–80			
Size, location, county growth	0.10921	3	$F(3,560) = 22.89^a$
Plus regional binaries	0.12128	6	
Regional increment	0.01207	3	$F(3,557) = 2.55$
Plus regional interaction	0.14478	15	
Interaction increment	0.02350	9	$F(9,548) = 1.67$

[a]Significant at the 0.05 level.

Source: Compiled by authors.

in mind, however, that our sample sizes are small, particularly in the West, and that other regional delineations would undoubtedly give somewhat different patterns of results.

To consider the other three variables together, Table 2–8 gives the regression of annualized population change for all villages on log

Table 2–8. Regressions of Annualized Population Change for All Villages, 1950–60, 1960–70, 1970–80.

Variables	Mean	S.D.	r	b	Beta
1950–60 (N=559)					
Annual village change	1.25	25.61			
Log initial size	6.19	0.89	0.23[a]	6.02	0.21[a]
Log accessibility	4.56	2.21	0.28[a]	1.53	0.13[a]
Annual county change	−0.80	19.87	0.46[a]	0.53	0.41[a]
(Constant)				−42.50	
R = 0.52					
R² = 0.28					
1960–70 (N=570)					
Annual village change	3.20	24.33			
Log initial size	6.12	0.96	0.07	1.18	0.05
Log accessibility	4.56	2.20	0.25[a]	1.34	0.12[a]
Annual county change	0.75	13.88	0.34[a]	0.51	0.29[a]
(Constant)				−10.51	
R = 0.36					
R² = 0.13					
1970–80 (N=564)					
Annual village change	10.16	27.97			
Log initial size	6.13	0.96	−0.09[a]	−2.62	−0.09[a]
Log accessibility	4.56	2.17	0.07	0.57	0.04
Annual county change	10.78	15.82	0.32[a]	0.55	0.31[a]
(Constant)				17.72	
R = 0.33					
R² = 0.11					

[a]Significant at the 0.05 level.

Source: Compiled by authors.

initial size, log of accessibility, and annualized change in the county.[3] (Size and accessibility were logged because of skewed distributions.) For the nation as a whole the results are consistent with the individual associations examined previously. In the 1950s initial size, accessibility, and county change all had significant net effects on annualized population change. The standardized regression coefficients (betas) indicate that annual county change is the most important of these variables followed by log initial size and accessibility.

By the 1960s the coefficient for initial size had dropped below significance, leaving county growth and accessibility. In the 1970s county growth continued to be important, but the accessibility variable dropped to insignificance, while the log initial size variable was again significant but with an opposite (negative) sign. Over this thirty-year period the multiple correlation coefficient dropped considerably from 0.52 in the 1950s to 0.33 in the 1970s. Thus, recent village growth appears to be less responsive to these factors than was true in earlier decades. This parallels findings with regression analyses using county population and net migration in previous studies of the nonmetropolitan turnaround (e.g., Heaton et al. 1981). Trends are not explained as well in the recent period with these indicators of position in the settlement hierarchy.

COUNTY GROWTH FACTOR ELABORATED

Throughout the preceding analysis, the importance of the county growth variable has been demonstrated. For each decade, as seen in Table 2-8, there is a positive association between county growth and village growth that is the strongest among the variables considered. By 1970–80, moreover, it is the only variable of the three that is particularly important in terms of the beta coefficients. This finding is consistent with a process of increasing social and economic interrelations among nearby population units, which is a rationale for metropolitan centered concepts such as the Urban Field (Friedmann and Miller 1965) or the Daily Urban System (Berry 1973). But in terms of population growth, the orientation here appears to be within the local area without regard for village accessibility to larger places.

This result indicates, however, that our examination of factors associated with village growth and decline should be extended to consider those elements that may contribute to county growth differentials. As noted before, it seems less likely that factors contributing to change in the village would lead to county change and more likely that the growth or decline of the county would affect the village or that external factors (since counties are hardly autonomous either) would contribute simultaneously to population change in the balance of the county and in the village. Although it is difficult to specify the precise causal process here, a better understanding of village population change should result by examining factors generally thought to be associated with county population change. Accordingly, we modified our model by replacing the county growth variable with several county-level characteristics that may affect the population growth and decline in villages as well as in the balance of the counties in which they are found.

Many variables have been considered to explain recent population changes for nonmetropolitan counties. A number are related to geographic location—that is, accessibility to metropolitan areas with resulting opportunities for greater social and economic interaction. The simple location variable included here is whether or not the county is adjacent to a 1960 SMSA. (Because it is highly correlated with and conceptually similar to metropolitan adjacency, the village accessibility variable has been omitted from this analysis.)

A major social trend in the United States since World War II has been the expansion and development of institutions of higher learning. Many of these institutions are located in nonmetropolitan areas and represent an important economic resource and potential stimulus for population growth. (Starting in 1950 students have been enumerated by the census where they are actually living, with those in dormitories counted there rather than at their home address.) Possible indirect effects of colleges and universities also should not be overlooked. These institutions have greatly increased the availability and quality of higher education in nonmetropolitan areas and have made the affected communities more attractive for further development.

Military activity was a major rural growth industry in the period following World War II. Military bases have been disproportionately located in nonmetropolitan areas, and they have employed many civilians as well as persons in the military. Since 1970 the number of armed forces personnel stationed in the United States declined about 20 percent. For the two earlier decades, however, we would expect our variable, presence of a military installation, to be positively associated with population change for nonmetropolitan counties.

As the demand for labor input in agriculture has decreased, nonmetropolitan counties with a high proportion of their work force employed in agriculture have tended to have substantial population loss. To a large extent this process appears to have run its course, as the number remaining in agriculture has shrunk to a small figure in most nonmetropolitan sections. We would expect the proportion employed in agriculture to be negatively associated with county growth but with a possible decline in the importance of this variable across the three decades.

Attracting new industry has generally been at the forefront of most community development programs aimed at reversing population decline (Summers et al. 1976). The decentralizing trend in U.S. manufacturing, particularly in the 1950s and the 1960s, has been a major factor in transforming the rural and small town economy. The percentage of the employed labor force in manufacturing industries is thus expected to be positively associated with population change.

An increasingly important activity in nonmetropolitan development has been the growth of recreation and retirement activities, often occurring together in the same localities. These are often referred to as "amenity" areas, usually having wilderness, mountains, lakes, seashores, or other attractive qualities. At least since Ullman's (1954) classic article on amenities, a physical setting conducive to recreation has been recognized as a factor in interregional population shifts. Whether growth in such areas represents a partial rejection of traditional economic incentives for movement in favor of migration to achieve a better quality of life, or whether this simply represents a new kind of economic development as part of our evolving service economy, is a matter of continuing debate (see Williams 1981; Heaton et al. 1981). Suffice it to say that increasing numbers of retired people are footloose, and many are choosing to move to more attractive areas. These are areas that also tend to attract many persons for vacations and recreation, so that an important secondary effect is the creation of new job opportunities in the service sector.

A completely satisfactory single variable to distinguish recreation and retirement counties is not available. Here we have taken the number of hotels and motels from the U.S. Censuses of Retail Trade for 1948, 1962, and 1972. These variables were regressed with the county population for 1950, 1960, and 1970, and counties were identified that had twice as many hotels and motels as one would predict on the basis of their population. Though some nonmetropolitan counties might have an unusual number of lodging places because of their location on transportation routes, most are, no doubt, in areas that attract a large number of visitors for recreation purposes. (Earlier work showed this variable not to be correlated with presence of an interstate highway (Fuguitt 1977).

Table 2-9 gives the results of the regression analysis with village population change on the county level factors and the log of village population size. For comparison, the right-hand panel shows the findings (leaving out log village size) with population change of the balance of the county as the dependent variable.

Location in a county adjacent to a metropolitan county was important for village growth in the 1950s but not in the two succeeding decades, paralleling the decline in the association of village growth with the accessibility score over the period. The first decade was also the time when the adjacency variable was most important in the regression with county growth (right-hand panel), and it too dropped to insignificance by 1970–80.

Presence of a college in the county has had no effect on growth for villages, though it was associated with county growth in the 1960–70 period, the time of major expansion of college enrollment throughout the country. The presence of a military population did associate with village growth in the 1950–60 period, when it also was most important as a variable positively associated with growth in the remainder of the county.

The results for percentage employed in agriculture show an interesting transition. For counties, this is an important variable negatively associated with growth. Contrary to expectations, its importance increased over the thirty-year period, although the shift of employment away from agriculture has meant that far fewer counties are highly dependent on this industry today. The county percentage employed in agriculture, however, was not associated with village growth until 1970–80, when it was also negatively associated. This indicates that until 1970 those villages serving as trade centers in agricultural counties were not more likely to decline in population (net of the other variables) even though such counties tended to be losing or growing less than other counties. Such a finding is consistent with a pattern of rural migration to population centers, including villages, in agricultural counties. By 1970–80, however, perhaps because of greater alternative growth opportunities for villages located elsewhere, villages in counties with high dependence on agriculture were more likely to decline or to grow less than other villages.

Table 2-9. Regressions of Annualized Village Population Change and County Population Change with County Independent Variables, 1950–60, 1960–70, 1970–80.

	Dependent Variables			
	Village Change		County Change[b]	
Independent Variables	b	Beta	b	Beta
1950–60				
Adjacent SMSA	8.47	0.17[a]	8.00	0.20[a]
College	2.85	0.03	3.25	0.05
Military	46.44	0.13[a]	114.06	0.42[a]
Percentage employed in agriculture	0.04	0.02	−0.26	−0.22[a]
Percentage employed in manufacturing	0.18	0.09	0.18	0.11[a]
Hotels	9.56	0.10[a]	9.93	0.14[a]
Log size	6.13	0.21[a]		
(Constant)	−45.64		0.54	
R	0.34		0.60	
R squared	0.11		0.37	
1960–70				
Adjacent SMSA	1.82	0.04	4.8	0.17[a]
College	5.15	0.06	10.24	0.21[a]
Military	12.28	0.04	17.26	0.09[a]
Percentage employed in agriculture	−0.13	−0.08	−0.29	−0.30[a]
Percentage employed in manufacturing	0.18	0.10[a]	0.23	0.21[a]
Hotels	1.11	0.01	6.33	0.15[a]
Log size	1.18	0.05		
(Constant)	−5.72		0.45	
R	0.19		0.59	
R squared	0.04		0.34	

Table 2-9. continued

Independent Variables	Dependent Variables			
	Village Change		County Change[b]	
	b	Beta	b	Beta
1970–80				
Adjacent SMSA	2.54	0.05	2.29	0.07
College	6.26	0.06	− 1.71	−0.03
Military	− 2.40	−0.01	− 20.76	−0.10[a]
Percentage employed in agriculture	− 0.37	−0.16[a]	− 0.54	−0.40[a]
Percentage employed in manufacturing	− 0.19	−0.09	− 0.03	−0.02
Hotels	8.29	0.10[a]	13.23	0.28[a]
Log size	− 2.56	−0.09[a]		
(Constant)	32.89		16.95	
R	0.22		0.47	
R squared	0.05		0.22	

[a]Significant at the 0.05 level.

[b]Annualized population change in county, with village, but excluding the village population.

Source: Compiled by authors.

The findings for manufacturing are parallel for counties and villages, with positive associations in the first two decades but not in the most recent one. In 1950–60 the coefficient for counties is significant, and that for villages approaches significance. In 1960–70 both village and county coefficients are significant and highest for the thirty-year period, whereas for 1970–80 the village coefficient is close to significance but with a negative sign.

The hotel variable indicates the importance of recreation for county growth throughout the period, with the value of the beta coefficient significant, and increasing from 0.14 to 0.28. This variable is less important for villages, with smaller betas significant only in 1950–60 and 1970–80.

In general, despite the high associations found between county growth and village growth in the preceding analysis, only some of the variables that were associated with county growth also were associated with village growth, and the proportion of variance explained for village growth is much less. Furthermore, the results were quite different from decade to decade, but this appears to reflect, at least in part, the transition in growth from the 1950s to the 1970s. In the 1950s level of dependence on agriculture was important for counties but not for villages, as already discussed. In the 1960s only manufacturing was significantly associated with village growth, whereas all variables were associated with county growth, and in the 1970s military had a significant negative coefficient for counties but not for villages. Much of the association found between the growth of villages and growth in the balance of their counties is apparently due to variables not measured here. Nevertheless, a comparison of the 1950s with the 1970s clearly reveals a shift away from urban hierarchy, metropolitan accessibility, and manufacturing variables that would be predicted to be important on the basis of classic settlement theory, with increased importance at the county level for the recreation variable.

GROWTH OF VILLAGES COMPARED TO OTHER POPULATION UNITS

By using a data file including the total population instead of our sample, it is possible to compare village growth with that for other population units. We compare growth "by place" (i.e., following the same places over time regardless of possible size-class changes) for nonmetropolitan incorporated centers 2,500 and over, and for those less than 2,500 at the beginning of a decade. Places not appearing in the subsequent census are excluded. Then the difference between these aggregate figures and the total population in nonmetropolitan areas gives the population outside incorporated places.

Table 2-10 shows the percentage change for places 2,500 and over, places less than 2,500, and the population outside such places for the United States over each of the past three decades. In order to guard against the results being explained by metropolitan spillover, the latest metropolitan definition is used, that for 1980. The results show a striking reversal of trends during the period. For 1950-60, metropolitan areas as a whole were growing fastest, followed by nonmetropolitan incorporated cities, and then incorporated villages under 2,500, with a 5 percent decline in the population living outside incorporated places. By the 1960s villages already were growing more rapidly than larger nonmetropolitan places, and the population outside places stabilized. Over the 1970–80 period the nonmetropolitan growth pattern had completely changed from the 1950–60 rank order, with the fastest growth outside incorporated places. Villages were then growing in the aggregate at a faster rate than the United States and metropolitan areas as a whole, and the population outside incorporated places was growing almost twice as fast as the nation as a whole. Not all of this "nonplace" population remained outside places or was even rural by 1980. Indeed, some was in 1980 urbanized areas, and some in places newly incorporated over the decade. Nevertheless, this is a remarkable transition, which must have important implications for the present and future role of the village in nonmetropolitan areas.

Table 2-10. Percentage Change in Metropolitan and Nonmetropolitan Incorporated Place and Nonplace Segments, United States, 1950–80.[a]

| | United States | Metro-politan | Nonmetropolitan | | |
			Total	Incorporated Places 2,500+	Incorporated Places LT2,500	Outside Incorporated Place
1950–60	18.5	26.0	1.7	13.3	6.3	− 5.1
1960–70	13.4	17.0	3.1	6.2	7.1	0.2
1970–80	11.4	10.3	15.1	7.7	12.4	20.7

[a]Metropolitan as of 1980.

Source: Compiled by authors.

ANOTHER VIEW: RESPONSES OF VILLAGE MAYORS

So far we have examined growth and decline by comparing the experiences of places distinguished by easily identifiable and readily available characteristics. This approach may lead to significant generalizations about villages in the changing rural and urban settlement structure, but of necessity lacks both the fine texture of what is happening in these places and the subjective element that can be obtained only by getting the reactions of community residents. As explained in Chapter 1, we have supplemented our analysis of secondary sources, such as U.S. census and Dun and Bradstreet data, with a telephone survey of mayors (or comparable officials) representing a subsample of 100 of our villages. We asked them, among other things, their views about population change and the causes of growth and decline. We complete this chapter, then, by reporting on information obtained in these interviews for the eighteen villages with the largest declines (5 percent or more) and the twenty with the largest gains (24 percent or more) over the 1970–80 decade.

Decline

Our analysis of decliners reveals a diversity of conditions and purported factors contributing to these declines. In fourteen of the eighteen villages, the officials interviewed perceived a decline. Of these, several reported simply outmigration of young people for jobs. Some more specific reasons given for lack of jobs included commuting distance, competition with larger places, problems in farming including the high cost of land, and school closures. Respondents from the declining places indicated that even though younger people were moving out, elderly people were moving in (one reported "lower taxes" and others "recreation and elderly housing" as primary reasons). All of these places had populations of less than 1,000 in 1980 and had experienced population declines of between 5 and 35 percent over 1970–80.

In all cases but one, retail activity either remained stable or declined. Generally, however, services in some way expanded in most of these places losing population, often in two or more services (i.e., water, fire protection, sewer, police). About half these decliners, however, reported a worsening financial situation: "tax base declining," "more low income people," "village worse off financially," and so forth. Five places indicated they were engaged in various activities to encourage investments in their villages, two of which have gained small manufacturers. (See Chapter 7.)

As would be expected from the preceding analysis, the declining places in this subsample tend to be small, remote, and in counties high in agricultural employment. For four of the five declining places over 1,000 in size, measurement of growth appears to be a problem; although they show a population decline according to census figures, they are purported by their mayors to be growing but outside their city limits. These larger declining places tend to have high accessibility scores and report a variety of increases in activities such as tourism and industry.

Growth

In reviewing the mayors' responses, there appear to be two categories of factors for growing villages, which could be termed, respectively, "consumptive" and "productive" advantages. The former includes the aesthetic and consumptive economic attractiveness of small towns, while the latter is related to the growth of industries and, hence, employment in or near these towns. On the whole, the twenty rapidly growing villages tend to fall into one category or the other.

Within the first category, villages are experiencing inmigration from rural and urban areas: Those from the rural areas are "retiring farmers," and those from urban areas are typically the elderly and young families, although some report that all ages are moving in "from everywhere." Reasons cited for the influx of new residents include: better or cheaper housing, lower taxes, better schools, local recreational opportunities, and escape from the ills of urban life. Of the twenty growing villages, ten mayors attributed their growth to these consumptive advantages.

The second category, consisting of the remaining ten cases, attributed their population increases primarily to increasing employment opportunities. Of the cases in this category, three experienced new or expanding activities in energy (in the West and Midwest) near their villages. In each of the cases in the South (four), the expansion of job opportunities was due to new garment manufacture. These villages apparently draw migrants from the surrounding rural areas and cite availability of highly skilled labor (usually women) as the main attraction for these industries. Two of these villages also reported migration from urban areas due to consumptive advantages, especially recreation. One village (in California) reported the opening of a poultry processing plant employing 3,000 new workers, and all of the inmigration reported was of a minority population.

SUMMARY AND CONCLUSIONS

This analysis of the 1950–80 period clearly demonstrates that villages have been part of the nonmetropolitan population turnaround. In the

1970s two-thirds of these incorporated places having less than 2,500 population grew, whereas only one-half grew during the 1950s. This is not due to the spread of new metropolitan areas or exclusively to spillover of activity from metropolitan areas. Moreover, the increase in levels of village growth appears to be widespread across the country, though it is not reflected in the North region (east of the Mississippi) as a whole.

We examined how population growth relates to the local and regional circumstance of the village by considering four basic factors: regional location, county growth, village accessibility to larger centers, and village initial size. There are increasing regional differences in growth levels, although the ranking of regions by growth has shifted to follow differentials for total population growth in 1970–80, with the West highest, followed by the South, Plains, and North in that order. Regional differences were statistically significant in only one decade, however, net of size, location, and county growth.

County growth was the most important variable in association with village growth across the three decades, and its importance relative to the remaining two variables (initial size and accessibility) appears to be increasing. Thus, though villages are often singled out as having particular problems in struggling for survival, they have at least over the past thirty years tended to share in the growth experiences of their surrounding areas. Nearness to larger cities was an important factor promoting growth in the 1950s and 1960s throughout most of the country, but this was not true in the 1970s.

Larger villages have had higher growth levels than smaller ones for many decades. This trend appeared to be slowing down when the 1960s were compared with the 1950s (Fuguitt and Beale 1976), and there is evidence here that overall this association reversed direction in the most recent decade.

Has the structure of village growth changed? Certainly in terms of the variables considered here. The last decade differed from the others in terms of region, with the strong growth increase in western villages, in the decline in the importance of accessibility and the reversal of the size of place—growth relationship. All of these are in the direction of overall deconcentration, the hallmark of the new nonmetropolitan population trend.

The rather consistent importance of county growth in these findings indicated the need to interrelate village growth with factors previously employed to explore levels of nonmetropolitan county growth in recent decades. Only some of the variables that were associated with county growth also were associated with village growth, and these differed by decade. There was, however, a shift away from urban-metropolitan hierarchy variables and level of manufacturing activity during the period, with the 1950s growth differentials largely consistent with traditional settlement theory, and the 1970s consistent with the new turnaround pattern.

Finally, there is the interesting finding that, although the association between initial size and overall growth shifts from positive to negative, Figure 2-5 reveals that the distribution of places across size groups by growth levels has a different relationship for the proportion of villages that are rapid decliners than for the proportion of rapid growers. This suggests that there may be different change processes for growing than for declining places. We calculated separate correlations and regressions for growing and for declining places (not shown) and confirmed the association between level of change and initial size noted in Figure 2-5—that is, a shift from positive to negative for growers but a continued positive association for decliners across the three decades.

Evidently, the long-standing centralization process whereby population change results in concentration in larger villages now applies primarily to situations where there is decline. Declining places are perhaps more likely not to have reasons for existence beyond central place retail activities (as in counties highly dependent on agriculture) and possibly manufacturing. This would result in a decline pattern favoring larger villages.

On the other hand, nonmetropolitan growth in the most recent decades was not associated so much with central place structure, since it was dispersed in nature, relating to factors such as recreation, energy development, and extended commuting, and was more likely to be found in nonagricultural counties. Smaller places might be more attractive to newcomers than larger ones, particularly if the primary reason for growth is to serve as residential centers in a general setting of population expansion. Indeed in a growth turnaround situation, smaller places that may have formerly declined could have more available housing and land for residential expansion. Recent related research has shown that some organizational impacts of population change processes are different for growing and declining nonmetropolitan counties and cities (Fuguitt and Kasarda 1981; Johnson 1982). We need to give more consideration to contrasts between growing and declining places and areas.

Another perspective was gained by telephone interviews with

mayors of twenty rapidly growing and eighteen declining villages. This detailed information is difficult to generalize but highlights the varied nature of local situations. The importance of what we have called "consumptive" growth factors reported for half of the rapid growers should perhaps be mentioned again, since it is consistent with the importance of amenity variables noted in much research on the nonmetropolitan turnaround (Heaton et al. 1981; L. Long and DeAre 1980). The fact that several larger declining places were actually in growth areas but were unable to annex lends a caution to the interpretation of our results, though it is difficult to hypothesize a plausible pattern of changing differentials in annexation that would substantially modify the findings discussed above. The findings are clear for villages as political units, but in general the more rapid nonmetropolitan growth outside incorporated places rather than inside is a most significant aspect of the turnaround.

A basic conclusion of this research is that the traditional structural correlates of village growth have been modified and are together no longer as important as they once were. At the same time one of these, county growth, has increased its relative importance. These indicators of the villages position in the settlement structure previously revealed a growth pattern for villages consistent with metropolitan and urban concentration. By 1970–80 this was no longer true except perhaps in the situation of population decline. The lowered multiple correlations indicate that the population fortunes of villages are tied less to their position in the urban/metropolitan hierarchy and more to local areas and individual characteristics that may make them more attractive to growth. This is part of a contemporary situation of widespread population deconcentration in which increasing numbers of people have a broader range of choice in deciding where to live.

An inference from these results is that the new patterns and increased village growth tendencies are being accompanied by change in the functions these places perform in the settlement system. As will be documented in succeeding chapters, there has been a notable shift away from trade center activities, but continued population growth appears to reflect increased functioning as residential communities. The apparent deconcentration of manufacturing even into remote locations also is evidently leading to increase in the village role relating to this activity. The increase in manufacturing and other related economic activities also is following a pattern more independent of the urban hierarchy than before—that is, not necessarily in counties already high in manufacturing employment (Till 1981;

L. Long and DeAre 1982). The mayors' survey illustrates the diffuse nature of contemporary settlement, in that only 15 percent of the mayors reported that most residents worked in their communities. At the same time, many of those villages with a high proportion of residents commuting elsewhere to work probably had industries that also attracted commuters from outside.

This leaves us with a final question. We have shown that villages are reviving in many areas, even if this is not the case for all of them everywhere. Yet the pattern of growth has changed, consistent with the overall turnaround process, suggesting that villages are growing as part of a general spread of deconcentrated settlement. Does this mean that some have lost or are losing many of the qualities that differentiate them from other units? These villages remain political units, but our findings here at least bring to mind the possibility that many could become more like some incorporated centers in metro-politan fringe areas—politically autonomous to a degree but almost functionally undifferentiated from their setting.

NOTES

1. Most of the theory and interpretations of population redistribution concerns migration, although a population also changes due to its levels of fertility and mortality. Unfortunately, there is no satisfactory way to estimate natural increase (births minus deaths) for these individual villages and separate a component for net migration. We must deal only with total population change, but it nevertheless seems likely that most of the variation in levels of growth among villages is due to different levels of net migration. For nonmetropolitan counties the correlation of total growth with net migration is high for all three decades. Also, natural increase would tend to work against a shift of places from decline to growth, since declines in population due to previous out-migration usually leave an older population having fewer births and more deaths. Of course, the migration of young people into an area may well have the effect of raising natural increase and so contribute to further growth.

2. The annualized measure of population change per 1,000 is based on the continuous compound interest formula $\ln(Pn/Po)/10 \times 1,000$, where $\ln$ is the natural logarithm, Pn and Po are end and beginning population values respectively, and 10 is the number of years between censuses. The results are in magnitude very close to a decade percentage change, but with the denominator equal to the mid-decade population rather than

the initial population. Consequently, such a measure does not exaggerate large changes from small bases and should be preferable to simple percent change for these small population unithe outcome was essentially no different from that reported in Table 2-8.

3. To make sure extreme cases were not affecting results unduly, we ran these regressions with the few cases growing more than 100 percent in a decade removed. The outcome was essentially no different from that reported in Table 2-8.

3 THE SOCIAL CHARACTERISTICS OF VILLAGES

INTRODUCTION

The comparative analysis of social and economic characteristics can provide a better understanding of villages and their place in the settlement system. Demographic characteristics such as age, sex, household composition, and migration give insight into the social structures of such communities and may well reflect past population growth and decline processes through natural increase and migration. Socioeconomic variables, such as those relating to education and income, provide objective social indicators of the "social well-being" or "quality of life" in these communities. Information on employment activity gives an indication of the economic roles of villagers, suggests level of well-being, and, to the extent residence and place of work coincide, reflects the economic functions of these small population units.

In this chapter we consider the 1970 social and economic characteristics of people living in incorporated villages and differentiated, in turn, by position in the settlement hierarchy, location with respect to larger places, and population change pattern over the past two decades. This approach, which is in the tradition of comparative community analysis, should contribute to our understanding of the nature of life in villages and the place of the village in the settlement structure of the nation. Although there have been similar analyses for cities and counties, the relevant information is not readily available for small villages, so these units have generally been neglected.

The results are presented in three sections. In the first we compare the village to other residence categories that together approximate a size of place or level of urbanization distinction for the nation. Many studies have compared places along the urban hierarchy, for example, in order to get a better understanding of the consequences of size and density for social structure and economic organization. To the extent that the urban hierarchy reflects a functional hierarchy, as in the central place or human ecological tradition, one also would expect systematic differences in the characteristics of residents. Indeed, Duncan et al. (1960) listed the study of correlates of community size as one of the three main empirical approaches to understanding the hierarchical aspects of systems of cities. Interest in this issue has been rekindled with the new population trends, as in concern about the amenities and disamenities of large size (Alonso 1973; Hoch 1976; Puryear 1977; Appelbaum 1978). Duncan and Reiss (1956), however, are almost alone in including villages in these comparisons, having examined a wide range of 1950 population characteristics for a set of size groupings that included incorporated places under 1,000 and places 1,000–2,500. Using unpublished census data, Fuguitt (1968) compared our basic sample of villages with nonmetropolitan urban and rural components on some 1960 population and housing characteristics, such as age, household composition, and housing quality. These studies generally revealed an intermediate position for the village between the urban and rural segments of the population on most characteristics.

In the second section we examine differences among villages in terms of the two additional basic properties, location with respect to larger centers and population growth and decline, and extend this in the third section to consider the nonmetropolitan turnaround. Again we must note that prior research in this vein related to the village is very limited. Location, however, has been an important dimension in the study of cities and counties. The activities and characteristics of a local community are thought to be influenced not only by its immediate vicinity but by its location with respect to cities of various sizes. Much work has focused on the place of nonmetropolitan places or counties in the wider metropolitan community (to name only a few: Bogue 1949; Duncan et al. 1960; Hathaway et al. 1968; Frisbie and Poston 1975, 1976). Hines, Brown, and Zimmer (1975) compared nonmetropolitan counties classed both by adjacency to a metropolitan area and level of local urbanization. We have already noted that prior to 1970–80, location near large cities has been associated with greater growth for small towns. Fuguitt (1968) also contrasted selected population characteristics of U.S. villages by metropolitan accessibility, as did Fuguitt and Field (1972) for Wisconsin.

In Chapter 2 we gave considerable attention to population growth and decline of villages as a dependent variable. A central problem in the comparative analysis of communities is to determine characteristics associated with population change experience. Studies comparing the characteristics of growing and declining cities include Ogburn (1937), Wu (1945), and Duncan and Reiss (1956). More recently, Brown (1976) contrasted growing and declining counties. Previous studies concerned with villages include Jenkins (1940), who contrasted the 1930 population characteristics of growing and declining agricultural villages for the Brunner sample of 140 such places; Fuguitt (1968), who examined U.S. villages in terms of 1960 age, sex, household composition, and housing; and Fuguitt and Field (1972), who studied villages in Wisconsin (the latter work considered size of place, location, and growth simultaneously in a cross-classification).

These sections of the chapter, then, represent the first effort to contrast a complete array of social and economic characteristics of U.S. growing and declining villages also classified by their location relative to larger cities. Further, by comparing places that changed growth patterns over the past two decades with those that did not, we can determine whether the characteristics of villages that are newly starting population growth are like those already growing or whether they are different in ways that reflect an alteration in overall growth processes.

DATA AND PROCEDURES

Unfortunately, 1980 characteristics data for U.S. villages are not yet available. To get 1970 characteristics data for villages we utilized the special version of the U.S. census fifth count summary tape for enumeration districts. We selected enumeration districts corresponding to (1) all incorporated places with less than 2,500 population in 1970 and located outside 1970 SMSA counties, and (2) all places that are members of the original village sample used in this research.

Recall that the sample includes places under 2,500 in 1960 nonmetro-politan areas, so it was selected from a universe almost identical to (1) above. The distributions by various characteristics for the two data sets were very similar, which confirms the representativeness of the sample of villages.

These census data are based on samples of households within enumeration districts, and given the small size of each unit it would not be appropriate to compare individual villages as was done in Chapter 2. In aggregate form, however, the data are comparable to information published in census volumes for the other population segments considered here.

Since the primary purpose of the first part of the analysis is to identify the position of the village in relation to other population classes in a settlement hierarchy, we simply aggregated the whole set of villages and summed the frequency in each variable category for the total group. These totals could then be compared with aggregated totals for the other segments considered, which were published in the 1970 census. Village totals were subtracted from the published rural nonfarm figures to yield a "nonvillage nonfarm" segment. Of the village population considered here, 98 percent is rural nonfarm.

For the second part of the analysis, enumeration district character-istics data were obtained for the 572 sample villages in 1960 nonmetro-politan areas and were aggregated for eight groups of these villages differentiated by 1960–70/1970–80 growth patterns (grow-grow, grow-decline, decline-grow, decline-decline) and whether they were above or below the median accessibility score.

Because of the large number of comparisons involved in these procedures and in the second part, the complex sample both of villages and households within villages, tests of significance have not been employed. Consequently, small differences between groups of villages should be interpreted with caution, particularly if they are not consistent with an overall pattern of results.

VILLAGES IN THE SETTLEMENT HIERARCHY

Here we consider the demographic, socioeconomic, and employment characteristics of the U.S. population by type of residence.[1] People living in nonmetropolitan incorporated places under 2,500 are com-pared with those in nonmetropolitan nonfarm, rural farm, and urban locations, along with metropolitan residents as a whole, using the

1970 Standard Metropolitan Statistical Area designation. The categories thus describe a kind of urban-metropolitan hierarchy, from metropolitan, to nonmetropolitan urban, village, nonvillage nonfarm, and rural farm, which will be examined in the sections to follow.

Demographic Characteristics

The most unique village characteristic is the predominance of older residents. Figures 3–1 and 3–2 show that villages have a higher proportion of older people than the metropolitan population or the nonmetropolitan urban, nonvillage nonfarm, or rural farm segments. There is a corresponding relative deficiency of village dwellers age 15 to 45 in comparison with all residence groups except the rural farm. Figure 3–2 shows that the 1970 rural farm age structure was very distorted, with concentration in the years 10–20 and 45–65, and deficiencies elsewhere.

Figure 3–1. Distribution by Age for Residence Groups, United States, 1970.

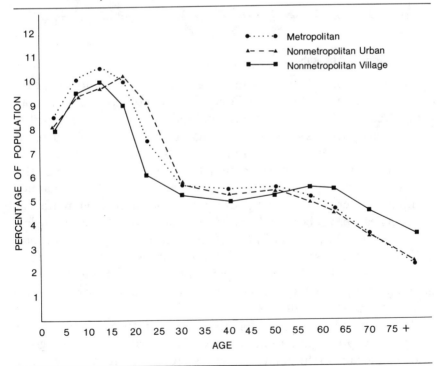

Source: Compiled by authors.

Figure 3–2. Distribution by Age for Nonmetropolitan Residence Groups, United States, 1970.

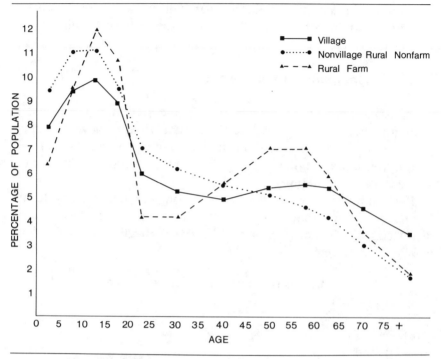

Source: Compiled by authors.

The surplus of older people in villages has long been noted. Years ago, T. Lynn Smith (1942) listed one of the functions of the village as being "America's Old Folks' Home." Other writers have noted a tendency for farmers to move to an agricultural service center upon retirement (Nelson 1961; Nesmith 1963). Undoubtedly, this is the reason for much of the concentration, but another reason must be the movement of younger people away from many villages. The dynamics of this are better understood by considering age-specific net migration rates. These have been calculated for the 1960–70 period using villages grouped by levels of 1960–70 population change and graphed in Figure 3–3.[2] We see that even declining villages give evidence of net migration gain for the elderly and that all but the most rapidly growing group of villages experienced net migration loss of young adults age 20–24 in 1970.

Data from the census question on residence in 1965 may be used to compare the proportional importance of recent migrants among the residence groups. Although differences are not great, it is seen that

Figure 3–3.   Net Migration Rates by Age for Village Categories of Population Change, 1960–70.

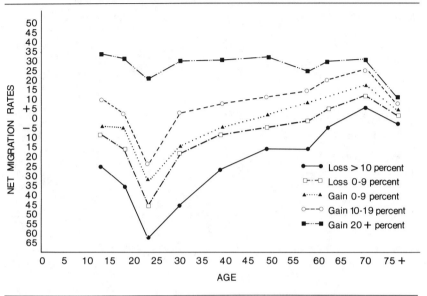

Source: Compiled by authors.

villages had a slightly lower proportion of newcomers from a different county or persons living in a different house in the same county than other groups except for rural farm. The farm category, however, shows the major difference among the groups, with very low levels of inmigration and local movement. This is consistent with the older age structures noted above for villages and farms, with the likelihood that farmers are homeowners and have a considerable investment in their farms, and with the fact that the number employed in farming was dropping rapidly at that time.

The proportion of primary individuals was highest in villages, according to Table 3–1. A primary individual in 1970 was a household head living alone or with another unrelated person. Also, the population per household was lowest—2.9—for the village. It appears very likely that these findings are associated with the high proportion of older people living in villages, although family and household data cross-classified by age are not available. Also, the proportion of people living in group quarters—that is, inmates of institutions, dormitories, and so forth (not shown)—was lowest in the village and rural farm segments and highest in the nonmetropolitan urban category.

Table 3-1. Demographic Variables by Residence Group, United States, 1970.

Demographic Variables		Nonmetropolitan			
	Metropolitan Total	Urban	Village	Nonvillage Nonfarm	Rural Farm
Different county in 1965 (percentage)[a]	20	23	18	19	7
Different house in 1965 (percentage)[a]	45	47	41	43	21
Primary individuals (percentage)	6	7	8	4	3
Population/household	3.1	3.0	2.9	3.4	3.4
Families with female head (percentage)	12	11	10	8	5
Families with children age less than 18 (percentage)	56	54	50	57	50
Children ever born[b]	3.0	3.2	3.4	3.5	3.7

[a]Population five years or more in 1970.

[b]Per woman 35-44 ever married.

Source: Compiled by authors.

The percentage of families having a female head displays a regular gradient that is highest in the metropolitan and lowest in the rural farm segment. The percentage of families having young children was highest in the nonfarm and low in the village and rural farm categories. This must reflect the concentration of older adults in the latter groups, for rural farm fertility was the highest and the bottom line of Table 3-1 shows a regular gradient down to the metropolitan segment, as measured by the number of children ever born per woman age 35-44 ever married. (Recent work on the latter relationship includes Rice and Beegle 1972 and Slesinger 1974.)

Socioeconomic Variables

The first row of Table 3-2 gives the proportion of persons age 25 and over who completed twelve years of school. Here villages stand midway between other rural and the urban and metropolitan categories. The next two rows show school attendance and employment data for young men age 16–21 years. The percentage of this group enrolled in school was lowest in the nonvillage nonfarm and next lowest in the village category. There is an inverse ranking (not shown) in the proportion of those not attending who did not graduate from high school. Thus the percentage of males age 16–21 who are high school dropouts was 16 in villages, 23 in nonvillage nonfarm, 13 in farm, 8 in nonmetropolitan urban, and 9 in the metropolitan group. To compound the problem, higher rates of unemployment were generally found in the three nonmetropolitan rural segments for

Table 3-2. Socioeconomic Variables by Residence Group, United States, 1970.

Socioeconomic Variables		Nonmetropolitan			
	Metropolitan Total	Urban	Village	Nonvillage Nonfarm	Rural Farm
Completing 12 years of school (percentage)[a]	55	52	45	37	41
Males 16–21 in school (percentage)	77	78	63	57	67
Other males 16–21 unemployed (percentage)[b]	25	22	28	32	27
Family median income	$10,474	$ 8,573	$ 7,418	$ 7,477	$ 6,720
Family income less than $5,000 (percentage)	13	24	31	31	36
Family income $12,000 up (percentage)	40	27	19	20	20
In poverty (percentage) total	11	16	19	22	20
Less than 65	11	14	16	21	20
65 and over	23	32	40	31	26

[a]Percentage of those 25 years up.

[b]Percentage of males 16–21 not in school who are unemployed.

Source: Compiled by authors.

males age 16–21 and not in school, whether or not they graduated from high school (line 3 of Table 3–2). Approximately 40 percent of the male school dropouts age 16–21 was unemployed in rural segments.

In terms of family income, a gradient from metropolitan down to rural farm prevails, except that the village appears to be slightly below the nonvillage nonfarm category. The median income for villages and for nonfarm was $3,000 less than the metropolitan total; moreover, the proportion of village and nonfarm families earning less than $5,000 was twice that of the metropolitan group, and the proportion earning more than $12,000 was one-half that for metropolitan residents according to Table 3–2. The positive association of income with city size has received considerable attention in the recent literature. According to one perspective, not universally accepted, this is compensation for the disamenities of living and working in larger places. Studies have indicated that differences in the cost of living do not completely explain the differential (see review and discussion in Puryear 1977).

The 1970 census included a classification of the population by poverty status. This poverty classification was based upon income thresholds adjusted for factors such as family size, sex of family head, number of children under age 18, and farm and nonfarm residence. (For details see U.S. census 1972.) To adjust for differences in the cost of living the poverty thresholds for farm families were set at 85 percent of nonfarm families within each of the other factor levels. One could argue, of course, that the cost of living in most nonmetropolitan villages is also lower than that in cities or metropolitan areas. No doubt a completely satisfactory measure of poverty to use for comparisons among residence categories as in this study is not yet available. Nevertheless, results using the census poverty classification are worth our attention.

The percentage of persons in poverty was lowest for the two more urban groups and highest for the rural groupings topped by the nonvillage nonfarm segment. The bottom rows of the table show the proportion of persons in poverty separately for two age groups. Of significance here is the finding that 40 percent of the village dwellers 65 and over were classed as in poverty, by far the highest among the residence groups. Not only was the village outstanding in the proportion of persons over 65, but it had the highest proportion of this age group below the census poverty threshold in the table. Subsequently the overall proportion of the elderly in poverty has dropped from 25 in 1970 to 15 percent in 1979 (U.S. Bureau of the Census, 1981: 448). It remains to be seen whether the relative concentration of such people in villages has continued through 1980.

Economic Activity

The percentage of males in the labor force was lowest in the village category, which one suspects was due to the higher proportion of people there of retirement age (see Table 3-3). Despite a deficiency of young adults, the rural farm male percentage was high—next to the metropolitan total—but this is not surprising since farmers leaving

Table 3-3. Economic Activity by Residence Group, United States, 1970.

Economic Activity		Nonmetropolitan			
	Metropolitan Total	Urban	Village	Nonvillage Nonfarm	Rural Farm
In labor force					
(16 years and over)					
Males (percentage)	78.3	73.8	70.6	71.4	76.3
Females (percentage)	42.8	41.8	37.8	36.0	29.2
Employed by occupation		Percentage Distribution			
Prof, technical, manager, clerical	44.6	39.6	33.9	28.3	16.9
Sales	7.6	7.2	5.7	4.7	2.8
Service workers	12.6	15.1	15.0	12.1	7.2
Craftsmen, operators	29.9	32.0	36.0	42.0	22.5
Farmers and farm labors	1.1	1.4	3.9	5.4	47.3
Laborers, nonfarm	4.2	4.7	5.5	6.5	3.3
TOTAL EMPLOYED	100.0	100.0	100.0	100.0	100.0
Employed by industry		Percentage Distribution			
Manufacturing, durable	16.0	13.0	12.6	16.6	8.2
Manufacturing, not durable	9.8	12.1	11.2	15.3	7.6
Wholesale, retail trade	20.7	21.5	21.5	16.8	9.5
Service industries	33.4	31.4	28.0	22.4	15.0
Other	20.1	22.0	26.7	28.9	59.7
TOTAL EMPLOYED	100.0	100.0	100.0	100.0	100.0

Source: Compiled by authors.

the labor force are likely to leave the rural farm category as well, even if they do not change their residences. The percentage of females in the labor force is a regular gradient, by level of urbanization, with the biggest difference being between rural farm women at the low end and the other categories. The village percentage, 37.8, is five points below the metropolitan total and approximately nine above the rural farm.

The occupational distribution for both sexes combined shows rather orderly gradients from rural to metropolitan (second panel of Table 3–3). Unfortunately, data on occupation or industry are not available by sex for villages. The two white collar occupation groupings at the top of the panel have the highest proportion in the metropolitan group and lowest in the rural farm. The two blue collar groupings (craftsmen; operators and nonfarm laborers) have the highest proportion in the rural nonfarm and lowest in the rural farm with metropolitan next lowest. The farm occupation categories are highest in the rural farm, as expected, and lowest in the metropolitan group. Service workers are an exception to the gradient, being highest in villages and nonmetropolitan urban places. Nevertheless, in terms of concentration in higher status occupations, the village is in the middle, between the nonvillage rural nonfarm and the urban and metropolitan categories. Worth noting also is the fact that less than one-half of the employed persons who lived on farms listed farming as their major occupation. The census rural farm classification, including everyone who lives on a farm, is far from a homogeneous grouping of full-time commercial farm operators and their families.

Differences between residence groups are less systematic by industry than by occupation (third panel of Table 3–3). Contrary to the assumption that industrialization is closely tied to urbanization and metropolitan development, the proportion employed in manufacturing was five percentage points higher in the nonvillage nonfarm than in any other category. As a precurser of the nonmetropolitan turnaround, there was a significant expansion of nonmetropolitan manufacturing employment in the 1960–70 period, and much of this was located outside cities (Till 1981). The village was almost as high as the metropolitan and urban nonmetropolitan groups in this proportion, but the rural farm was considerably lower. There was a difference in manufacturing employment between metropolitan and nonmetropolitan, in that 37 percent of metropolitan residents employed in manufacturing were in nondurable products, whereas this was true for approximately 48 percent of those in manufacturing in the four nonmetropolitan residence groupings.

The village was highest, along with nonmetropolitan cities, in the percentage employed in wholesale and retail trade. Retail trade is, of course, a major function of most villages. The service industries, such as finance, insurance, real estate and business, and repair services, do show regular gradients, with few exceptions, from rural farm up to metropolitan, both individually and in the combined group shown here. The "other industries" category includes agriculture and shows a reverse gradient between residence groups, with more than one-half of the employed rural farm persons included in this grouping.

VILLAGE CHARACTERISTICS BY ACCESSIBILITY AND GROWTH

Having compared the population characteristics of villages with other population settlement types, the remaining task is to consider groups of villages that differ in terms of accessibility and population growth experience. For this section and the one to follow, we return to the original sample of U.S. villages as our data base. They have been sorted by the four 1960–70/1970–80 growth patterns and dichotomized approximately on the median of the accessibility score used in Chapter 2. Table 3-4 gives the number of villages in each cell, the aggregate populations, and the mean size of village. (The fifth count aggregations deviate slightly from the complete counts shown here because the former source is based on household sample data.) We see that the populations in these cells are reasonably large, so that sampling variability should not be a problem in interpreting the results at least for moderate-size differences.

The third panel of the table shows there are considerable differences among the cells in the average size of villages. Because of the large number of comparisons involved and the small cell sizes that would result, we did not further subdivide the villages so as to control for size. With this broad approach, made necessary by the nature of the data, we must be cautious about assuming that any differential characteristics found are primarily consequences of urban accessibility or growth and decline. But we can say something about what accessible, growing, declining, and turnaround places are like, including the fact that accessible places, and growing places over the first ten-year period, were on the average larger in size in 1970 than those in the other groups.

Table 3–4.   Number of Villages, Total Populations, and Mean Village Size, Sample Villages by Growth and Location.[a]

	GG	DG	GD	DD	TOTAL
		1960–80 Growth Patterns			
Number of Villages	203	154	89	106	552
Accessible	127	61	54	33	275
Not accessible	76	93	35	73	277
Total Population	199,739	80,311	71,805	62,902	414,757
Accessible	127,910	34,808	42,781	22,284	227,783
Not accessible	71,829	45,503	29,024	40,618	186,974
Mean Village Size	984	522	807	593	751
Accessible	1,007	571	792	675	828
Not accessible	945	489	829	556	675

[a]Includes villages under 2,500 in 1960 and reported in censuses of 1970 and 1980.

Source: Compiled by authors.

The results of the classification for selected population characteristics are given in Table 3–5. We will begin by comparing villages of sustained growth (column 1) with those experiencing chronic decline (column 4) at the same time, classified by their accessibility to larger places. In addition to percentages, Table 3–5 gives average difference scores in order to summarize the effects. Differences in accessibility are averaged for the GG and DD groups for the first score, and differences between the GG and DD groups are averaged across accessible and nonaccessible situations for the second. Separate averages are reported for accessible and nonaccessible villages in the two instances where the growth difference was not consistent. In general, accessibility is more important than growth in distinguishing different levels of the social and economic characteristics considered here.

Sustained growth villages (column 1) have a higher proportion of young people than corresponding villages with extended decline (column 4), and for both of these categories accessible villages have a higher proportion of young people than those that are not accessible. The pattern for those age 18–64 is similar, but these relations are reversed for the percentage age 65 and over, with higher proportions in nonaccessible than accessible villages and in declining villages compared with those that continued to grow.

Since migration is the major determinant of whether a village grows or declines and is usually selective on the basis of age, one would expect growth to have more impact on age structure than location. Indeed, this was found by Fuguitt and Field (1972) for Wisconsin villages in 1960.

Inspection of the table, however, indicates that whereas the growth differences are consistent across the accessibility levels, they are more pronounced for nonaccessible villages. Evidently, decline in accessible locations is not accompanied by the characteristic migration selectivity leading to an older age structure even to the extent shown by nonaccessible villages that have grown over the past two decades.

Educational attainment for the population age 25 and over is measured as before by the percentage completing twelve or more years of school (usually equivalent to graduating from high school). There is a growth effect but a larger positive accessibility effect. Since older people generally have less education and declining and remote villages generally have more older people, these results are partly, but evidently not entirely, due to differences in age structure, as evidenced by a standardization procedure.[3]

Villages in nonaccessible areas have a considerably higher proportion of people with annual incomes of less than $5,000 and a somewhat lower proportion with annual incomes $12,000 and over as of 1970. Generally also places growing over the twenty-year period have higher income patterns than those declining, a finding consistent with virtually all research on growing and declining communities cited previously. But an exception here is that growing remote villages have a higher proportion at the poverty level (less than $5,000 annual income) than declining remote villages. No reason for this small exception is evident, but it at least suggests that growing remote places may have more income inequality than other areas and brings to mind some of the reservations that have been expressed about the presumed benefits of rural economic development for the general population (Whiting 1974a; Summers et al. 1976; Lonsdale and Seyler 1979).

Labor force participation of men and women is higher in the accessible villages and in growing villages. The accessibility effect is larger for men than women, but the growth effect is about the same for both sexes. The percentage in white collar occupations (professional and technical, managerial, clerical) is higher in growing places, as has been found in prior research (see Fuguitt and Kasarda 1981), but it is also higher in remote rather than accessible locations. The

Table 3–5. Village Population Characteristics by Growth Patterns and Accessibility.

	1960–80 Growth Patterns				GG–DD Comparisons[a] Average Difference	
	GG	DG	GD	DD	Accessibility	Growth
Percentage less than 18						
Accessible	34.0	31.3	34.9	33.8	1.9	1.3
Not accessible	33.2	32.0	34.9	30.8		
Percentage 18–64						
Accessible	53.0	50.1	51.5	52.5	1.7	0.6
Not accessible	51.4	47.7	48.5	50.8		
Percentage 65 and over						
Accessible	13.0	18.6	13.6	13.7	− 3.6	− 1.9
Not accessible	15.4	20.3	16.8	18.4		
Percentage 12 or more years schooling						
Accessible	48.4	42.2	45.7	47.2	6.3	2.0
Not accessible	42.9	42.8	42.7	40.1		
Percentage families income less than $5,000						
Accessible	24.9	30.9	23.9	25.2	−10.0	− 0.3
Not accessible	35.8	39.3	40.0	34.2		1.6
Percentage families income $12,000 up						
Accessible	22.8	19.4	23.9	20.0	5.6	1.8
Not accessible	16.2	12.5	14.5	15.4		
Percentage males in labor force						
Accessible	73.9	69.0	74.0	73.3	5.1	2.5
Not accessible	70.7	64.7	63.2	66.4		
Percentage females in labor force						
Accessible	39.6	37.5	39.5	38.9	1.7	2.1
Not accessible	39.3	33.0	39.5	35.9		

Table 3-5. continued

| | 1960–80 Growth Patterns | | | | GG–DD Comparisons[a] Average Difference | |
	GG	DG	GD	DD	Accessibility	Growth
Percentage professional, technical, manager, clerical						
Accessible	33.5	31.2	30.9	30.9	− 1.8	2.6
Not accessible	35.3	33.4	37.4	32.7		
Percentage in manufacturing, durable						
Accessible	14.6	17.3	18.1	23.2	10.7	− 4.8
Not accessible	7.7	7.1	6.4	8.7		
Percentage in manufacturing, not durable						
Accessible	13.4	10.4	17.5	12.0	1.3	2.1
Not accessible	12.8	6.2	4.3	10.1		
Percentage in wholesale, retail trade						
Accessible	21.1	21.2	18.0	20.0	− 2.0	0.7
Not accessible	22.7	23.1	23.9	22.4		
Percentage in service industries						
Accessible	26.7	26.3	24.7	23.5	− 3.7	3.2
Not accessible	27.9	31.7	36.1	29.6		− 1.7

[a] Indicated differences are averaged across levels of other variables. Where the direction of the differences is not consistent, scores were calculated for each direction.

Source: Compiled by authors.

latter might be contrary to expectations but was found true also for villages in Wisconsin (Fuguitt and Field 1972) and is better understood after consideration of the industry percentages of Table 3-5. Here we see that accessible villages have a higher concentration of employment in manufacturing, whereas remote villages have a greater concentration in the trade and service industrial categories. This is consistent with the hypothesis to be examined in Chapter 6—that accessible villages concentrate less on trade and services because of competition with nearby larger centers.

There is a difference between the two types of manufacturing in terms of growth and decline. Durable manufacturing was concentrated in declining and in accessible villages. The accessibility effect, as measured here, is about twice that of the growth effect. Differences among the percentages in this panel are particularly large, with accessible villages that declined between 1960 and 1980 having 23 percent of their labor force employed in durable industries in 1970, whereas this was true of only 7.7 percent of the growing nonaccessible villages. On the other hand, nondurable manufacturing differed much less among the growth-accessibility categories. Growing villages had a slightly higher proportion of their populations employed in nondurable manufacturing than did declining villages regardless of location, and the accessibility difference is slight.

These findings indicate a diversity in the role of manufacturing for villages. Villages with a high proportion of their residents in durable manufacturing, a prime factor in traditional urban-industrial expansion over this century, tend to be located near large cities, and as is true for large cities, such a concentration is no longer associated with population growth. According to the diffusion, "trickle down," or filtering hypothesis, deconcentration of industry should be primarily in labor-intensive, routine production, often of nondurable goods such as textiles (Thompson 1969). Here we see that there is little accessibility difference for nondurable manufacturing and that it is a factor associated with growth rather than decline for nonmetropolitan villages. We should add, however, that post-1970 work indicates slower growth in nonmetropolitan manufacturing in the 1970s than the 1960s and recent relative increases in growth in less labor intensive, more high-wage manufacturing (Heaton and Fuguitt 1979; Petrulis 1979; Till 1981).

Growing villages also had a slightly higher proportion employed in trade than declining villages, but the accessibility effect was negative, again indicating the greater importance of trade for villages away from large cities. The pattern is inconsistent for service industries, as growing accessible villages had more concentration in services than declining accessible villages but declining remote villages had proportionally more service employment than remote villages that grew over the twenty-year period. In fact, among the sustained growth and extended decline groups, the remote declining villages had the highest proportion in services, an unexpected result, given the recent widespread growth in service employment. A separation of this variable into the four types of service occupations given in the tabulations (finance, insurance, business, and repair; professional and related; educational; public administration) shows that this is true separately for each of the private and public service industry groups. Fuguitt and Field (1972) found this relation among public services for villages in Wisconsin, and some years ago Maki (1968) noted that declining rural areas are usually characterized by higher per capita expenditures for public services. Perhaps it is more difficult to transfer services, particularly public services, out of declining communities than is true for other activities.

VILLAGE CHARACTERISTICS AND THE TURNAROUND

In the preceding section we contrasted sustained growth villages with those declining over the twenty-year period. But since villages have shared in the recent increase of nonmetropolitan growth, we now shift attention to a consideration of the characteristics of those places involved in the turnaround (for a similar analysis of county growth patterns, see Brown and Beale 1981).

So far we have not looked at the two middle columns of Table 3–5, which show results for villages that grew in one of the two decades but declined in the other. Given the rather small differences found between villages that have either grown or declined over the entire twenty-year period, most being consistent with previous work, what would we expect the turnaround villages to be like? In perhaps the earliest systematic comparison of growing and declining cities, Ogburn (1937) concluded that his analysis suggested the view that growing places have greater economic opportunities. An association between growth of villages and economic opportunity is suggested by findings that growing villages have populations with higher incomes, greater labor force participation, and higher educational status. Similarly, differences in occupational and industry status may be interpreted as reflecting expanding or stable and contracting economic opportunities. For example, much of the job growth in nonmetropolitan areas in the 1960s was in nondurable manufacturing, and the proportion

Table 3–6. Patterns of Differences for Population Characteristics, Turnaround Growth and Turnaround Decline Villages.[a]

	Turnaround Growers		Turnaround Decliners	
	GG Closer than DD	DD Closer than GG	DD Closer than GG	GG Closer than DD
Percentage less than 18				
Accessible		1[b]		1[b]
Not accessible	equidistant			1[b]
Percentage 18–64				
Accessible		1[b]	1[b]	
Not accessible		1[b]	1[b]	
Percentage 65 and over				
Accessible		1[b]	1	
Not accessible		1[b]		1
Percentage 12 or more years schooling				
Accessible		1[b]	1[b]	
Not accessible	1			1
Percentage families income less than $5,000				
Accessible		1[b]		1[b]
Not accessible	1[b]			1[b]
Percentage families income $12,000 up				
Accessible		1[b]		1[b]
Not accessible		1[b]	1[b]	
Percentage males in labor force				
Accessible		1[b]		1[b]
Not accessible		1[b]	1[b]	
Percentage females in labor force				
Accessible		1[b]		1
Not accessible		1[b]		1[b]

Table 3–6. continued

	Turnaround Growers		Turnaround Decliners	
	GG Closer than DD	DD Closer than GG	DD Closer than GG	GG Closer than DD
Percentage professional, technical, manager, clerical				
Accessible		1	1	
Not accessible		1		1[b]
Percentage in manufacturing, durable				
Accessible	1			1
Not accessible	1[b]			1[b]
Percentage in manufacturing, not durable				
Accessible		1[b]		1[b]
Not accessible		1[b]	1[b]	
Percentage in wholesale, retail trade				
Accessible	1[b]		1[b]	
Not accessible	1[b]			1[b]
Percentage in service industries				
Accessible	1		1	
Not accessible		1[b]	1[b]	
PATTERN SUMS	7 1	18	11	15

[a] Indicates correct comparison for each pair.

[b] Value for turnaround group outside range of GG and DD.

Source: Compiled by authors.

employed in this activity is positively associated with growth. Nationally, most new jobs have been in service industries, and this is reflected here in the contrast between growing and declining accessible places. (National trends, however, do not explain the results for services in nonadjacent villages.)

As reviewed in Chapter 2, the nonmetropolitan turnaround appears not to be driven so much by new manufacturing (at least not in areas already high in manufacturing) as by service expansion, particularly relating to retirement and recreation, and by opportunities directly or indirectly associated with energy development in selected areas. Also, we found that villages turning around were more likely to be smaller and less accessible than others. To the extent this is a new pattern, we might expect that the turnaround villages would be dissimilar in social and economic structure to the villages they join in growth— that is, the villages that grew over the entire 1960–80 period. If it does not represent new economic and social forces, on the other hand, one might predict that turnaround growth villages would reproduce the old patterns. If the latter were true, a turnaround growth village should have 1970 demographic, socioeconomic, and employment characteristics more like the sustained growth villages than sustained decline villages.

Table 3–6 summarizes the patterns for the groups of turnaround villages. For the turnaround growth villages, a number 1 in the first column means that for this characteristic these villages as a group are more like the villages they are joining in turning to growth (GG) than the villages they left (DD); a number 1 in the second column means they are more like the villages they left than those they joined. Similarly, for the turnaround decline villages, a number 1 in the third column means these villages as a whole are more like the villages they joined in the 1970–80 period (DD), and a number 1 in the fourth column means they are more like the villages they left when they shifted to decline (GG).

For the turnaround growers, out of the twenty-six comparisons in the table, only eight fail to support the view that the new growers, as might be expected from a new trend, are more like the villages they left than those that they joined. Indeed for sixteen comparisons the turnaround percentage is not only closer to the percentage for sustained decliners than for sustained growers, it is outside the range of these two groups (indicated by the letter *b*).

Variables for which the group of turnaround villages are more like the sustained growers include the percentage with twelve or more years school (nonaccessible villages), durable manufacturing, trade, services (accessible villages) and percentage with income less than $5,000 (nonaccessible villages). For eighteen other age, education, occupation, and income variables they are more like the villages they left by moving from decline to growth, and one comparison was equidistant between the GG and the DD groups.

In short, on the basis of characteristics usually identified with growth, these data indicate that one would have done a rather poor job predicting which villages among those that declined in the 1960s would change to growth in the 1970s. In fact, on most characteristics they appeared (as a group) to be more different from sustained growers than were those that continued to decline as indicated by the letter *b*. This even suggests a converse prediction strategy: Declining villages at the extreme of villages identified with decline are the best candidates for turnaround growth. Undoubtedly, the fact that turnaround villages are also smaller than others as a rule helps to explain these differences in characteristics, but this does not make the pattern appear any less unusual.

On the other hand, the results for the turnaround decline villages are more ambiguous. Of the twenty-six comparisons, fifteen are closer to the sustained growth group, and eleven closer to the sustained decline group. For seven of the thirteen variables the results for accessible villages, moreover, are different from those for corresponding nonaccessible villages. Thus, although a few more comparisons fall in the right-hand column, the results for the turnaround decliners do not support the new pattern argument to the extent found for the turnaround growers.

As was true for the turnaround growers, most of the percentages (19 of 26) among turnaround decliners were outside the ranges of the sustained growers and the continued decline groups. This at least suggests that villages changing from growth to decline or from decline to growth are somewhat unusual in their characteristics in comparison with those that do not.

SUMMARY AND DISCUSSION

In the comparison of social and economic characteristics, the village stands out from other settlement types in the urban hierarchy as extreme on the following conditions: (1) Villages have older populations; (2) villages have a greater proportion of primary individuals rather than families in households; (3) the incidence of poverty among people over age 65 is highest in villages; and (4) employment in wholesale and retail trade is higher in villages. On most other characteristics, the village falls either between the urban and other rural or among the other rural segments as opposed to the urban group.

The higher proportion of older persons in villages is no doubt associated with the prevalence of single person households there, and age structure differences may be reflected in the income comparison also. Villages have traditionally been centers of trade in retail and service activities, commonly linked with agricultural hinterlands. With declining support for these business activities, many have declined in income, if not closed their doors completely, in recent years as documented in Chapters 4 and 5. The higher frequency of people over age 65 in poverty at the time of the 1970 census may be, in part, due to a concentration of retirees who were self-employed as either small business operators or farmers. Retirement pensions other than social security are uncommon in these cases and may be a factor in the comparatively low incomes of the retirement age group.

A gradient consistent with the urban hierarchy, as noted in Duncan and Reiss (1956), is evident in the tables for education, income, labor force participation, occupation, and service industries for 1970. The urban to rural gradient is most often disrupted by the measure for the rural nonfarm category, which is probably the most diverse of all population segments included here. This category is high in manufacturing, craftsmen and operators, poverty, school dropouts, and low in educational status. It should be noted that this group includes residents of unannexed urban fringe settlements, residents of unincorporated places, and nonfarm families living in the open country.

In terms of quality of life, the American village represents the pattern of conditions often noted as characteristic of more rural as compared with urban areas. Although these data are aggregated over all villages and ignore the wide variation that surely exists among these places, the general pattern is evident. Incomes are lower and the incidence of poverty higher in villages than in their urban counterparts. Unemployment is higher and education levels are lower, and there is a greater proportion of high school dropouts among males in villages than in urban communities. A comparison with Duncan and Reiss (1956) shows that many of these differences have persisted over at least twenty years.

Despite these negative quality of life features and although measurement is beyond the scope of this study, most villages still probably have cleaner air, less water pollution and congestion, fewer problems of waste disposal, and less crime than most large cities. The income differences, although striking, make no allowances for differences among types of communities in the cost of living. We would suspect, furthermore, that many village dwellers would feel even more deprived if they had to live elsewhere.

We also differentiated groups of villages according to two other basic elements of the settlement structure—accessibility to larger places and population growth or decline. Some differences among groups of villages parallel those found between all villages and other population units. Just as villages as a whole have more elderly than other residence groupings, as noted above, so do remote, declining villages have more elderly than other village types. They also have fewer high school graduates, even adjusting for age, lower male and female participants in the labor force, proportionately fewer employed in nondurable manufacturing, and fewer families with higher incomes. Generally growing, accessible villages are at the opposite extreme.

Patterns show turnaround-to-growth villages are generally more like long-term declining than growing villages. Indeed, our comparison suggests that if anything they are somewhat worse off in social and economic characteristics than villages that continued to decline. This is consistent with the view that the nonmetropolitan turnaround is a new trend, since we know, as reviewed in Chapter 2, that the new growth has been in formerly declining and depressed low density areas and that villages shifting from decline to growth are concentrated relatively among the smaller, more remote places in contrast with earlier decades. We will give further attention to the recent increase in nonmetropolitan population as it affects the village, particularly in Chapters 7 and 8.

NOTES

1. Composition by race is not included as a demographic variable here since previous work for 1960 showed nonmetropolitan villages to be predominantly white: 93 percent for the United States, 97 percent or more in the North and West, and 82 percent in the South (Fuguitt 1968).
2. Census survival ratios were used to estimate age-specific mortality, and the net migration for an age group was estimated as the difference between observed population in 1970 and the population expected on the basis of the 1960 population ten years younger and the age-specific mortality estimate.

3. The fifth count tabulations give educational status for three age groups,
    25–44, 45–54, and 55 and over. We calculated percentages directly
    standardized by age, using the age structure for all villages combined as
    the standard. The standardized percentages yielded difference scores
    approximately one-half as large as the original ones (3.7 for accessibility,
    1.0 for growth).

4 ECONOMIC ACTIVITIES IN VILLAGES

In addition to their residential role, villages perform key economic roles that provide both employment and goods and services to rural dwellers. Changes in rural population, primary industries, and the social life of rural residents have caused many adjustments in the economy of village communities. The period since 1950 has been especially dynamic, witnessing many major innovations in agriculture and other primary industries and significant increases in mobility among rural residents.

In this chapter we look at the variety of economic activities in villages by sector and how these activities have changed over time. The analysis in the first part of the chapter demonstrates the frequency and distribution of activities among villages for the 1950–70 period and is based on data from Dun and Bradstreet.[1] Trends in economic and other service activities for the 1975–80 period follow this section and are based on the national survey of village mayors.

Comparative research on the economic structure of American villages on a national scale has been almost nonexistent in the literature. In 1927 Brunner published a study of economic characteristics for a national sample of villages from agricultural areas of the United States (Brunner et al. 1927). Concerned primarily with agricultural villages, Brunner described the village economy as a system that served nearby farmers in two ways: first, as a center for marketing, storage, and other services designed to dispose of surplus agricultural production, and second, as a center for retail goods and other services necessary to the livelihood of farm and village people. The first role of the village—that of marketing or disposal of farm produce—gave rise to the grain elevators, produce warehouses, creameries, cheese factories, canning factories, and other familiar facilities designed to collect, process, and distribute farm products. The village served as a collection point and first-stage processing center for goods on their way to more distant markets, and its marketing activities supported employees engaged in wholesale handling and processing activities.

The complementary role noted by Brunner, that of a service center, brought the "main street" to the village as a shopping center or "trade" center, as farmers accustomed to exchanging produce for merchandise often called it. The village, therefore, was a link to the world beyond the farm and served as an intermediary between the farmer and the larger urban centers.

Although Brunner's description of the village economy was focused on agricultural activities, the concept can be enlarged to include other primary industries, such as forestry, mining, fishing, and other natural resource developments in rural areas. In each case the villager performs an intermediary role between the producer and consumer of primary production, and the facilities differ according to the nature of the product (e.g., grain elevators in agricultural areas, portals and processing plants in mining areas, and sawmills and lumber mills in forest areas). The role of the village in nonagricultural primary industry situations is not apt to be structured around individual producers, since the industries are commonly large companies in mining and forestry activities, but is similar to that of the farm community in that it provides shopping facilities for people in primary occupations.

Manufacturing activities in villages have provided an employment base that itself was often dependent on primary production. Much of the manufacturing found in earlier villages involved the processing of local raw materials such as food products, wood, and fiber products. This form of secondary industry was in many situations seasonal, varying with the natural rhythms of the harvest of raw materials and in such cases did not serve as a permanent employment source. Instead it was often an employer of farm wives, itinerants, and students during the summer months.

The evolution of villages in this country has followed the development of primary industrial activities in most cases and has been subject to the fluctuations of success and failure in those industries. Since agriculture probably accounted for a majority of villages in their initial development, fluctuations in farm production, farm prices, scale of operation, and characteristics of farm operators have been noticed in most village economies (see Brunner and Lorge 1937).

As marketing and distribution centers, we can assume that villages emerged as needed or as supported by the primary sector and in relation to the location of other competing centers. The pattern of village location and characteristics of villages at any time should reflect, in part, the status of primary production and the competition among centers in an area. As marketing and processing centers for primary products, development of villages has responded to production characteristics such as volume, perishability, and transport needs of primary products. For example, more villages may have been necessary in a dairy area due to the perishability and bulk of milk than in a grain producing area, and thus a greater density of villages may have emerged in dairy regions than in grain farming areas, depending, of course, on the productivity of the land in each case.

Changes in technology and scale of production have continually altered the role of villages in primary industries. Numerous changes in the nature and volume of agricultural products, along with scale increases in both production units and processing plants, have resulted in continued adaptation among agricultural villages. Many activities common in villages in the past, such as blacksmiths, harness repair, and small-scale processing plants, have become obsolete while new businesses related to large-scale production were added (Paulsen and Carlson 1961). These new activities include bulk fertilizer stations, equipment dealerships, and other services dependent on the volume and techniques of modern agricultural production.

As centers for consumer goods and services, villages have developed in relation to population distribution and population characteristics in rural areas. The service center role of the village could be expected to result in a pattern of trade centers in response to market population distribution, location of competing centers, and transport facilities in the equilibrium framework devised by Christaller as central place theory (Berry and Pred 1965; Christaller 1966). An increase within the village trade area in the number of consumers would allow a corresponding increase in the number of businesses in the village. In theory, a survey of village business activity at any time will demonstrate the condition of equilibrium at that time, within the limits of adjustment capabilities. The distribution of retail and service business outlets should reflect the relative distribution of the population or of consumer demand. Similarly, the processing and handling facilities should reflect the value or volume of production in primary products in the local vicinity in the context of current technology.

Major changes have occurred in both population distribution and demographic characteristics and also in primary and secondary industries in rural areas, causing adjustments in village economic and social life. We will examine the status of the various economic activities in villages during a time of major adjustments in an attempt to understand the patterns of change and its causes.

BUSINESS ACTIVITIES SINCE 1950

The immediate postwar period witnessed significant change in rural society as manufactured goods, particularly automobiles, tractors, and other durable goods, became widely available to rural people. It was also a time of increased participation in larger city activities resulting in and further reinforced by the migration of young people from rural to urban areas. To examine changes, data on business activities in the national sample of villages were obtained from the Reference Book of Dun and Bradstreet for the years 1950, 1960, and 1970, and from the survey of current mayors in a subsample of 100 villages as of 1980.

To better understand the geographical pattern of village business activities and trends, the sample was divided along census divisions into regions similar to the breakdown used in Chapter 2 and outlined on the map in Figure 1-1. The major categories of business activities listed by Dun and Bradstreet for the total U.S. and the North, South, and West regions are found in Table 4-1 along with the number of establishments in each category and the percentage change during the two decades.

The service center role of villages was paramount during this time as measured by the number of establishments. Retail activity outnumbered all others with over 60 percent of all business establishments in all three years; however, it declined during both decades in contrast to all other categories of economic activity except services. This differs from the pattern observed by Brunner and Kolb (1933) in the early part of the century. They noted a steady increase in the number of retail establishments per village from 1910 to 1930. The village seems to have reached its high-water mark as a retail center during the 1930-50 era, probably immediately after the war when manufactured products became more readily available and local merchants flourished.

The retail sector in villages has no doubt been affected by a declining farm population throughout the country and by outmigration of young people to urban centers (Banks and Beale 1973). The increased scale of farming has displaced many farm families that shopped in village stores in the past. In addition to population decline in the village trade area, the mobility of the rural population has increased with the availability of automobiles, and equally as important, the speed, comfort, and relative efficiency of the modern automobile and modern highway routes have encouraged mobility.

The automobile has been seen as a threat to village merchants since it was first introduced in rural areas (Vogt 1917; Hawthorn 1926; Converse 1928). The villagers feared it would enable farmers to journey to nearby cities for greater variety and better prices for goods. This fear was realized in some cases but was often short lived. Farmers returned to trade in the village, where merchants rallied by offering greater variety and by operating their businesses more efficiently (Brunner and Lorge 1937).

The increased mobility of the modern farmer (and villager) carries with it several conditions that were not present in the earlier situation. At least five of these can be summarized as follows:

1. The rate of automobile travel has increased to the point that a person can average twice the distance in the same time as in the late 1930s. Added to this is the factor of comfort, with air conditioned and heated autos, AM-FM radio, and more recently stereo tape systems and citizens'-band radios, each of which makes the duration of the journey more bearable and increases the travel range of the rural dweller. This may bring within convenient reach a medium-size city or even metropolitan area complete with the urban amenities and variety of shopping not available in the small town or village.

2. The relative distance to urban centers has also decreased with the development of large regional shopping centers on the periphery of cities that reduce travel time to the shopping district of the city

Table 4-1. Inventory of Economic Activity in Sampled Villages.

Economic Activity	Total United States			North			South			West		
	1950	1960	1970	1950	1960	1970	1950	1960	1970	1950	1960	1970
Retail												
Number of establishments	11714	9721	8958	6395	5058	4685	4216	3603	3329	1103	1060	944
Mean per village	22.5	18.7	17.2	21.3	16.9	15.6	24.6	21.0	19.4	22.0	21.2	18.8
Total percentage change	—	-17.0	-7.8	—	-20.9	-7.3	—	-14.5	-7.6	—	-3.9	-10.9
Service												
Number of establishments	2511	2368	1430	1548	1361	795	693	737	477	270	270	158
Mean per village	4.8	4.5	2.7	5.1	4.5	2.6	4.0	4.3	2.7	5.4	5.4	3.1
Total percentage change	—	-5.7	-39.6	—	-12.0	-41.5	—	6.3	-35.2	—	—	-41.4
Wholesale												
Number of establishments	491	745	663	271	445	396	161	396	195	62	89	72
Mean per village	0.9	1.4	1.3	0.9	1.5	1.3	0.9	1.3	1.1	1.2	1.8	1.4
Total percentage change	—	51.7	-11.0	—	64.2	-11.0	—	145.9	-50.7	—	43.5	-19.1
Agriculture Production and Service												
Number of establishments	511	519	470	180	181	173	279	280	243	52	58	54
Mean per village	1.0	1.0	0.9	0.6	0.6	0.6	1.6	1.6	1.4	1.0	1.1	1.0
Total percentage change	—	1.6	-9.4	—	0.5	-4.4	—	0.3	-13.2	—	11.5	-6.8
Manufacturing												
Number of establishments	1043	1072	1169	559	594	647	356	351	400	128	127	122
Mean per village	2.0	2.0	2.2	1.8	1.9	2.1	2.0	2.0	2.3	2.5	2.5	2.4
Total percentage change	—	2.7	9.0	—	6.3	8.9	—	-1.4	13.9	—	-0.7	-3.9

Table 4–1. continued

Economic Activity	Total United States			North			South			West		
	1950	1960	1970	1950	1960	1970	1950	1960	1970	1950	1960	1970
Building contractors												
Number of establishments	570	875	1064	384	551	691	126	241	301	60	83	103
Mean per village	1.1	1.7	2.0	1.2	1.8	2.3	0.7	1.4	1.7	1.2	1.6	2.0
Total percentage change	—	53.5	21.6	—	43.4	25.4	—	91.2	24.8	—	28.3	24.0
Mine												
Number of establishments	101	130	95	55	62	56	41	63	34	5	5	5
Mean per village	0.2	0.2	0.1	0.2	0.2	0.2	0.2	0.4	0.2	0.1	0.1	0.1
Total percentage change	—	28.7	−26.9	—	12.7	−9.6	—	53.6	−46	—	—	—
Forest												
Number of establishments	5	1	3	1	0	1	4	1	2	0	0	0
Mean per village	0	0	0	0	0	0	0	0	0	0	0	0
Total percentage change												
Number of villages with economic data [a]	520	520	520	299	299	299	171	171	171	50	50	50

[a] Of the 572 villages in the total sample this is the number that were listed by Dun and Bradstreet all three years. Where villages were extremely small or adjacent suburbs of larger places, the listing had been combined with the larger place and therefore was not available.

Source: Compiled by authors.

(see Cohen 1972). The rural shopper may stop at the edge of the city and obtain most of the variety in retail goods once available only in the congested downtown.

3. Competition from larger cities has increased with awareness in rural areas of the latest fashions and fads, due, at least in part, to the medium of television and its spread to a majority of households. As new styles and innovations are introduced, they usually begin at the top of the urban hierarchy and trickle downward, reaching the village store later than larger centers. The awareness of innovations, however, often precedes local availability due to media advertising and urban-centered entertainment on television, and rural people will travel to the larger city to obtain the goods not yet found in local stores.

4. Advertising by urban competitors is often designed for chain or franchise outlets and thus is standardized and more efficient and far-reaching than the local store advertisements or local media. The scale economies of the chain store and franchise occur in part due to standardization, which also lowers costs. These savings, along with the lower per unit profits due to larger volume trading, give the urban stores a competitive edge.

5. Finally, mechanization in modern agriculture and in other primary activities has increased the leisure time available to rural people. This encourages more travel either for recreation or shopping, increases awareness, and enables visits to more distant places, a condition that probably builds upon itself (i.e., with each trip to the city, the next one becomes easier due to increased familiarity).

The plight of the village merchant in many areas has therefore been one of increasing competition with urban retailers for a declining population of consumers. Returning to Table 4–1, the data show the trend in both retail and service activities since 1950 that has been experienced by villages throughout the country. The total number of retail establishments declined by 17 percent during the 1950–60 decade and by a lesser rate during the 1960s. Service establishments declined less in the first decade than between 1960 and 1970, in part due to the increase in service firms in the South region between 1950 and 1960, which offset losses in the North. The two activities together, however, constitute the bulk of consumer-oriented business firms in villages, and together they declined by 15 percent between 1950 and 1960 and by 14.4 percent in the 1960s.

Wholesale business increased in villages between 1950 and 1960 followed by a decline between 1960 and 1970, although the loss did not offset the gain in the earlier decade and the net result was an increase between 1950 and 1970 in wholesale establishments. The pattern was consistent throughout the country, with the greatest relative gain and loss occurring in villages in the South. The increase in wholesale activities was largely in farm products as raw materials, including dairy, poultry, meat, and grain. Increased farm production during this period may have led to the increase in wholesale dealers in villages, thereby strengthening that role of the village community.

Agricultural production and service firms were relatively stable throughout the twenty-year period, with a slight decline in the latter decade. The small net change, however, includes declining numbers of cotton gins in the South and of poultry hatcheries, while other agricultural business firms were increasing in such activities as dairies, poultry, and animal specialties.

The only consistent increases in business establishments were in the manufacturing and construction categories. Probably most important is the increase that occurred in manufacturing because it represents basic employment within the village and has been a much sought-after industry by rural communities in recent years. The net increase during both decades suggests that some villages have been successful in attracting manufacturing firms to rural areas to offset declines in primary occupations.

The net increase in manufacturing shown in Table 4–1 disguises declines in some traditional manufacturing activities such as food processing (especially canning, butter, cheese), lumber mills, and newspaper publishing, while increases occurred in animal feeds, textiles, and concrete and concrete products. Table 4–2 contains a breakdown by type of manufacturing industries and shows an increase in textile and apparel industries along with a diversified category labeled other manufacturing. The traditional raw material-oriented industries that dominated manufacturing in the earlier village as reported by Brunner et al. (1927) are still important, but villages have gained in industries that have less concern with either raw materials or rural markets and that are attracted by low land and labor costs that offset locational disadvantages. These tend to be fabricating or apparel industries, which seek inexpensive labor such as farm wives and other female workers in rural areas where labor

Table 4–2. Number of Manufacturing Firms in Sampled Villages.

Type of Manufacturing	Total United States			North			South			West		
	1950	1960	1970	1950	1960	1970	1950	1960	1970	1950	1960	1970
Food, kindred, and tobacco	265	263	214	167	165	129	78	76	70	20	22	15
Textile and apparel	79	95	130	11	17	23	47	54	86	21	24	21
Lumber and wood products, furniture, paper, and allied products	214	212	196	68	78	79	111	104	84	35	30	33
Printing and publishing	193	184	163	123	108	103	45	50	42	25	26	18
Other manufacturing	292	318	466	190	226	313	75	67	118	27	25	35

Source: Compiled by authors.

unions have been slow to develop. Inexpensive labor is not the only reason industries choose villages, however, and issues of community environment, low taxes and land costs, and even transport connections, which have improved for many villages, are apt to be involved in the decision also (Little 1972). Villages can offer a pleasant environment for manufacturing and a competent labor force, if not from within the local community then from nearby villages or rural open country residents who will commute.

Referring back to Table 4-1, we see that the number of building contractors nearly doubled in villages between 1950 and 1970. Most of these firms were general building contractors, but gains were experienced in most major building trades, probably in response to both farm and suburban-rural construction needs of the time. Modern scale increases in farming have often required an increase in physical plant to accommodate innovations in livestock feeding and housing and in machine, grain, and feed storage. Farm housing has also been changing as farmers have replaced old farmhouses with modern dwellings resembling those in suburban areas. Prior to the current economic recession, housing and other construction increased rapidly in near-urban villages and rural residence situations, enabling construction firms to prosper where access to the urban fringe is good.

Although responsible for rapid growth in many energy resource areas during the 1970s, mining activities represented a minority category of business in villages as measured by the number of firms during the 1950-70 period (Table 4-1). Listed was a variety of mineral ores including iron, copper, lead, and zinc, along with bituminous coal, which was the most common mining activity and also the most subject to decline. It dropped from 61 establishments in 1950 to 44 in 1960 and 23 in 1970. Most of these were found in the Appalachian region. Declines in coal were offset by increases in natural gas and petroleum mining activities and also in stone quarries and construction sand and gravel. Together, the mining activities represented a small portion of village business firms at each time, as did forestry activities, which were almost nonexistent in these places. It should be noted that the Standard Industrial Classification includes logging and sawmill firms as manufacturing, thereby excluding these common activities from the forest category. Forestry and mining will therefore not be included in the further analysis of economic activities by major category for the 1950-70 period.

DISTRIBUTION OF VILLAGES BY BUSINESS ACTIVITY

Another way to look at change in the economic system of villages is to examine the proportion of places with various numbers of businesses over time. The proportion of places having a given number of business establishments has not remained constant for most activities and represents a fluctuation in the pattern of business offerings within the urban system. The share of each line of business that was found in various size classes has shifted for most activities with growth or decline in the total number of establishments.

Figure 4-1 presents the proportional distribution of villages by number of establishments for the major categories of economic activity in the total sample. A downward trend in the distribution of retail and service activities has been consistent during both decades and indicates a loss of establishments throughout the system of places. As the proportion in the lowest size class increased each decade, the proportion in the largest class decreased. Thus a shift toward a system of smaller retail clusters has occurred. The village with more than sixty retail stores in 1970 has become much less common in the system, while the village with no more than ten stores has increased to nearly 50 percent of the sample.

Service activities in villages are much like retail activities in their consumer market orientation and consist primarily of repair shops for common items. These have experienced a shift similar to retail in their distribution among villages, with increasing proportions of villages in the lower number-of-establishment groups. The proportion of villages having no services increased to nearly 30 percent in 1970 from a low of under 15 percent in 1950. The size group 11-15 almost disappeared between 1960 and 1970 after relative stability between 1950 and 1960. The greatest change in the proportional distribution of places occurred in the first decade with retail activities and in the second decade with the service group, although the shift was in the same direction.

The incidence of multiple establishments of wholesale activities in villages increased during the first decade and then decreased slightly by 1970, while the distribution of places with three or more construction firms increased each decade. Manufacturing retained a nearly constant distribution among the villages throughout the total period with a majority of places having two or less firms at each time. It is

Figure 4–1. Percentage of Villages by Number of Establishments of Each Economic Activity Each Year.

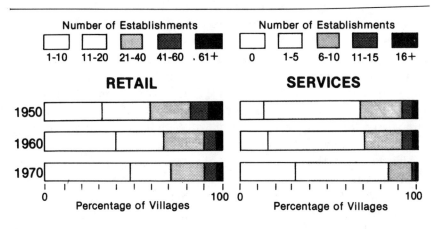

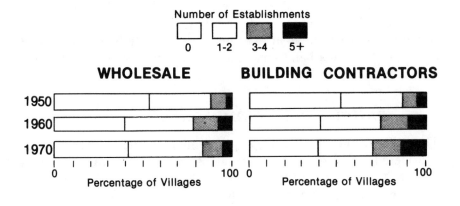

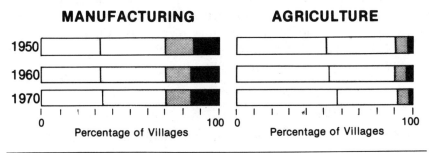

Source: Compiled by authors.

important to note, however, that fully 15 percent of the places fell into each of the upper levels with 3–4 and 5+ manufacturing firms. This demonstrates that manufacturing has been relatively important in the village throughout the time period since 1950 and that the proportional distribution of places by number of firms has remained consistent while the number of firms has increased.

Agricultural activities experienced a trend similar to the retail and service distribution, with an increase in the proportion of places with no establishments and a slight decline in the incidence of more than three firms. By 1970, over 55 percent of the villages had none of these activities compared to about 50 percent in 1950.

The change in the number and type of business activities in villages noted in Table 4–1 has thus been accompanied by a change in the distribution of these activities among places. A greater number of villages with a smaller number of business firms has been the trend with retail, service, and agricultural activities, while stability or growth in the proportion of places with a larger number of firms has prevailed in manufacturing, construction, and wholesale activities. The trade center role of the village appears to have given way to production related activities in the relative distribution of places by activity. A village drawn at random in 1970 would have been apt to have had fewer retail and service and more production related firms than it had in 1950.

PATTERNS OF ECONOMIC CHANGE

The shifts in the distribution of economic activities among villages considered above represent aggregate distributions at each time and describe the net result of many individual cases of growth and decline. It is also necessary to compare villages as to the’ı direction of change in number of economic activities. Villages were divided into categories of initial number of establishments for which the number of places that gained, remained stable, or declined in number of establishments were plotted for each major category of activity (Figure 4–2). The graphs show the proportion of villages in each initial size class that experienced net gain, loss, or stability during the decade.

Retailing

The number of places that lost firms dominated all size categories in retail business (Figure 4–2). The graph shows that over three-fourths

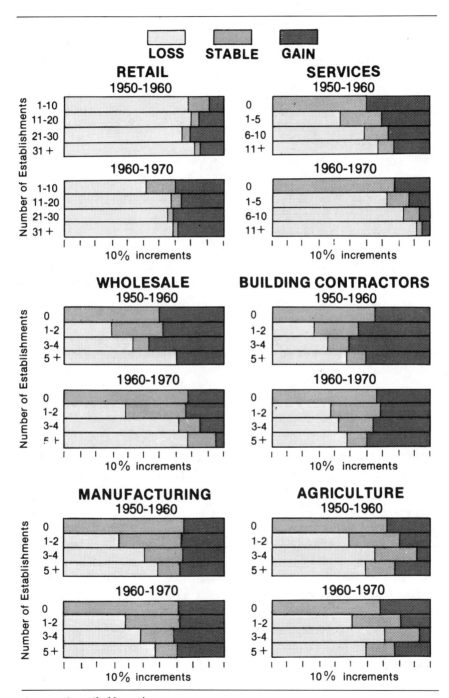

Source: Compiled by authors.

of all villages in each size category lost retail establishments during the 1950–60 decade and over half in each size category lost during the latter decade. The reduced rate of loss in the second decade was accompanied by an increased proportion of places that gained establishments. Some fluctuation in retail activity was the norm among villages, as indicated by the relatively low number that remained stable each decade. The proportion of places that gained establishments was quite similar for each size class during each decade but increased substantially from an average of 16 percent during 1950–60 to nearly 30 percent between 1960 and 1970. Corresponding to this increase in places that gained is a slight reduction in the number and proportion in each size class that lost establishments during the second decade. There was little difference by size in the pattern of decline as measured here, although as a group the smallest villages had proportionally fewer losing than the other size categories.

The overall pattern of change in retail establishments by initial number was one of net loss predominant at all size levels, diminishing slightly during the second decade. A consistent minority of the villages gained retail establishments in all size categories, however, suggesting that initial number of establishments was not the major determining factor in explaining the pattern of net loss and gain at this level of measurement.

Services

The graph of villages for service activity in Figure 4–2 arranges villages according to slightly different categories of initial size than was used for retail activity, and includes a zero category to show the number of places with no service activity at the beginning of each decade. Obviously, villages in the zero category could not lose establishments, so these bars are coded only for stability and gain.

Again, the predominant trend was loss as represented by the number of places losing in each size class. In contrast to retail activity, the number of places losing increased in the second decade in all size groups. Loss was more prevalent among larger places in each decade, as indicated by the percentage values for each bar, which show increasing frequency of loss with increasing initial size. In contrast, the proportion of places showing net gains in each size class diminished with increasing initial size, as did the proportion that remained stable.

Wholesale

Among the less common business activities in villages, wholesale establishments actually increased during the 1950–70 period as was shown in Table 4–1. The distribution of gaining and losing places in Figure 4–2 also demonstrates this trend. The number of places gaining wholesale establishments was greater than the number losing in all but the largest size class during the first decade. Overall, 32 percent of the villages gained wholesalers during the first decade. The proportion gaining declined, however, to 17 percent of the villages in the 1960–70 decade. A significant trend was for places with fewer wholesale firms to gain, especially during the first decade. However, a majority of those with no wholesale firms at the beginning of each decade remained without these at the end of the decade as indicated by the graph. The greatest rate of decline was during the second decade in the largest categories, where an average of 79 percent of places with three or more firms had a net loss of wholesale firms.

Construction

The pattern of change for building contractors was much like that for wholesale firms. Gains were common for all size groups because this activity was increasing in frequency among the villages over both decades. Forty-one percent of the places in each category gained between 1950 and 1960, and 36 percent gained between 1960 and 1970. The growth was primarily in general building contractors, although specialized contractors such as plumbing and heating also increased. This growth was more common in villages close to larger urban centers perhaps related to the growth of settlement in the urban fringe. Increased construction in agricultural areas, particularly of storage facilities and livestock shelters, was also a likely cause of this expansion, which nearly doubled the total number of construction firms (Table 4–1).

Manufacturing

For manufacturing activity, the pattern of change was similar during both decades. The pattern of places gaining, losing, or remaining stable by initial number was highly consistent over both periods. Growth occurred among 25 to 29 percent of all places during the 1950s and increased to 32 percent during the 1960s. The distribution of losing places was not uniform among the village groups, with the places with more manufacturing firms having a higher relative frequency of loss and less stability than those with fewer firms. There seems to be a "floor effect" here where the probability of loss is less in villages having a smaller number of firms present. Manufacturing firms in rural areas are often small in size and of a somewhat "footloose" variety that can benefit equally from a variety of locational settings. These characteristics are especially common among the newer firms acquired as perhaps the third or fourth manufacturing industry in the village and thus more subject to closure as economic conditions dictate.

Agriculture

Agricultural production and service activities had a similar distribution of places among the change categories in each decade. The villages with no firms at the beginning were the most stable group, although nearly one-fourth of these gained each decade. The loss of agricultural firms was most common among the 3 to 4 size category relative to the number in the group, with 65 and 70 percent of these places losing at least one of their firms during the two decades respectively.

This trend reflects a pattern of decline during both decades in such agricultural service establishments as cotton gins, poultry hatcheries, and grist mills, along with a reduction in the number of dairies and other agricultural business activities. Gains in fertilizer and chemical dealers, irrigation services, and other production related activities did not offset the losses of other more traditional activities in the village community.

POST-1970 BUSINESS ACTIVITIES

To assess post-1970 business activities, mayors in our subsample of 100 villages were asked to report the number of establishments present for each type of activity from a list read to them and, further, to give the number of establishments that were gained or lost in their community during the past five years (1975–80). Business activities that were examined are listed in Table 4–3.

The list of activities on the survey question was not exhaustive and did not include the wide variety and detailed breakdown that Dun and Bradstreet includes in its Reference Book. The survey addressed professional services including medical doctor, dentist, lawyer, veterinarian, and hospital, which were not included in the data for the previous years.

The predominance of retail and service business is evident in Table 4–3, with nearly three-fourths of all establishments of surveyed businesses falling into this category each year. The decline in retail establishments was still occurring during the late 1970s, although this different data source suggests the decline was at a somewhat lower rate than in the previous decades. Forty-two percent of the surveyed villages reported a net loss in retail and service establishments between 1975 and 1980. This contrasts with about 75 percent during each of the previous decades, using the Dun and Bradstreet source. The shorter time period may be partly responsible for the lower rate of decline in establishments as compared with the previous ten-year periods, although the lower rate of loss for the five-year period is sustained even if annualized rates are compared and the percentage of mayors reporting net gains in retail establishments 1975–80 was the same as in the decade of 1960–70. This suggests an improved condition for village retail activities—that is, a less severe decline and a greater number of gains than in previous decades.

Other business activities that declined were wholesale and mining, although neither was common to begin with and the loss was only one establishment in each case. Since this loss was not offset by gain in any village, the result was simply a decline of one firm in each activity.

A moderate gain was experienced in finance, insurance, and real estate business as measured by the number of establishments. This represents a gain of 6 banks, 4 savings and loan offices, and 12 real estate offices among the 100 villages. Insurance agencies remained stable in number during the 1975–80 period.

The greatest increases among the different activities, as reported by the mayors, were in manufacturing and professional services (Table 4–3). Manufacturing establishments increased by 42 percent, with a gain of 19 firms among the 100 villages. Only one village lost

Table 4–3. Economic Activities in Villages, 1975–80.[a]

Activity	Total Number of Establishments		Percentage of Change	Percentage of Villages Reporting			
	1975	1980		Net Loss	Stable	Net Gain	
Retail and service	1637	1567	– 4.3	42	32	26	
Wholesale	31	30	– 3.2	1	99	0	
Manufacturing	45	64	42.2	1	85	14	
Mining	27	26	– 3.7	1	99	0	
Finance/insurance/ real estate	278	299	7.6	6	77	17	
Professional services	211	249	18.0	8	66	26	

[a]Based on a national survey of 100 village mayors.

Source: Compiled by authors.

manufacturing, and most of those with manufacturing firms in 1975 remained stable during the five-year period. The gain in manufacturing represents a continuation of a growth trend witnessed during the 1960s (Table 4-1) and suggests a growth of employment opportunities in village communities that may be partly responsible for the renewed growth in population.

Professional services increased by 18 percent or 38 positions during the five-year period (Table 4-3). A total of twenty-six villages reported net gains in this category, while only eight experienced a net loss. Gains were found in medical doctor, dentist, veterinarian, and lawyer categories, and hospital remained stable (Table 4-4). This is an encouraging finding, especially in the area of medical and dental services, which have been recognized as lacking in many rural areas. The proportion of places having the other services also increased, indicating a greater distribution among villages than was found previously.

CONCLUSION

These patterns demonstrate the dynamic process of business growth and decline in American villages since 1950. The postwar period has witnessed many changes in rural society that have affected the village

Table 4-4.   Professional Services in Villages.

Activity	Percentage of Places with at Least One Establishment		Total Number of Establishments	
	1975	1980	1975	1980
Medical doctor	36	38	75	77
Dentist	26	31	40	48
Lawyer	25	34	61	78
Veterinarian	19	21	26	37
Hospital	9	9	9	9

Source: Survey of 100 mayors.

communities. Many economic adjustments have resulted in closure of firms, particularly in the "service center" sector of the village economy. The recent trend toward increase in industry and professional activities and the apparent reduced rate of decline in retailing suggest a possible future end to the decline phase and a parallel to the recent population revival. The following chapters will examine in greater detail the village as a "service center" to determine how this important aspect of rural communities has survived the period of adjustment and in which direction it is going today.

NOTE

1. The Dun and Bradstreet Reference Book has been a standard data source for small town business. We examined the validity of this source (see Appendix A) and found it to be consistent and reliable through 1970. Due to increased franchise business units, we do not feel this source can be used with confidence for villages after 1970. The listing procedure of Dun and Bradstreet includes franchise outlets under the owner's address, which, in many cases, is not the same as the business location. Since many establishments come and go in less than a decade, our approach here no doubt fails to reveal all the fluctuations in retail or other types of activities.

5 VILLAGE RETAIL AND SERVICE ACTIVITIES

The previous chapter demonstrated that the dominant economic activity of the American village has been in the retail and service sector even though a considerable decline of these activities has occurred since 1950. As might be expected, therefore, an extensive literature of empirical research on economic activities in small towns and villages has concerned the retail/service sector. Important objectives have been to understand the distribution of those activities among places and, to a lesser extent, the change over time in this order.

The village has traditionally been viewed as part of a larger integrated system of centers offering goods and services of varying scale and specialty in response to both market demand and location relative to competing centers. In this chapter we will observe the specific offering of retail goods and services in villages over the 1950–80 time period to better understand both the structural change within the trade center role of the village and how this relates to observed changes in the larger settlement system as discussed in Chapter 1.

The study of functional classification among centers has been the subject of much theoretical and empirical effort in the literature on trade centers. Beginning with the work of Kolb (1923), rural sociologists have attempted to classify communities into categories of varying complexity of "structural differentiation." Later classification efforts have used Guttman scaling to measure the hierarchical differentiation of places on the basis of economic, political, medical, and other services available in them (Hassinger 1957; Fuguitt and Deeley 1966; Hamilton et al. 1976).

Following the early work of Christaller (1966), geographers have sought to establish empirically whether the hierarchical concept is valid and how places can best be classified. An excellent review of this literature can be found in Marshall (1969), who concludes that most attempts have failed to establish the existence of a hierarchy with discrete classes of centers. A reliance on arbitrary decisions in methodology and a failure to acknowledge the spatial aspects of Christaller's hierarchical concept have prevented a true test of its empirical validity. A majority of these have emphasized the lower-order service centers and the change in their specific offerings over time (e.g., Landis 1932; Chittick 1955; Anderson 1961; Hodge 1965). These research efforts raised questions such as whether hierarchical structure actually exists in all systems and in what form and how societal and demographic trends affect the locational and structural arrangement of retail activities (Marshall 1969).

Our unit of analysis prohibits a study of the overall system hierarchy as conducted in previous research because we are looking only at the lowest order of places—that is, one class or level of the total urban hierarchy. Furthermore, a sample of centers does not allow a study of the spatial interrelationships among centers since not all are present in the study. We will, however, compare places within the village level and look at the stability of functional complexity among these places over time.

The importance of functional complexity in the process of retail change is uncertain. In a study of villages in the Canadian provinces of Saskatchewan and Manitoba, Zimmerman and Moneo (1971) discuss the decline in business activities among small places as a function of the size of the center as measured by the number of business establishments. Considering the smallest places the most vulnerable to competition from other larger centers, they propose a gradual demise of the smaller centers and thus a change in the frequency distribution of centers by size toward a higher proportion of larger places. Their comparison of frequency distributions for several intervals between 1910 and 1966 showed, however, that the proposed shift did not occur in their data. Instead, the smallest category, with less than ten business establishments, retained the highest proportion of places throughout the period. This finding suggests a uniform distribution of business change over the size classes, or a sufficient balance of growth and decline among all places, to retain the size distribution.

On a disaggregated level, we would expect that in a process of decline as demonstrated in Chapter 4, functions that are more specialized within the village size class would be lost before more common goods and services, as predicted by Parr and Denike (1970) and demonstrated by Adams (1969) in a study of selected Wisconsin and Missouri villages. Christaller's concept of the range of a good or service as the maximum distance that people will travel to obtain it can help us understand the process of change among individual functions (see Berry and Garrison 1958). In theory, the range of a function increases with rank—that is, a common or "low order" function has a shorter range than a less common activity. In the village, we are comparing common activities such as groceries and hardware with "higher order" functions such as jewelry or sporting goods.

In recent years, the range of most functions has no doubt increased with improvements in transportation, causing increased competition among adjacent centers offering the same activity, since in theory their market areas will overlap. Bell et al. (1974) demonstrated this overlap using estimated market areas for places in southern Minnesota. Assuming that less common activities have a larger range and that this range will extend proportionally with each innovation in transportation, then the less common activities in the village will suffer greater competition from adjacent centers than more common functions. Furthermore, this competition will be predominantly from larger centers where the function is usually offered through larger outlets and in repeated establishments.

Another useful aspect of central place theory is the concept of a minimum threshold population requirement to support retail and service activities. Each function has, in theory, a minimum population required within its range or market area to support a profitable business operation. This threshold population requirement increases with rank from low-order to high-order activities—that is, a grocery store has a lower threshold requirement than a florist, presumably because a higher percentage of the population resident in the market area will purchase groceries than flowers. In some situations declining population may fall below the threshold required for certain activities, beginning with the higher order functions and followed by less common functions. In the case of the village, a declining farm population and continued outmigration of younger people from both farm and nonfarm settings have reduced the number of people and very likely the overall consumer support as the remaining population ages. Villages should therefore become centers of even lower order as decline occurs.

In viewing the urban system from the perspective of the village we would also expect an introduction of new establishments of activities that are diffusing through the system. These activities would logically be new merchandising or service functions with an expanding market to include rural areas. Recent examples would be fast-food franchises, electronic games, and offset printing and copying. In the process of diffusion, these functions will typically move downward from larger to smaller cities, reaching the village only after becoming established in larger places (Berry 1972; L. Brown 1981), although Hudson (1969b) has shown that some innovations may move from large to small places within the immediate hinterland simultaneous to their movement to other cities of similar size.

As new functions appear in the village, they automatically become "higher order goods" because they are less common among places of this size. They may eventually become well established and ordinary where they are met with a sufficient and stable demand such as automobile and television dealers experienced in earlier times. We should therefore expect, in the process of functional change, to see more fluctuation among less common activities as villages lose and gain these somewhat tenuous functions.

Another process may be occurring, however, where decline is predominant. Hart et al. (1968) have explored the process of decline among midwestern villages and found evidence of a tendency in villages to share their market with adjacent villages in a form of "dispersed city" as proposed earlier by Burton (1963). They found what they termed "outsized functions" among these villages that were larger in scale than expected on the basis of village size and presumably of higher order (see also Dahms 1980 for a Canadian example). If such a process were occurring throughout American villages—and this seems highly plausible given the recent tendency toward deconcentrated settlement and increased mobility of rural residents—we should expect some irregularities whereby certain functions survive that serve neighboring communities while others, including more common functions, decline. This process places neighboring villages in a complementary position as opposed to the competitive situation posited by central place theory and thus differs sharply from the generally accepted model of retail location based on spatial competition.

Previous theoretical and empirical literature therefore suggests alternative outcomes for villages in a process of adjustment to changing market conditions for retail and service functions. On the one hand we should expect the loss of higher-order functions resulting from increased range and threshold conditions, but with a possibility, although limited, of new activities entering the village where markets are expanding. On the other hand, in a process of "dispersed city" formation, villages will generally lose functions but not necessarily from their higher-order activities. The first alternative would result in the retention of a hierarchical structure of retail trade centers as demonstrated in empirical work by Brush (1953), Hassinger (1957), and Fuguitt and Deeley (1966), whereas the dispersed city process would result in a less orderly pattern of losses and gains of activity and some evidence of decay in the traditional hierarchy with individual villages sharing a larger market. Bell et al. (1974), using Hassinger's data for Minnesota and additional data for Iowa, conclude that the latter process has occurred. They used Guttman scaling to test for the retention of a hierarchical structure of central place activities over time and found a slight reduction in the coefficient of reproducibility when comparing consistent functions.

It is difficult to test for the dispersed city formation in our data for the national sample because we do not have information for adjacent villages and cities. We will look at the pattern of change by functional rank and at the consistency of the hierarchical arrangement of functions among villages over the 1950–80 period. If the dispersed city is replacing the established order of competing centers, we should find disintegration of the hierarchy over time as opposed to an orderly process of decline with a hierarchy intact. We will explore these issues in the national sample after a brief introduction to the village as a shopping center.

THE VILLAGE AS A SHOPPING CENTER

The most visible aspect of the village community in the United States is, or has been, the "main street" business district. It is a microscale model of the central business district in larger cities and has, with minor variations, a consistency of form that is recognizable throughout the country. The "main street" is the shopping center of the village and contains most of the retail and service business establishments found in the village. The importance of local and regional accessibility to the village shops is evident in the spatial pattern of the main street within the village network. It commonly lies either in the center of the residential area of the village along a segment of a main artery of traffic or perpendicular to a main highway or railroad track, as in villages of the plains (Hudson 1977). In most villages the main street is intersected by at least one important avenue of traffic, which forms a center of focus for business activities.

The main street is the core of the business community of the village. Isolated establishments will be found away from the main street, but the majority of firms will be found here. The complexity and size of the business district will vary considerably within the size class considered in this study, that is, less than 2,500 population. The smallest village may have none or only a few business activities, and rather than a main street as such it may focus on a "crossroads" with little development beyond it. In contrast, the largest village will have a well-developed pattern of business and residential activity with necessary supporting services and utilities.

Casual observation in many villages today reveals a transition in the village business district just as it is evident in the central business districts of larger cities. Many stores are empty and many former banks and other prominent buildings are used for less important activities or are vacant. ' .though some new stores can be found in village communities, the more common trend has been decline.

Retail Establishments and Functions

Turning now to the sample of villages and the data from Dun and Bradstreet, we see that these observable symptoms of decline are supported in the data (Table 5-1). A distinction is made in the retail/service sector between "functions" and "establishments." A function is a specific activity or line of business such as hardware or auto body repair, while an establishment is an outlet or firm engaged in that function. The number of functions in a village, therefore, represents the number of different activities available, and the number of establishments is the total number of stores or firms. A village with three gas stations and one grocery store would, therefore, have two functions and four establishments. In cases where a single entrepreneur offers two or more functions at the same location (e.g., a restaurant and a gas station), each line of business is counted as a separate establishment.

Looking at the first two panels of Table 5-1 we see that between 1950 and 1960 the average number of establishments declined in the total sample and in all three regions at a substantial rate and that the percentage of places losing establishments during this decade was over three-fourths (79 percent) for the total sample. The 1960–70 decade resulted in a further decline of establishments as measured by the means, and the proportion of places losing was again over three-fourths (76 percent) in the total sample.

Perhaps even more serious is the high rate of decline in functions during this time period. The average dropped from thirteen per place

Table 5-1. Retail and Service Establishments and Functions by Region.

	Date	United States	North	South	West
Mean number of establishments	1950	27	27	29	25
	1960	23	22	25	21
	1970	18	18	21	16
Percentage of villages losing establishments	1950–60	79	81	73	82
	1960–70	76	77	71	80
Mean number of functions	1950	13	13	10	14
	1960	12	12	11	12
	1970	10	10	10	10
Percentage of villages losing establishments	1950–60	60	61	46	76
	1960–70	76	77	71	80
Mean number of establishments per function	1950	2.1	1.8	2.7	1.8
	1960	1.8	1.6	2.3	1.7
	1970	1.6	1.5	2.0	1.6

Source: Compiled by authors.

to ten during the two decades, and the pattern was widespread with fully 60 percent and 76 percent of the sampled villages losing functions during the two decades respectively. These high rates of decline demonstrate the severity of the problems facing village residents and merchants. These declines represent loss of employment and income for the merchants and a loss of shopping and service opportunities for village residents.

The rates of loss of functions were highest among western villages during each decade. Western villages averaged fewer establishments each year (Table 5-1) but had a greater or equal number of functions compared with northern and southern villages. In contrast, southern villages averaged a greater number of establishments each year than villages in other regions and had a lower incidence of loss than the other villages during both decades. Duplication of establishments was also greater among southern villages, as indicated by the lower number of functions each year. Comparing the means in the bottom panel in Table 5-1 we can see that the surplus of establishments over functions declined each decade and was greatest in the South during all three years. It seems rather anomalous that the villages with the greatest duplication in establishments, suggesting smaller-scale outlets, should have had the lowest rate of establishment loss. Recent trends toward increasing scale of common goods retail outlets would suggest the opposite pattern.

The reduction in the average ratio of establishments to functions demonstrates that it is the duplicate establishments that close first in the process of decline, followed by complete loss of the function in more severe cases. For the village resident, the variety of alternatives is reduced before the function disappears altogether in situations where decline is occurring.

Distribution of Villages by Establishments

Following the work of Zimmerman and Moneo (1971), we examine next the distribution of villages by the number of establishments at each time (Figure 5-1). We can see an establishment distribution similar to that reported by Zimmerman and Moneo but a more pronounced pattern of change in this distribution between 1950 and 1970 than they reported in the earlier period for Canadian villages.

Figure 5–1. Frequency of Villages by Number of Business Units.

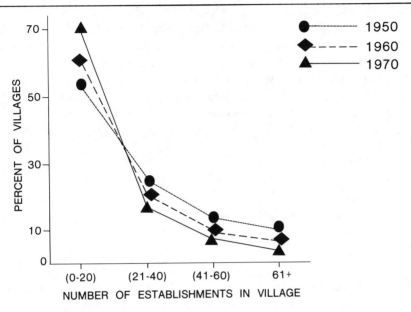

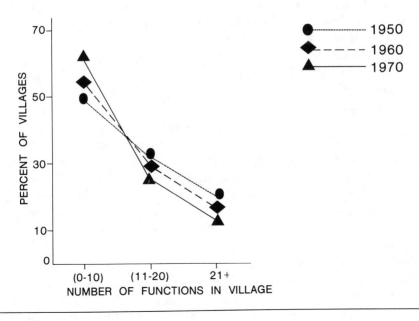

Source: Compiled by authors.

There was a shift toward fewer villages with a larger number of establishments and proportionally more with a small number over the time period. This shift was noticed using both the establishment and function measures (Figure 5-1). The percentage of villages with less than twenty establishments or less than ten functions increased each decade, while the corresponding proportions in the larger size categories declined. This change in the size distribution of villages suggests as Zimmerman and Moneo found, contrary to their expectations, that decline in retail and service activities has occurred among large as well as small villages resulting in a downward shift of villages from all levels.

Changes in Individual Activities

It is necessary to look at specific business activities in a disaggregated manner to understand what lies behind the changes observed in Table 5-1 and Figure 5-1. All business activities that appeared in the sampled villages under retail and service categories are listed in Table 5-2. These activities are ranked by the number of villages with at least one establishment of the activity as of 1950, the beginning of the period of study.

Looking first at the percentage of villages with each activity, we can see that the ranking indicates the importance of basic functions such as groceries, service station, and hardware compared to the less common activities such as jeweler, meat market, florist, and department store. The consistency of functional offering among villages was quite low, possibly because of the wide range in size among places under 2,500 population. Only eight out of forty-seven functions were found in more than half of the sampled villages in 1950, and this number declined to seven in 1960 and only three in 1970 (Table 5-2).

The normal business trend was decline, as represented by the data in Table 5-2. Nearly two-thirds of the business activities were found in fewer villages in 1960 than in 1950, and this rate increased to nearly three-fourths during the 1960-70 decade. Of the activities that did not decline, most were either stable or experienced only modest gains. It is interesting to note that these functions were largely of the less common variety, such as electrical repair, florist, and sporting goods, suggesting the possibility of expansion of these functions to include rural markets.

By 1970 most activities had declined in their frequency of occurrence and the ranking of functions was disrupted as some declined more sharply than others and a few increased in frequency. As a measure of change in the importance of functions over each decade, an index of retention was developed and is shown in the right-hand columns of Table 5–2. This index is the percentage of the 1950 occurrence that was found in 1960 and similarly, the percentage of the 1960 occurrence found in 1970, such that a function found in 50 percent of the villages in 1950 and in 25 percent in 1960 would have a retention rate of 50 percent. The index was compiled for each decade and for the entire 1950–70 period.

The rate of retention varied by function and by decade. Some functions such as service stations, banks, and clothing stores were highly consistent, while others, such as tavern and auto repair, varied greatly by decade. The retention rate was not clearly related to rank in either decade, since decline was common at all levels. The highest relative gains, although experienced in only a few villages, were found among the less common activities. Electrical repair, radio and television dealers, florists, sporting goods, and farm supply stores were found in less than one-fifth of the sampled villages in 1950 but showed substantial gains in occurrence during the twenty-year period. Looking at these activities, we can speculate as to their growth.

The increase in electrical repair seems to reflect a trend toward mechanization involving electrical machinery and appliances on the farm and in rural homes, providing a demand for this service. Radio and television stores have increased in number, because of innovations in and increased usage of products commonly handled in these establishments. These developments, along with repair services, kept dealers busy, even while other activities were declining.

Sporting goods represent another line of merchandise that has grown to meet an expanding demand, probably resulting from increased leisure time and disposable income among rural residents. In some rural areas recreational development has been an important stimulant to the local economy including the retailing of sports-related merchandise (McCarthy and Morrison 1979).

Florists represent an activity that has not been common in villages yet experienced consistent growth in each decade. This trend could reflect a need for space that brings urban florists out to nearby villages to avoid high land prices or high taxes in urban areas. It

Table 5–2.   Individual Business Activities in Sampled Villages.

Business Activity	Percentage of places with Activity			Index of Retention		
	1950	1960	1970	1950–60	1960–70	1950–70
Groceries	99	97	93	0.98	0.96	0.94
Service station	90	87	81	0.97	0.93	0.90
Auto repair	68	57	27	0.84	0.47	0.40
Eating place	68	51	47	0.75	0.92	0.69
Hardware	60	53	46	0.88	0.87	0.77
Drug	56	51	41	0.91	0.80	0.73
Lumber	55	49	45	0.89	0.92	0.82
Bank	51	54	55	1.06	1.02	1.08
Feed	47	43	37	0.91	0.86	0.79
Farm implement	43	37	33	0.86	0.89	0.77
Tavern	40	42	20	1.05	0.48	0.50
Auto dealer (new)	38	32	26	0.84	0.81	0.68
Petroleum	37	40	38	1.08	0.95	1.03
Mortuary	35	34	23	0.97	0.68	0.66
Appliances	35	28	19	0.80	0.68	0.54
Clothing	34	31	30	0.91	0.97	0.88
Furniture	33	28	28	0.85	1.00	0.85
Welding	33	18	7	0.56	0.39	0.21
Variety	32	26	26	0.81	1.00	0.81
Fuel	27	21	18	0.78	0.86	0.67
Laundry and dry cleaning	26	26	17	1.00	0.65	0.65
Bowling	23	15	8	0.65	0.53	0.35
Hotel	22	25	25	1.14	1.00	1.14

(Continued on next page)

could also reflect a growing market in the rural area caused by certain demographic trends of the past few decades. The prolonged outmigration of young people from rural areas has separated many children from their parents and relatives still living in rural areas. Since florists have developed networks of communication and sales to alleviate the sending of flowers from distant locations, a convenient way for outmigrant family members to extend and receive good wishes at holidays and other special occasions has been through the sending of flowers. This may well have stimulated the market for the village florist, often in the face of a declining local demand for these services and products.

Farm supplies stores represent a diverse category of goods related to gardening and farm activities, typically on a small scale. These

Table 5–2.   continued

Business Activity	Percentage of places with Activity			Index of Retention		
	1950	1960	1970	1950–60	1960–70	1950–70
Jeweler	20	15	12	0.75	0.80	0.60
Auto parts	20	20	24	1.00	1.20	1.20
Liquor	20	11	11	0.55	1.00	0.55
Electrical repair	18	26	28	1.44	1.08	1.56
Confections	16	5	5	0.31	1.00	0.31
Radio and television	13	17	16	1.31	0.94	1.23
Dairy	12	7	3	0.58	0.43	0.25
Bakery	12	9	8	0.75	0.89	0.67
Meat	11	11	7	1.00	0.64	0.64
Florist	9	13	16	1.44	1.23	1.78
Plumbing	9	7	6	0.78	0.86	0.67
Farm and garden supplies	9	20	23	2.22	1.15	2.56
Sporting goods	7	9	10	1.29	1.11	1.43
Auto body repair	6	7	5	1.17	0.71	0.83
Paint	6	4	3	0.67	0.75	0.50
Fruit	5	3	1	0.60	0.33	0.20
Laundromat	5	4	3	0.80	0.75	0.60
Department store	5	4	4	0.80	1.00	0.80
Antique	5	8	7	1.60	0.86	1.40
Used autos	5	7	9	1.40	1.29	1.80
Watch repair	4	3	2	0.75	0.67	0.50
Electronic supplies	4	3	1	0.75	0.33	0.25
Photographer	3	5	2	1.67	0.40	0.67
Furniture repair	3	4	2	1.33	0.50	0.67

Source: Compiled by authors.

stores have increased from presence in only 9 percent of the villages to 23 percent over the twenty-year period. The increase might be partially related to the rise in rural nonfarm population whose residence often includes the space for gardening or part-time farming activities. If so, this increase would probably have been most common in near-urban locations where the part-time farms are most common (Johansen 1979). The increase might also reflect greater demand for farm supplies, which relates to the increased productivity of farm land despite the smaller number of farm units. The larger scale of farm units has reduced the number of farms in most rural areas. At the same time, total farm output has grown, giving support to production-related services and supplies in small towns, while most activities that are dependent on the number of farmers, such as clothing stores, have declined (Paulsen and Carlson 1961).

THE STRUCTURE OF RETAIL ACTIVITIES

Villages, as defined in this study, would fall at the bottom level of most attempts to classify the urban system. They have provided the basic goods and services commonly needed by their resident and nearby populations. Yet within this size class of places with 2,500 or fewer residents, we can see a considerable variation in the number and variety of retail and service activities.

The Retail Hierarchy

As a first step toward understanding the structure of the distribution of retail and service activities within our villages, we ranked the forty-seven various functions found in the villages by the number of villages that offered them. This rank was then compared with the ranking of villages by the number of functions offered in each one as diagrammed in Figure 5-2. Although too cumbersome to show here, the resulting pattern approximated a Guttman type hierarchy with errors at all levels of size. The larger villages with the most functions had the greatest number of higher order (less common) activities as one would expect, but outliers appeared at all levels of village size as did the absence of common functions in villages where one would expect them.

To summarize the lengthy table resulting from the comparison described in Figure 5-2, we have prepared Table 5-3. This table combines the forty-five most common functions into nine consecutive groups of five and the villages into categories ranked by the number of functions in the village separately in 1950, 1960, and 1970. The body of Table 5-3 contains the mean number of the five functions in each group that was found among the villages in each functional size category. For example, among the largest villages (those with 26 to 35 activities) the average place had 4.94 of the five functions in group 1

Figure 5-2. Ranking Procedure Used to Group Activities.

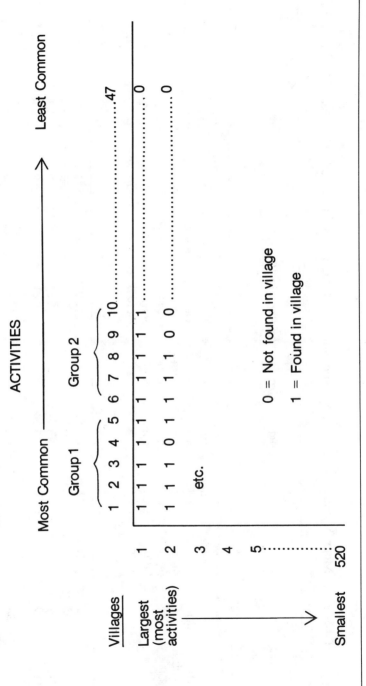

Source: Compiled by authors.

Table 5–3. Mean Number of the Five Functions in Each Group Present by Total Number of Functions in Village.

Number of Functions per Village in 1950	Number of Villages	1950 Functions Grouped by Rank in 1950[a]								
		1 — Grocery, Service stations, Auto repair, Eating place, Hardware	2 — Drugs, Lumber, Bank, Feed, Farm implements	3 — Tavern, Auto dealer (new), Petroleum fuel, Mortuary, Appliances	4 — Clothing, Furniture, Welding, Variety store, Fuel	5 — Laundry and dry cleaning, Bowling, Hotel, Jewelry, Auto parts	6 — Liquor, Electrical repair, Confection, Radio/television, Dairy	7 — Bakery, Meat, Florist, Plumbing, Farm and garden supplies	8 — Sporting goods, Auto body repair, Paint, Fruit, Laundromat	9 — Department store, Antiques, Used autos, Electrical supply, Photographer
26+	46	4.94	4.65	4.25	3.86	3.92	2.51	1.80	1.23	0.90
21–25	53	4.80	4.33	3.63	3.46	2.62	2.17	1.02	0.60	0.48
16–20	71	4.60	3.94	2.94	2.62	1.62	0.88	0.65	0.32	0.29
11–15	90	4.20	3.02	1.88	1.47	0.81	0.76	0.45	0.16	0.22
6–10	146	3.62	2.64	1.96	0.72	0.32	0.38	0.14	0.10	0.06
0–5	90	2.73	0.45	0.30	0.22	0.17	0.01	0.04	0.03	—

Table 5-3. continued

1960
Functions Grouped by Rank in 1960[a]

Number of Functions per Village in 1960	Number of Villages	1 Grocery, Service stations, Auto repair, Bank, Hardware	2 Drugs, Eating place, Lumber, Feed, Tavern	3 Petroleum fuel, Farm implements, Mortuary, Auto dealer, Clothing	4 Appliances, Furniture, Electrical repair, Laundry and dry cleaning, Variety store	5 Hotel, Fuel, Farm and garden supplies, Auto parts, Welding	6 Radio/television, Bowling, Jewelry, Florist, Meat Market	7 Liquor, Sporting goods, Bakery, Antiques, Plumbing	8 Auto body repair, Dairy, Used autos, Photographer, Confectionary	9 Department store, Laundromat, Paint, Furniture repair, Electrical supplies
26+	40	4.95	4.4	4.75	4.46	2.88	2.82	1.84	1.64	0.93
21–25	41	4.56	3.97	3.95	3.39	2.29	1.95	1.09	0.83	0.53
16–20	64	4.37	3.78	3.29	2.30	1.68	1.07	0.56	0.29	0.19
11–15	85	4.15	2.02	1.92	1.34	0.96	0.55	0.40	0.18	0.18
6–10	123	3.38	1.84	0.76	1.03	0.80	0.24	0.15	0.09	0.06
0–5	143	2.03	0.26	0.22	0.14	0.14	0.05	0.07	0.01	0.03

Table 5-3. continued

| | | 1970 Functions Grouped by Rank in 1970ᵃ | | | | | | | | |
Number of Functions per Village in 1970	Number of Villages	1 Grocery, Service station, Bank, Eating place, Hardware	2 Lumber, Drugs, Petroleum fuel, Feed, Farm implements	3 Clothing, Auto repair, Furniture, Electrical repair, Auto dealer	4 Variety, Hotel, Auto parts, Mortuary, Farm and garden supplies	5 Tavern, Appliances, Fuel, Laundry and dry cleaning, Florist	6 Radio/ television, Jewelry, Liquor, Sporting goods, Used autos	7 Bowling, Bakery, Meat market, Welding, Antiques	8 Plumbing, Auto body repair, Department store, Dairy, Confectionary	9 Paint, Laundromat, Photographer, Furniture repair, Fruit
26+	23	4.93	4.46	3.52	3.95	3.65	2.48	1.60	1.04	0.95
21–25	35	4.81	4.28	3.11	3.14	2.85	1.68	1.37	0.49	0.34
16–20	50	4.51	3.60	2.38	2.46	2.08	1.30	0.76	0.36	0.16
11–15	84	4.28	2.89	1.58	1.44	1.22	0.61	0.39	0.27	0.10
6–10	128	3.49	1.82	0.61	0.62	0.76	0.32	0.08	0.15	0.04
0–5	176	1.74	0.45	0.23	0.18	0.25	0.05	0.06	0.02.	0.01

ᵃFunctions were ranked by the number of places in which each was found.
Source: Compiled by authors.

(Table 5–3). The mean per village decreases to the right across the table toward less common activities and also down the table in all groups toward villages with fewer functions. This pattern is consistent in the table for 1950, 1960, and 1970, although the specific functions in each group did not remain the same.

The table for each year demonstrates a strong relationship between number of functions in a village and the ranking of activities (Table 5–3). A perfect Guttman hierarchy is not the case here, however, since the mean values indicate that none of the categories of villages had achieved all of the functions expected according to their rank (e.g., the village size category 26–30 should have had a mean of five for all functional groups through at least the twenty-sixth function). This was not found in any year. Similarly, villages with five or less functions should not have had any of the functions ranked higher than the five in group 1 to form a perfect scale, yet positive mean values were found for higher ranked groups in all three years (bottom line of Table 5–3 for each year). These occurrences are called "positive errors" in Guttman terminology. To summarize the consistency of these error patterns over time, we computed the percentage of functional occurrences that were positive errors among each size class. The percentages varied from eight for the villages with 26–35 functions in 1950 and 1970, to 31 and 42 percent among the 0–5 category of places in 1950 and 1970 respectively. The smallest places had a slightly greater positive error pattern at the end of the twenty-year period, which suggests the possibility of an increased number of outsized functions. The total number of positive error occurrences, however, remained an identical 23 percent from 1950–70 for all size classes.

It has been stated that the process of decline in a central place system results in a shift of functions from low to higher levels in the hierarchy when population falls below threshold level or other factors such as metropolitan competition operate (Berry 1967; Parr and Denike 1970). Close examination of Table 5–3 reveals that of the forty-five functions arranged in rank order in 1950, eleven had moved up the hierarchy to higher level groups by 1970, and thirteen had moved to lower level groups during the twenty-year period. We must realize that the village communities studied here altogether represent the lowest level in most hierarchical classifications, yet it is interesting that movement within this group of places was so balanced.

Functions that moved up the hierarchy, include: auto repair, tavern, mortuary, appliances, and welding. Among functions moving down the hierarchy, were bank, sporting goods, farm and garden supplies, florist, and hotel. It seems that functions experiencing a growth or diffusion in society still trickle down to these small centers even during a period of major decline in more established activities. The activities increasing in frequency include products or services that accompany trends in modern rural society where demand is yet strong due to development in the village market area such as recreation, hobby farming, and, in some cases, population growth.

Despite the movement of villages among the size classes and the shifting of activities among the functional groups, the relationship between village size and the presence of the various activities remained very much the same throughout the twenty-year period. The mean values in Table 5-3 were highly correlated among the three years despite fluctuations in rank among both functions and villages, which indicates a stability in the pattern of the hierarchical scale over time within village level functions.

As mentioned earlier, Bell et al. (1974) discovered a highly stable pattern of hierarchical order among selected functions in two midwestern study areas. Using Guttman scaling they noticed a slight reduction in the coefficient of reproducibility over time. We selected the five comparable functions from our data (which were clothing, furniture, drugs, hardware, and grocery) and computed Guttman's coefficient of reproducibility for 1950–70 using the Dun and Bradstreet data and the mayors' survey results for the sample of 100 villages. Table 5-4 compares these results. Although the time period of our study differs somewhat from theirs, the trend appears to be different among the national sample. The coefficient of reproducibility increased consistently indicating a stable and slightly improved orderly hierarchy among U.S. villages between 1950–80 on these functions. This seems to indicate, as does Table 5-3, that the hierarchical order has not been decaying during this period of considerable change in functional offerings.

Change in Activities by Size

We established earlier in this chapter that over the period of study a majority of retail and service functions declined in occurrence and

Table 5-4. Coefficients of Reproducibility from Guttman Scaling of Selected Functions.

Data Source	Date	Coefficient
Minnesota[a]	1951	0.984
	1970	0.981
Iowa[a]	1960	0.902
	1970	0.899
U.S. Sample (N = 100)	1950	0.872
	1960	0.864
	1970	0.900
	1980	0.927

[a]As reported in Bell et al. (1974) from Hassinger's study of trade centers in Minnesota and their data for Iowa communities.

Source: Compiled by authors.

that most of the villages experienced a net loss of these activities. It is true, of course, that individual activities were gained by some villages while declining from others and, similarly, that villages with a net loss of functions may have gained some while losing others. To understand the trends underlying the patterns of net change observed, we have selected certain activities for detailed analysis. The activities were selected to represent both common and uncommon functions, and their growth and decline in occurrence is compared to village size in Figure 5-3. The selected functions are ordered in Figure 5-3 by rank in 1950 as listed in Table 5-3. These include drugs, mortuary, clothing, radio-television, and farm and garden supplies.

The graphs in Figure 5-3 show (1) the percentages of villages that had each function at the beginning of the decade but lost it during the decade and conversely (2) the percentages of villages that began the decade without each function but gained it during the decade; both are plotted by the total number of functions at the beginning of the decade. The rate of loss for most activities was inversely related to village size as measured by number of functions, while the pattern of gain was directly related to size for most of the five selected functions considered in either decade.

As would be predicted in a declining central place system, there was a very high rate of loss among the few small villages (those with less than five activities) that had acquired or retained these functions, and this high rate of loss extended to larger size classes for the less common functions each decade (e.g., radio-television and farm and

Figure 5–3. Frequency of Growth and Decline of Selected Functions by Total Number of Functions in Village.

● Percent of villages that lost function during decade.

▲ Percent gaining function that did not have it in beginning of decade

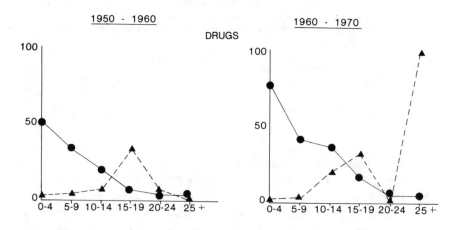

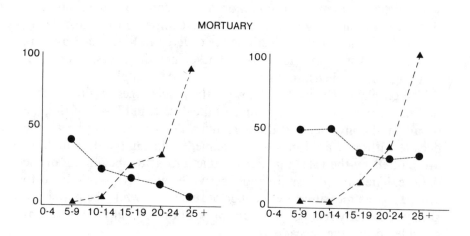

Figure 5–3.   continued

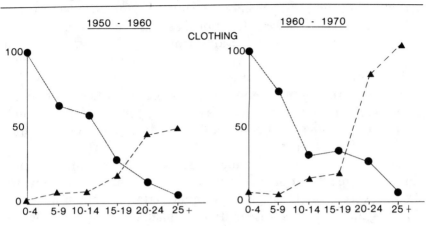

CLOTHING

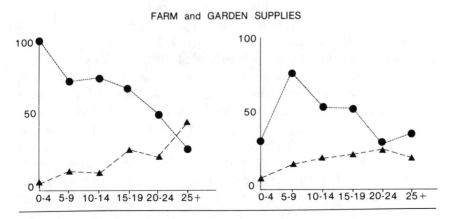

RADIO and T.V.

FARM and GARDEN SUPPLIES

Source: Compiled by authors.

garden supplies) (Figure 5–3). The point at which the two curves of percentage gaining and percentage losing cross for 1950–60 seems to indicate a correspondence to functional rank, since it moves generally to the right in the sequence of graphs from drugs to farm and garden supplies, although for 1960–70 the lines do not cross for the two highest ranked functions. The smaller places had an increasingly high rate of loss throughout this sequence of ranked activities. In contrast, the villages with the most functions suffered fewer losses, although the rate of loss increased between decades for all of these activities among the largest places.

Just as we would expect higher rates of decline among small villages where a function is unusual or out of its normal ranking, we should expect that large places without certain common activities should gain these. The distribution of places gaining functions in Figure 5–3 supports this notion, although error exists in the pattern. In all cases, the frequency of gain increased with the total number of functions, although the slope of this curve was steeper for common activities such as mortuary and clothing than for radio-television and farm and garden supplies. The small percentage of large villages gaining drug stores during the first decade represents only a very small absolute number since nearly all villages with more than fifteen functions already had this activity.

POST–1970 TRENDS

Using data from the telephone survey of mayors, we can see the 1975–80 pattern of occurrence and change for some of the functions considered in this chapter. Activities included in the survey are listed in Table 5–5 ranked by the percentage of places with each in 1975. The functions listed represent common goods and services similar in rank to those listed in Table 5–2 based on Dun and Bradstreet sources. Of the sixteen functions listed, ten were found in fewer places in 1980 than in 1975, and twelve had fewer establishments at the end of the five-year period. Despite the different data source and the shorter time period represented in Table 5–5, these figures suggest that the trend of retail decline did not end during the 1970s and that the celebrated turnaround in population among small towns was not matched by an overall growth in retail activities.

Table 5–5 represents the net result of gain and loss in each case and therefore disguises the specific performance of individual activities. The percentage of places that gained, remained stable, or lost each activity is listed in Table 5–6 for all functions included in the survey. The functions are ranked by the percentage of places with each in 1975 as they were in the previous table. We should expect here that less common functions would have higher rates of loss if the system is becoming more centralized, as was discussed earlier. What we see is a pattern of change that is somewhat relative to rank, although not in a completely consistent manner. The greatest losses and gains were found among the most common functions. This suggests higher turnover among these activities as previous research has shown. In a study of Illinois retailers, Star and Massel (1981) found low survival rates (under 50 percent) for groceries, eating places, and taverns, among other activities, during the 1974–79 period. In contrast, they found relatively high survival rates for farm implement dealer, auto

Table 5–5.   Retail/Service Activities in Villages, 1975–80.

Retail/Service Activity	Percentage of Places with at Least One Establishment		Total Number of Establishments	
	1975	1980	1975	1980
Gas station	94	92	303	279
Grocery	93	91	189	181
Eating places	87	87	203	206
Auto repair	80	79	166	162
Tavern	70	68	175	173
Hardware	69	69	104	98
Bank	61	65	66	72
Feed	58	59	85	84
Lumber	51	48	61	54
Clothing	51	48	91	85
Drug	38	39	56	54
Hotel	35	31	63	58
Auto dealer	33	30	59	50
Furniture	28	28	36	38
Farm implements	23	21	32	32
Jeweler	13	12	14	13

Source: Survey of 100 mayors.

dealer, jeweler, and furniture—the less common functions on Table 5-6. We might expect, therefore, that in the small town low-order goods and services will come and go with somewhat greater frequency than less common functions whose losses are not matched by new stores opening up (e.g., auto dealers) (Table 5-6).

Another possible reason for the retention of some higher-order activities while more common functions decline, as shown in Tables 5-2 and 5-6, is the tendency for villages to specialize in certain "outsized" functions, as Hart et al. (1968) have suggested. This can occur where villages lie close enough to each other to share the market area as a form of dispersed city. In the process of decline, each village may lose some activities but will retain certain functions that complement the mix of goods and services found in the other centers.

Table 5-6. Percentage Distribution of Villages by Pattern of Change for Individual Activities, 1975–80.

Activity	Loss	Stable	Gain
Retail/Service			
Gas station	21	72	7
Grocery	20	70	10
Eating place	16	69	15
Auto repair	16	72	12
Tavern	7	88	5
Hardware	10	85	5
Bank	1	93	6
Feed	3	94	3
Lumber	7	93	0
Clothing	11	83	6
Drug	7	88	5
Hotel	5	95	0
Auto dealer	10	89	1
Furniture	2	94	4
Farm implements	3	93	4
Jeweler	1	99	0
Finance/Insurance/			
Real Estate			
Insurance	6	89	5
Real estate	2	86	12
Savings and loan	1	94	5

Source: Compiled by authors.

These may become larger and more important than other business activities in the village, thus the term "outsized." This process, if happening, seems to evolve from competition among centers yet results in a complementary situation. The surviving functions in each village would need to share the total market area and thus could not duplicate activities in other centers sharing the same market. The idea seems best suited to a situation where population decline causes insufficient market support for existing centers to offer a complete array of functions, but it could also apply where some traditional customers are attracted away from the local shopping centers to larger cities.

The continued decline in retail business evident in the survey data for 1975–80 probably stems from a multitude of factors, as discussed in Chapter 4. Responses to a question addressed to the mayors are quite revealing, however, in demonstrating the plight of the typical small town. Mayors were asked, "Where do most people in your community go to shop?" The responses are totaled in Table 5–7 for selected goods and services. The high rate of shopping (as perceived by the mayors) in other cities or towns for even common goods such as groceries and auto repair points to the problem of holding a potential market population that has become increasingly mobile.

Table 5–7. Responses to Question "Where do most people in your community go to obtain . . . ?"

	Local Village	Other City or Town	Both
	(Percentage of Respondents)		
Groceries	25	63	12
Appliances	16	81	3
Medical care	14	76	10
Banking	51	41	8
Auto or appliance repair	32	50	18
Religious services	91	6	3

Source: Survey of 100 mayors.

SUMMARY AND CONCLUSIONS

In summary, the analysis in this chapter has revealed some regularities within the retail and service sector of business activities in American villages that conform to the structural organization posited in central place theory. Variations were noticed among the particular activities in their frequency of occurrence and in their pattern of change that were related to their overall rank and to the total number of functions in the village. Villages commonly offered goods and services such as groceries, hardware, and banking, while only occasional outlets of more specialized activities were found among places of this size range.

The particular functions found in villages were somewhat uniformly associated with the size of the village as measured by the total number of functions offered, such that the occurrence of ranked groups of activities was highly correlated with size of place. We also saw that change in the frequency of occurrence varied among the activities and that the number of functions in a village was a factor in determining the pattern of function growth and decline. Larger villages tended to gain activities at a higher rate and lose them at a lesser rate than smaller villages, and this was true regardless of the rank of functions. This did not, however, offset the overall shift among the villages toward smaller functional size, as shown in Figure 5-1. There were fewer places with more than ten functions in 1970 than in 1950.

Our results have demonstrated an orderly process of change within the array of functions found in villages that seems to discount the idea of a disintegrating hierarchical order through the process of decline. Yet the patterns of change among functions are not clearly related to their rank in the system, and certain adaptive, complementary trends could be occurring. Needed is a study of this process among adjacent centers to determine the extent to which the dispersed city pattern is emerging among villages.

As a whole, villages suffered a serious loss of retail outlets during the period of study. With over three-fourths of all sampled villages losing establishments between 1950 and 1970, the importance of the village as a shopping center has clearly been diminished. The village has also lost in the selection of retail activities that were normally associated with places of this size, since over three-fourths of the functions listed in 1950 were found in fewer places in 1970.

The post–1970 turnaround in population trends experienced in many villages, as reported in Chapter 2, was not matched by a revival of retail business, as reported in the survey of mayors. Although a few functions increased in frequency among the subsample of villages, a majority declined between 1975 and 1980 as they had in previous decades.

The implications of these trends for the residents of rural areas seem to suggest a declining level of local service opportunity. As the villages lose their shopping districts, the people living in and near them must travel farther to obtain those activities. It is, of course, true that residents have chosen to travel to larger cities to obtain goods and services available in their local villages, which helped to hasten the decline of the village merchants. The next chapter will explore the causes of the patterns of change observed here and attempt to explain both the variations among villages in the net patterns of change in retail and service activities and the relationships between such activities and village population.

6 VILLAGES AS RESIDENTIAL AND TRADE CENTERS

The previous chapters have addressed either the demographic or the economic aspects of village communities looking at characteristics and processes of change within these attributes. In this chapter we bring together village population with village business activities to study their interrelationships in both static and dynamic comparisons.

Previous research has shown that village communities in rural America emerged largely as service centers and residential centers for people engaged in primary occupations. Many of these communities have experienced fluctuations of growth and decline in population and business activity in response to employment changes in primary occupations such as mining and forestry or through mechanization in agriculture, which eventually reduced the market population for village services (Brunner et al. 1927; Johansen and Fuguitt 1973). The particular experience of each place as either a service or residential center has depended largely on its supporting economic base and its location relative to other centers of employment and service activities. The shifts in both retail activities and population reported separately in earlier chapters can be viewed as possible evidence of change in the relative importance of each of these roles in today's village.

A principal research theme has been the association of place population size with the number of central place activities in an attempt to establish the form of this relationship and its consistency among different systems (Stafford 1963; Berry 1967; Kenyon 1967; Marshall 1969). Empirical studies have demonstrated a strong positive linear association between place population and the number of retail/service establishments and functions, in a variety of locational settings. The specific linear function describing the association has varied somewhat among published empirical examples and has been shown to vary over time within a random sample of Wisconsin villages (Johansen and Fuguitt 1973). In the Wisconsin sample the number of business activities corresponding to a given population size declined between 1939 and 1970. This finding suggests a possible explanation for differences in the exact form of the linear association found in other empirical studies reported by Marshall (1969), which are based on data from slightly different time periods.

A change in the relationship between population and retail/service establishments can result only from a differential rate of change between the two variables. We know from Chapters 4 and 5 that retail and service activities have declined sharply in many villages since 1950. Population also declined in many places but not as frequently nor as severely as business activities did, and population increase was more common than business increase in villages during the post-1950 period. We should expect, therefore, a shift in the regression of business activities on population during this time, toward fewer business activities corresponding to a given population size.

An assumption that seems to prevail in most research on business/population relationships is that place population is directly correlated with the generally more inclusive market area population, which is an important factor in determining the level of business activity in a place. Berry (1967) gave empirical evidence of a relationship between both place population and market area size and number of central functions supporting the validity of this assumption. A retail business may also support a segment of the population resident in the village because it provides jobs. With an increase in the residential desirability of rural village communities, however, an increasing proportion of the resident village population can be considered strictly as potential market support for village merchants. Other factors influencing village or market area population growth—such as expansion of industries or expansion of schools or other public institutions—would in turn create additional support for village merchants.

In this chapter we examine the association between the residential and trade center roles of the village at each point in time, looking first at the aggregate relationship and later at individual functions and the population associated with single and multiple establishments of each. The latter association will allow us to address the issue of population increments required for the first and second establishment of each function as a form of population threshold analysis. Later in the chapter we develop models of the relation between change in retail establishments and population change over each decade, incorporating also accessibility of the village to larger places and change in the number of industrial activities.

TRENDS IN THE POPULATION-TRADE RELATIONSHIP

The association between the population of a village and the number of retail and service establishments and functions is examined first using a regression analysis of retail establishments or functions on population. The resulting association for the total sample is plotted in Figure 6-1 for the years 1950, 1960, and 1970.

As expected, village population was highly correlated at each time both with number of establishments and functions, but the relationship shifted toward the population axis (Figure 6-1). Thus, for a given population, there were fewer establishments and fewer functions in later years. The change in slope evident in both graphs suggests

Figure 6-1. Relationship between Village Population and Business Activities at Each Time.

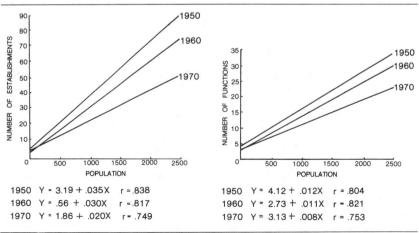

1950 Y = 3.19 + .035X   r = .838
1960 Y = .56 + .030X   r = .817
1970 Y = 1.86 + .020X   r = .749

1950 Y = 4.12 + .012X   r = .804
1960 Y = 2.73 + .011X   r = .821
1970 Y = 3.13 + .008X   r = .753

Source: Compiled by authors.

that larger villages have witnessed greater loss in economic activity corresponding to a given population size during the latter decade.

This condition can be demonstrated by comparing corresponding levels of economic activity with a given population size for each time—that is, by considering the regression line as the mean of the distribution of establishments among the population size categories. The number corresponding to a place of 2,000 population was about 70 establishments in 1950, 60 in 1960, and 40 in 1970. The comparable figures for a place of 500 were 20, 15, and 11.8. The decline in number of establishments for the place of 2,000 population amounted to an average of −14 percent and −33 percent respectively, and the decline for the place of 500 would be −25 percent and −21 percent in the two decades. The number of business units was not, however, the only variable that changed in this model. We know from the previous analysis that population increased in many of these villages while business units generally declined. The relationship, therefore, represents change in both variables and shows a movement toward fewer business units per unit of population, especially in larger villages.

Population-Retail Ratios by Region

Another way to examine this trend is to compare the ratios of population to business units to see if they have increased over time. Table 6-1 clearly demonstrates the increase in this ratio for both establishments and functions. Here the population per establishment was calculated for each village and the averages across the villages are reported in this table. For the total United States the average population associated with a given function increased from 58.4 to 83.8, or over 43 percent between 1950 and 1970. For establishments the increase was 26 or 89 percent.

The trend toward increased population per business was found throughout the country, but regional differences were quite pronounced at each time (Table 6-1). The population function ratio was lowest in the North and highest in the South during all three years with western villages falling in between. This suggests that, relative to their population size, northern villages had a greater variety of functions than villages in the other regions and resembled, therefore, the classic "trade center" or "central place" more than the other villages. Southern and western villages were not as well served with functions relative to their population size during this time period.

Table 6–1. Population and Retail Establishments and Functions by Region.

	Total United States	North	South	West
Mean Population Size				
1950	662	651	715	614
1960	694	687	750	620
1970	745	721	845	663
Mean Number of Establishments				
1950	27	27	29	25
1960	23	22	25	21
1970	18	18	21	16
Mean Number of Functions				
1950	13	13	10	14
1960	12	12	11	12
1970	10	10	10	10
Mean Population per Function				
1950	58.4	47.5	76.6	64.8
1960	65.6	57.9	80.9	62.2
1970	83.8	74.1	102.0	83.0
Mean Population per Establishment				
1950	29.1	26.9	30.1	39.3
1960	39.0	38.8	39.1	40.0
1970	55.0	54.0	56.2	56.4

Source: Compiled by authors.

The population/establishment measure reveals a slightly different regional pattern. Here the northern villages remain the best served, but the South did not have the highest ratio as was the case with functions. The population/establishment ratio was consistently highest in the West, which suggests that southern villages had a more limited variety of retail and service activities than the other villages but that their offering of establishments was better than in the West. This indicates a greater duplication of establishments among functions offered in southern villages, which was substantiated by a ratio of establishments to functions that also was highest in the South as shown in Chapter 5 (Table 5-1). Southern villages are larger in population on the average than others due to traditionally higher population requirements for incorporation, therefore some of this regional variation could be due to a relative lack of small places, which tend to have lower ratios of establishments to functions. The difference among the regions in the population/establishment ratio was considerably smaller by the end of the twenty-year period, however, indicating greater uniformity among American villages in their number of retail/service outlets relative to population, despite continuing differences in their complement of functions.

Threshold Population Analysis

These aggregate relationships indicate that considerable change has taken place in the association between village population and business activities. The ratios have shifted toward fewer business units relative to population, and although the ratio can change in this direction from a variety of growth or decline differentials in the two variables, the net result is that for most villages, population has grown more, or declined less, than retail business. A look at individual business activities will demonstrate this association for specific functions.

Functions are ranked in Table 6-2 by the average resident population associated with the single establishment of each for the total sample in 1950. This can be interpreted as a minimum threshold population for each activity, as defined in Christaller's theory (Christaller 1966) and reported in other studies for selected sets of urban places (Berry and Garrison 1958; Yeates 1968; Foust and DeSouza 1975; Hamilton et al. 1976).

What we see in Table 6-2 is a ranking of functions, based on the average population associated with one establishment, that very closely resembles the ranking of these activities in Table 5-2 (Chapter 5) on the basis of the total number of places with each activity. The average population of villages with one establishment varied from a low of 305 for a service station to 1,453 for a photography studio. The value had increased for nearly all functions by 1970, and the rank order changed somewhat during these twenty years (Table 6–2). For example, the average population associated with one service station increased by 152 between 1950 and 1970, and the increase was considerably greater for many less common functions. An increase in threshold size has also been reported by Hamilton et al. (1976) for a wider range of town sizes in the state of Idaho.

The average population of villages with two establishments of each function was higher, as expected, in almost every case (Table 6–2 columns 3 and 4), but due to the variation in population size relative to business activities, an occasional function was associated with a lower average population for two establishments than for one (Table 6–2). This was the case with plumbing, electrical supplies, hotel, and paint and wallpaper in 1950 and welding and used autos in 1970.

Inferring the threshold population concept from this measurement we can see that the increment in population required to open a second establishment of any function was smaller than that required or associated with the first one (compare column 5 with column 1, and column 6 with column 2, Table 6–2). This was true both in 1950 and 1970, and for most functions the population increment corresponding to the second establishment was substantially lower than that of the first one. This suggests that for these smallest members of the urban system, the association between population and establishments is not linear for most functions; instead, the change in business units may be described as an exponential growth curve perhaps conforming to a logistic curve when larger places are included. It may be that the relationship between village population and total market area population is not directly proportional—that is, that an increase in hinterland population or traffic volume is not matched equally by village residents, which causes a growth in business establishments disproportionate to village population growth.

Due to the small size of villages, more than two establishments of all but the most common activities was rare; therefore, an analysis of the association beyond the second establishment would not be reliable. Because of this limitation we chose not to use regression analysis to estimate threshold populations as has been done in other empirical work for a wider range of community sizes (Berry and Garrison 1958; Kenyon 1967; Foust and DeSouza 1975). The population values reported in Table 6–2 are larger for most activities than those derived from regression analyses for comparable dates in two statewide studies based on towns in Wisconsin and Idaho respectively (Foust and DeSouza 1975; Hamilton et al. 1976). This difference may

Table 6–2. Population Associated with Specific Functions.

Business Activity	Average Population Associated with 1 Establishment		Average Population Associated with 2 Establishments		Average Additional Population Associated with Second Establishment	
	1950	1970	1950	1970	1950	1970
Service station	305	457	451	629	146	172
Grocery	321	418	438	570	117	152
Eating place	546	816	787	1163	241	337
Hardware	623	960	1071	1369	448	409
Auto repair	653	1008	736	1155	83	147
Feed	663	822	1019	1164	356	342
Tavern	683	744	846	994	163	250
Petroleum fuel	713	870	1071	1168	358	298
Lumber	714	836	1193	1561	479	725
Drug	718	1013	1357	1686	639	673
Farm implements	746	931	889	1343	143	412
Welding and repair	748	1499	954	881	206	− 618
Auto dealer (new)	779	1023	981	1390	202	367
Liquor	784	1294	1123	1570	339	276
Appliances	818	1096	1251	1739	433	643
Clothing	874	1025	1122	1331	248	306
Fruit and vegetables	901	1531	1383	NA	482	NA
Bank	919	1038	1575	1953	656	956
Bowling	929	1390	1328	1434	399	44
Fuel (other)	935	1128	1102	1514	167	386
Furniture	958	1158	1239	1454	281	296
Plumbing	964	1012	959	1883	− 5	871
Farm and garden supplies	984	975	1205	1143	221	168
Used autos	1001	1272	1599	1069	598	− 203
Mortuary	1009	1263	1455	1689	446	426
Confections	1015	989	1464	NA	447	NA
Electrical supplies	1038	1414	918	NA	−120	NA
Auto parts	1042	1040	1452	1311	410	271
Sporting goods	1045	1172	1096	1297	51	125
Variety	1045	1344	1337	1598	292	254
Meat and fish	1046	1235	1307	1805	261	570
Electrical repair	1078	1594	1378	NA	300	NA
Furniture repair	1102	1816	1527	NA	425	NA
Dairy products	1110	1386	1773	2251	663	865
Radio and televisions	1111	1195	1305	1754	194	559

Table 6-2. continued

Business Activity	Average Population Associated with				Average Additional Population Associated with	
	1 Establishment		2 Establishments		Second Establishment	
	1950	1970	1950	1970	1950	1970
Laundry and dry cleaning	1139	1463	1524	2311	385	848
Hotel and motel	1142	1154	1118	1628	− 24	474
Antiques	1172	1453	1331	2342	159	889
Paint and wallpaper	1192	1602	1150	2617	− 52	1015
Watch repair	1230	1680	2102	1736	872	56
Jewelry	1250	1669	1595	2030	345	361
Auto body repair	1252	1513	NA	NA	NA	NA
Department store	1297	1768	1326	1957	29	189
Florist	1321	1405	1350	1818	29	413
Laundromat	1339	1995	2241	2813	902	818
Bakery	1361	1722	1653	2186	292	464
Photography studio	1453	2049	NA	2121	NA	72

Source: Compiled by authors.

be a result of the greater diversity of village communities represented in the national sample used in this study and the inclusion of only the places less than 2,500 in the data presented here.

Trade-Population by Accessibility and Industry

Variation in the number of business activities or establishments relative to population size can be associated with characteristics of villages that include their proximity to larger competing centers and the presence of other non-central place activites such as mining or manufacturing. Villages that are highly accessible to larger cities typically are influenced by those cities in the form of a substantial commuter population and competition from urban shopping centers that is greater than is found in more remote settings. Such places, along with other villages with institutions, factories, and mining activities, should have greater populations corresponding to a given number of retail and service functions than places whose principal purpose is to serve a hinterland population with goods and services

(Berry 1967). We should, therefore, expect an inverse association between urban accessibility and the number of business units controlling for population size, and also an inverse association between specialized functions such as manufacturing and other basic economic activities and the number of retail and service business units relative to population size.

Table 6–3 contains results of a regression analysis designed to show the effect of urban accessibility on the number of business units relative to population size. The index of urban accessibility (see Appendix A) and village population size were used as independent variables in models with the number of establishments or functions as dependent variables for each year of observation. We can see that while controlling for population size, greater urban accessibility resulted in fewer business units among villages each year, as expected. Furthermore, the strength of this association increased over time, as would be expected given the likely increase in incidence of commuting among village populations. The survey data for 1980 was also consistent with previous observations. Variations in urban accessi-

Table 6–3. Regression Analysis of Retail and Service Units by Population and Accessibility.[a]

| Dependent Variables | Standardized Coefficients | | |
	Population	Urban Accessibility	R
Number of Retail and Service Establishments			
1950	0.85[a]	−0.05	0.85[a]
1960	0.86[a]	−0.10[a]	0.84[a]
1970	0.83[a]	−0.13[a]	0.81[a]
1980	0.77[a]	−0.20[a]	0.75[a]
Number of Retail and Service Functions			
1950	0.82[a]	−0.06	0.81[a]
1960	0.86[a]	−0.07	0.85[a]
1970	0.84[a]	−0.10[a]	0.82[a]
1980	0.63[a]	−0.17[a]	0.61[a]

[a]Significant at 0.05.

Source: Compiled by authors.

bility were therefore responsible for some of the variation in the association between population size and number of business units, since this locational dimension contributes to larger populations and fewer services simultaneously. Residuals from the regression in Figure 6-1 may be explained in part by location relative to larger centers, with those falling below the line having greater urban accessibility than the positive residuals.

The role of other economic activities—in this case, manufacturing, construction, agriculture, and wholesaling, for 1950, 1960, and 1970, and manufacturing, wholesale, and mining for 1980—are considered together in Table 6-4 with a similar analysis. According to Berry (1967), we would expect an inverse relationship between these "non-central place" activities and the number of business units net of population size, due to their role in supporting a resident population that is not directly engaged in the retail sector. This was certainly not the case during the 1950-70 period, as demonstrated in Table 6-4. On the contrary, a significant positive association was found in these years indicating instead a supportive role on the part of basic industries. The data for 1980 do not produce the strong association

Table 6-4. Regression Analysis of Retail and Service Units by Population and Other Economic Activities.[a]

| | Standardized Coefficients | | |
| | Population | Other Economic | R |
Dependent Variable			
Number of Retail and Service Establishments			
1950	0.56[a]	0.38[a]	0.88[a]
1960	0.50[a]	0.45[a]	0.89[a]
1970	0.40[a]	0.53[a]	0.88[a]
1980	0.72[a]	0.03	0.72[a]
Number of Retail and Service Functions			
1950	0.55[a]	0.34[a]	0.84[a]
1960	0.60[a]	0.32[a]	0.87[a]
1970	0.54[a]	0.38[a]	0.86[a]
1980	0.58[a]	0.04	0.61[a]

[a]Significant at the 0.05.

Source: Compiled by authors.

found in earlier years but were consistent in the direction of this relationship. This finding conforms to a more common notion that basic industries contribute a multiplier effect that leads to growth in the nonbasic sector of the community (Alexander 1954; Pred 1966).

These results suggest that the retail sector in villages has been bolstered by basic activities, whereas villages accessible to larger centers tend to have fewer businesses than one would expect based on their populations. The effect of basic industry on retail business probably operates, in part, through its effect on population growth or retention—that is, industry can support residents of villages and elsewhere within their market area, who in turn support local stores. A certain amount of business may also be generated directly by industries, especially for local repair services. These relationships will be examined in the section to follow.

MODELS OF THE CHANGE IN RETAIL ACTIVITIES

The static relationships just described fall short of giving us an understanding of the process of change among these variables. For this reason we turn now to an analysis similar to that reported in Johansen and Fuguitt (1979), in which change in the number of retail/service business units is the main focus. Village population change is an explanatory variable in this analysis along with urban accessibility and change in the number of industrial firms, as used in the preceding section. It is helpful to review some earlier attempts to analyze change in retail activities in order to better understand the complexity of the relationships between these variables.

Change in retail business activities in villages can be viewed as part of an overall shift within a system of cities and villages in response to increased mobility among rural residents and to changing patterns of population distribution. Parr and Denike (1970) predicted a decline in village retail and service activities, where competition from urban centers and rural population decline have occurred. Earlier efforts have argued the importance of these conditions in affecting retail change (e.g., Landis 1932; Chittick 1955; Anderson 1961).

Lentz and Johansen (1975) developed a probabilistic model to simulate the process of retail decline for small towns within the trade area of a single city. An empirical application of the model for the Charleston, West Virginia, trade area supported the effect of location relative to the larger center, initial population size, and economic base activities as determinants of the pattern of retail decline for smaller centers over the 1940–70 interval. Villages with greater urban proximity, smaller population size, and limited or declining economic base activities suffered a greater loss of retail activities.

Other studies have examined the bivariate associations among the variables considered here. Population change in villages has been shown to have a direct relationship with proximity to larger urban places in several studies of village communities (Hart and Salisbury 1965; Hodgson 1972; Fuguitt and Beale 1976; Roseman 1977; see also Chapter 2). This relationship is understood to be a response to employment and other opportunities available in villages near cities through commuting, whereas more isolated villages lack this locational advantage.

A few research efforts have tested the effects of urban proximity on the stability or change in economic activities in villages over time. In a study of villages in Louisiana, Smith (1933) found that nearness to larger cities resulted in a greater disappearance of trade centers during the 1901–31 period (disappearance here meant loss of all retail functions). Hodge (1965) found in Saskatchewan that between 1941 and 1961 trade centers within ten miles of a large city declined sharply in number of services, while more remote centers were less vulnerable to decline.

Finally, a positive association of change in village population and change in business activity has been reported by Hassinger (1957), who used a Guttman scale to determine a hierarchy of retail activities in villages in southern Minnesota and related change within the hierarchy to change in population between 1939 and 1951. In a study of Illinois villages during the 1940–60 period, Folse and Riffe (1969) found a similar relationship between the two trends with the lowest rate of loss in business activities occurring in villages that experienced population growth.

The next step is to examine the interrelations among population change, retail change, and urban accessibility for villages. Because of empirical evidence, one might expect urban proximity to be associated with population change in villages while it bears an inverse relationship with change in retail and service business activity. Although a village near a city is viewed by many as an attractive residential setting, its urban accessibility is apt to present the local merchant with greater competition than he would have in a more remote location. Retailers in larger cities can offer greater variety and lower prices through volume trading and can benefit from scale economies in merchandising and advertising as members of franchise or chain organizations.

Yet, as population growth of a village is enhanced by urban proximity, this increase in potential customers may serve to support some local stores despite competition from nearby cities. On the other hand, village merchants in a remote location might suffer a loss of the necessary threshold population and be forced to close despite relative freedom from big city competition. In considering the overall relation between urban accessibility and retail activity, therefore, previous research and theory would lead us to posit conflicting effects: a negative direct effect, with villages more accessible to cities having greater declines in retail activity, but a positive indirect effect, since villages that are more accessible to cities are more likely to grow in population and growing places are more likely to sustain retail activity. The following analysis examines this complex relationship over the 1950–80 period for the random sample of U.S. villages, including the data from the survey of mayors in the subsample of 100 villages.

Path analysis is used here to structure the relationships in order to determine the direct and indirect effects of the independent variables on retail change. To measure change in population and business activities, we used residuals from the regression of initial with end-of-period values. For example, population change from 1950 to 1960 for a village is measured as the residual from the regression of 1960 population on 1950 population for the sample of U.S. villages. This variable has a correlation of zero with initial size and avoids problems due to small initial size in the measure of change (see Bohrnstedt 1969).

Model I: Change in Trade and Population with Accessibility

Figure 6–2 is a path diagram of the association between urban accessibility, population change, and change in retail business units. Table 6–5 contains the resulting path coefficients using both the establishment and function measures of change in retail business for the 1950–70 period and the data on establishments only for 1975–80, based on the survey of mayors. As noted in Chapter 4, mayors were asked about trends in establishments from a short list, including

Figure 6-2. Path Diagram for Model I.

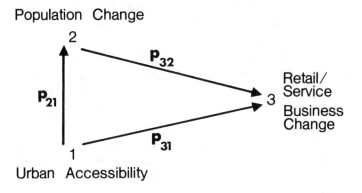

Source: Compiled by authors.

Table 6-5. Path Coefficients for Model of Change in Trade and Population with Urban Accessibility.[a]

	Path	Path	Indirect	Direct	Total
	P_{21}	P_{32}	$P_{32}\,P_{21}$	P_{31}	$r_{31} = (3) + (4)$
Dependent Variable	(1)	(2)	(3)	(4)	(5)
Change in Retail Establishments					
1950–60	0.13^b	0.37^b	0.05	-0.09^b	-0.04
1960–70	0.15^b	0.27^b	0.04	-0.05	-0.01
1975–80	0.16	0.15	0.02	-0.11	-0.09
Change in Retail Functions					
1950–60	0.13^b	0.29^b	0.04	0.03	0.07
1960–70	0.15^b	0.15^b	0.02	-0.02	0.01

[a]Trade, Population, and Accessibility represented by subscripts 3, 2, and 1, respectively, in the coefficients. See Figure 6–2.

[b]Significant at 0.05.

Source: Compiled by authors.

twelve functions representing the range of ranked functions obtained using Dun and Bradstreet. Column 1 contains the correlation coefficient for urban accessibility and population change, which was moderately positive in each time period. Column 2 (P_{32}) is the beta coefficient for change in population with change in retail units net of accessibility. This was positive as expected during 1950-60 and 1960-70 using both the establishment and function measure of change in business units, and also during 1975-80 on establishments. (In the 1975-80 line of Table 6-5 population change is for the 1970-80 decade).

The direction of causality implied in this model is from population to retail business—that is, that an increase in the resident population will support the retail sector either in the form of growth or reduced decline. We recognize the reverse causal link between retail change and population change where growth in the retail sector can support residential growth. Paths in both directions cannot be estimated with our data, however, so our model considers village population as a supporting market for retail activities with its population size not dependent upon these activities. This assumption has become more plausible in modern villages where the residential population is increasingly dependent on commuting, basic industry employment, or retirement income for support. Furthermore, the resident population employed in the retail sector does constitute a market for retail goods and services and cannot be ignored as a supporting factor.

The direct effect of urban accessibility on retail change is shown as P_{31} in Table 6-5. This was expected to be inverse due to the competing forces of larger cities, and this proved to be the case in four out of five examples, although the coefficients were small in all cases. The indirect effect of urban accessibility through population change is $P_{32} P_{21}$ (column 3) and shows a weak positive relationship in all cases. Consequently, we can see that urban accessibility does seem to have conflicting effects via its direct and indirect paths toward retail change although the coefficients are not high. The total effect of urban accessibility (column 5) is therefore represented by a low value in all cases.

This analysis suggests that of the two variables, the most important factor in village retail change has been population change. This was true for both the change in number of establishments and the change in functions, although the strength of the association diminished over the 1950-80 period (Table 6-5, column 2). It is interesting that the survey data for 1975–80 results in coefficients that are consistent with the 1950–70 findings despite the difference in the data source and the shorter time period.

Model II: Change in Trade, Population, and Industries

The assumed importance of basic industrial development in stimulating local community growth goes almost without saying, having been a principal factor in regional development strategies throughout the world. Regional economic models project multiplier effects from developments in basic industries that will directly increase personal and community wealth through increased tax revenues (Tweeten and Brinkman 1976; Chapter 8). Industrial developments are also projected to benefit the tertiary sector directly through increased demand for goods and services resulting from increased disposable income in the community and from a demand for goods and services from the industry directly. Further benefits to local merchants are proposed through the increased tax revenues to the local government, thus either reducing the local merchants' share or creating additional public funds to allow improvements in the local infrastructure.

Evidence of multiplier effects of new industrial developments in nonmetropolitan communities has been documented in several studies of industrial growth (Wadsworth and Conrad 1966; Brinkman 1973; Shaffer and Tweeten 1974; Tweeten and Brinkman 1976). These studies demonstrate monetary benefits from new industrial growth at the community level and support the premise that changes in retail activities should be directly correlated with change in industrial activities.

The model proposed here is designed to parallel the accessibility model using level of industrial activity, as indicated by the sum of the number of manufacturing, wholesale, construction, and agricultural establishments in the village. Change in this level is measured as the residual of beginning with end-of-period sums (Figure 6–3). In contrast to the static relationship shown earlier between industrial firms and the population/retail association in villages, we would expect a positive effect of industrial change on retail change because of its potential for direct demand for goods and services and its

Figure 6-3.   Path Diagram for Model II.

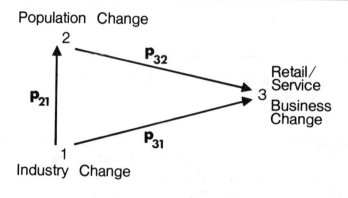

Source: Compiled by authors.

contribution to local tax revenues. A positive indirect effect through population change is also expected due to the potential for increased employment from industrial expansion and, conversely, decline in employment with industrial decline, which can affect population change directly and therefore retail change indirectly.

Table 6-6 contains the path coefficients resulting from the model of industrial change. Here we can see a consistently strong positive direct effect of industrial change on retail change with the exception of the 1975-80 survey results, although the latter weak association was not inverse. (Table 6-6, column 4). As industrial firms increased, so did retail business units net of population change. Population change was directly related to retail change in this model also, as it was in the model with urban accessibility (column 2 in Tables 6-5 and 6-6).

The positive association between population change and industrial change was quite strong in 1950-60 and 1960-70 and was also positive using the survey data compared with the 1970-80 population change, as shown in column 1 of Table 6-6. This suggests an indirect effect of industrial change on retail change through population change given the strong association between population change and retail change (P_{32} column 2). The indirect effect of industrial change ($P_{32} P_{21}$) is shown in column 3 and resulted in only a moderate positive coefficient in either decade for either measure of retail business change. The importance of industrial change was therefore

Table 6-6. Path Coefficients for Model of Change in Trade, Population, and Industry.[a]

Dependent Variable	Path P_{21} (1)	Path P_{32} (2)	Indirect $P_{32} P_{21}$ (3)	Direct P_{31} (4)	Total $r_{31} = (3) + (4)$ (5)
Change in Retail Establishments					
1950–60	0.25[b]	0.29[b]	0.07	0.29[b]	0.36[b]
1960–70	0.19[b]	0.19[b]	0.04	0.38[b]	0.42[b]
1975–80	0.09	0.12	0.01	0.07	0.08[b]
Change in Retail Functions					
1950–60	0.25[b]	0.23[b]	0.06	0.28[b]	0.34[b]
1960–70	0.19[b]	0.10[b]	0.02	0.26[b]	0.28[b]

[a]Trade, Population, and Industry represented by subscripts 3, 2, and 1, respectively, in the coefficients. See Figure 6–3.

[b]Significant at 0.05.

Source: Compiled by authors.

more pronounced as a direct effect than through its impact on population change.

Changes in the numbers of industrial firms in the villages, particularly those related to manufacturing, can create an influx of employees to the community for daily employment who live elsewhere but find it convenient to shop near their place of work. Such intrarural commuting patterns are becoming common as industries have moved into smaller towns and villages causing a daily influx of potential shoppers. These forces, along with the direct support by industries for local services, can create advantages in the retail sector of village communities.

The total effect of industrial change on retail activities is shown in column 5 of Table 6–6. This combined effect was consistently positive. Although weak in the 1975–80 survey data, it was of sufficient magnitude in all other examples to allow the inference that industrial growth is good for retail business in villages and that this is true even when accounting for population growth that may be due to other causes. The relatively short time period 1975–80 that the survey covered may not have been adequate to allow the effect of new industry to appear in the retail sector. The consistency of the industry effect during the 1950–70 period suggests it should continue through the 1970s.

Model III: Change in Trade, Population, and Industry with Accessibility

To understand their combined effects, the variables accessibility and industrial change were both included along with population change in a third model of retail change shown in Figure 6–4. In this case we can see that urban accessibility may have an indirect effect on retail change through population change and industrial change. We would expect the direct effect of urban accessibility to be negative based on the competition principle. The indirect effects through population should be positive following the results of the previous model including accessibility and population change. We would also expect the indirect effect through industry change to be positive, since the second model showed industry to be positively associated with retail change and because there is a recognized tendency for industrial expansion in construction, manufacturing, and wholesaling to choose sites near larger urban places where possible.

Table 6–7 contains the path coefficients for the combined model. Using the establishment and function measures of retail change for the two decades and the survey results for change in establishments between 1975–80, we see that the expected relationships were realized in nearly all cases.

In the case of urban accessibility, its direct effect on retail change P_{41} (Table 6–7, column 3) was inverse and of slightly greater magnitude than in the previous model. It had a moderate positive indirect effect through industrial change ($P_{42} P_{21}$) during the first two periods and a similar positive indirect effect through population change ($P_{43} P_{31}$) during all three periods, including the survey data.

Industrial change also retained its positive direct effect on retail change (Table 6–7, column 4), and the strength of this association was not diminished by adding accessibility to the model. Its indirect effect through population change ($P_{43} P_{32}$) was also positive during all periods as expected.

Figure 6–4.   Path Diagram for Model III.

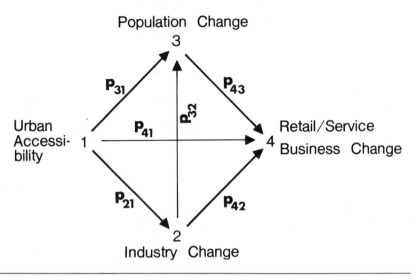

Source: Compiled by authors.

Table 6–7.   Path Coefficients for Model of Change in Population and Industry with Accessibility.[a]

Dependent Variable	Path P_{21} (1)	Path P_{31} (2)	Path P_{41} (3)	Path P_{42} (4)	Path P_{32} (5)	Path P_{43} (6)
Change in Number of Establishments						
1950–60	0.19[b]	0.09[b]	−0.14[b]	0.32[b]	0.23[b]	0.30[b]
1960–70	0.23[b]	0.11[b]	−0.14[b]	0.41[b]	0.17[b]	0.21[b]
1975–80	−0.15	0.18	−0.11	0.05	0.11	0.14
Change in Number of Functions						
1950–60	0.19[b]	0.09	−0.02	0.28[b]	0.23[b]	0.23[b]
1960–70	0.23[b]	0.11	−0.07	0.27[b]	0.17[b]	0.11[b]

[a]Trade, Population, Industry, and Accessibility represented by subscripts 4, 3, 2, 1, respectively, in the coefficient. See Figure 6–4.

[b]Significant at 0.05.

Source: Compiled by authors.

Of the three independent variables in the model in Figure 6–4, industrial change and change in population were the most important in determining the direction and magnitude of retail change in villages prior to 1975–80. Urban accessibility did show a negative relationship in all but one case, indicating the likelihood that competition from urban retailers does affect the village merchants and reduce their ability to compete for resident rural population.

Stepping back in the model to population change, we see a consistently positive, although diminishing, association with industry change (P_{32}) and a positive association with accessibility net of industry change (P_{31}). This suggests that industrial growth and relative location remain independently important in village population change, although possibly at a somewhat lesser rate in the case of urban accessibility in recent years, as shown in Chapter 2 with the full sample.

DISCUSSION

We have explored in this chapter some associations between village population and village economic activities, emphasizing the interrelationship between population and the retail service sector. It seems that the villages have retained their population to a greater extent than their retail stores during the 1950–70 period, as indicated by the change in the ratio of population to business units and the shift of the regression axis toward fewer retail units per population unit. The population threshold estimates were also shown to have increased since 1950 for nearly all functions indicating a universal pattern among the various activities.

In the analysis of change in retail/service activities, we observed a consistent and rather strong association between village population change and business change. This was true in all three models and for all time periods. Knowing the seemingly divergent trends of modest population growth and retail decline during much of the post-1950 time period, we can assume that this association describes variations in decline of business with variations in growth of population for many villages. The positive association does suggest, however, that the turnaround in village population trends observed in Chapter 2 could help revive the trade center activities in villages once again, although the threshold population required for each additional function during the 1980s is apt to be much larger than it was earlier.

The importance of village location relative to larger cities on retail change was only marginal in the total effect since the competition for retailers from nearby cities seems to have been offset by the locational advantages supporting population growth. Neither association was particularly strong.

An important and somewhat encouraging finding in the analysis of change was the role of industrial activities in the process of retail change. Developments in manufacturing and other basic industries clearly were related to the process of retail change as measured here during the 1950–70 period. Yet the weaker association during the 1975–80 period may suggest a changing association here. It could, however, result from the difference in the nature of the data (i.e., survey versus Dun and Bradstreet listing) or from the shorter time period of observation. The finding for 1950–70 contradicts previous discussions about the affect of non-central place functions on retail/population relationships and suggests that efforts to attract industry to village communities have been worthwhile on the part of local merchants. Evidence here, although not conclusive, indicates that the "trade center" role of the village has, therefore, been enhanced by industrial development, which unlike urban accessibility can possibly be altered by communities through various strategies. Further work is needed to examine the importance of these developments in the current village economy. The next chapter will explore some attempts to attract new industries to villages and the results that were reported by several communities since 1975.

7 LOCAL PROMOTION, EXPANSION OF COMMUNITY FACILITIES AND VILLAGE GROWTH

The decline or stagnation of the rural small town has long been viewed as a problem requiring remedial action at the local, regional, or national level. For many years, efforts have focused on promoting local activities that could lead to growth, the most common being some action to encourage the development of industry. Typically, this has been seen as a viable replacement for lost trade center functions, given the decline of the population identified with agriculture (Nesmith 1963). Broader views of development have been emphasized in more recent years, including planning on the basis of multicounty areas (Powers 1969) and the growth center approach. Assuming the importance of economies of settlement scale, it has been argued that promoting growth in and around selected middle-size or larger cities has far greater chance of some success than the direct competition between thousands of middle-size towns, and even tiny villages, for the locations of manufacturing firms (Borts 1968; Hansen 1970; Commission on Population Growth and the American Future 1972). This was seen not only as a solution to problems in rural areas but also as a means to ease problems of urban and metropolitan congestion (Morrison 1973).

Substituting rational regional planning for competitive efforts among small communities to attract growth, however, has proved difficult. Perhaps a classic anecdote in this connection was told to one of the authors by a local community development agent. He reported that one community organized itself and succeeded in attracting industry in indignant response to the challenge posed by having a neighboring rival community officially identified by regional planners as the growth center for the subregion.

In any event, with the 1970s came the nonmetropolitan population turnaround coupled with decreased government expenditures supporting rural and area development. Consequently, although local growth promotion continues, it has been joined in some instances with efforts to slow down growth (White 1978; Baldassare and Protash 1982). Multicounty regional units have had relatively little impact on county or local autonomy, and not much has been heard in recent years about the growth center approach.

In this chapter we consider the promotion of growth at the local level, the expansion of community facilities as a related activity, and possible consequences in terms of economic and population growth. The data source is our mayors' survey of 100 villages, which is a systematic subsample of the basic village sample, so that the results should be representative of U.S. nonmetropolitan incorporated places under 2,500 in size.[1]

First we will review the extent to which mayors report activities encouraging commercial and industrial development and the improvement of community facilities, and we will also examine the types of villages that are most likely to engage in these activities. Next, the promotion of business and improvement of facilities will be associated with their possible consequences—the reported growth in retail trade, industry, professional services, and population.

Prior to this chapter we have described and contrasted villages and considered their changes over time. The story has been one of growth and decline in retail trade, industry, and population. By utilizing simple properties such as size, local and regional location, and county characteristics, village composition and change have been examined in the context of the nation's settlement structure.

Thus, up to now there has been no consideration of ongoing social processes in the communities—that is, those corporate activities pursued by their citizens for governmental, public, and private goals. More needs to be learned about how these activities are influenced by the position of the village as a unit of settlement and how they in turn affect the village. This is a central consideration, particularly since it is generally assumed that local communities as well as larger areas, through their own actions, may affect their future. For example, the key to success, however defined, in a community is often seen to be vigorous local leadership. Also, the study of social processes has been a continuing area of work in the community studies literature. More specifically, there has been an emerging interest in what has been termed "community mobilization," which pays primary attention to actions within the community and especially those related to the promotion of growth (Molotch 1976a; Humphrey and Krannich 1980; Lyon et al. 1981; Baldassare and Protash 1982; Krannich and Humphrey 1983).

At the same time there is the theme of dependency and integration of small communities with the larger society. Much that affects the village is seen to be beyond that place's local control through purposive action (Vidich and Bensman 1968; Warren 1972). Although in earlier chapters we have not assumed that purposive action at the village level is necessarily fruitless, much of this work deals with the possible importance of some of these external influences as indexed by various aspects of position in the larger settlement structure. As Humphrey and Krannich (1980:583) assert, however,

> . . . state programs, local entrepreneurial efforts and national corporate activities cannot be carried out in specific localities without local support. Furthermore, it is reasonable to assume that localities actively engaged in growth promotion will have more visibility and enhanced attractiveness to public and private organizations in complex industrial societies.

VILLAGE PROMOTION ACTIVITIES

Following this line of work, we consider aspects of local mobilization in our sample of mayors' responses. What kinds of activities are reported that would support or promote growth? Next, we examine whether variations in the extent of growth promotion can be attributed to aspects of the settlement structure. What properties of the village setting, if any, are associated with its "mobilization potential"?

We developed an index of growth mobilization that includes items relating to the promotion of commercial and industrial development.[2] Activities conducted in the sampled villages are listed in Table 7-1 and range from relatively simple efforts such as organizing a committee to attract industry, done by almost one-half of the places, to major activities such as the development of an industrial park (less than one village in five). The first six of the efforts were listed in the structured interview schedule; the seventh includes all other activities in an open-ended question that followed. Specific examples of these other activities as stated by the respondents are:

> Trying to spruce up the center of town—the retail sector. An empty theatre is being made into a civic center.

> Trying to take over the mobile home manufacturing company that has left town.

> We've tried, but we have a stumbling block. We don't have any sewer. We have a development corporation that has bought land for lagoons and sold them to the city.

> The development corporation brought in a nursing home and a tool and die company. They have been real active.

> Adopted a new master plan to set aside retail and industrial activities. Created an industrial development corporation. New zoning for business.

> There is a Community Pride Program. It is a group of individuals that help clean up buildings and offer suggestions for how to use the buildings. All of this is to attract business.

> Applied to FAA (airport master plan) for a grant. Money not yet received.

> We publish a brochure through the Chamber of Commerce that serves the central part of our county. Once a year we take an advertisement out in a local paper that is distributed throughout the state. The town doesn't have a sewage system, and that is our major drawback. We can't really do much about attracting industry until we do.

> Working with Northwest Council of Local Governments. Applying for a block grant to pave the street and extend water service.

> We have an industrial development corporation that makes money available for loans to new businesses and industries.

> We've zoned in the last five years. We've set aside property for industry, but we really don't want industry. We want to be a bedroom community for ———. We want new residents but not industry.

The promotion scale was formed simply by adding the number of the seven items reported for each village. For villages applying for

Table 7-1. Promotional Activities of Villages, 1975–80.

Activity	Percentage
1 Organized a committee to seek new industry or business	46
2 Cooperated in a county or regional effort to expand business	43
3 Started or carried out a program to improve the downtown area	37
4 Applied for public funding from county, state, or federal sources to attract new or expand existing business and industry	25
Received such funding	5
5 Advertised the community in local, regional, or national magazines or newspapers	20
6 Developed an industrial park or community center	18
7 Conducted other activities to attract new or expand existing business and industry.	24

Source: Survey of 100 Mayors. N = 99 because one village had disincorporated by 1980.

public funding (item 4) two points were given instead of one if the request had been successful. Scale reliability was acceptable, with Cronbach's alpha equal to 0.71 (Bohrnstedt 1970).

Only 28 percent of the villages scored zero, thus some form of growth promotion was pursued by almost three villages out of four. The extent to which this was done cooperatively with other political units is unclear, though only a little more than one-half of the mayors who reported any promotional activities included being involved in a county or regional effort to expand business (43 percent of all villages). The pervasiveness of efforts to expand or attract new business supports the position of Molotch (1976a) and others that growth is a dominant theme in local political action and perhaps is one of the few goals about which community leaders show a broad consensus.[3]

EXPANSION OF COMMUNITY FACILITIES

Efforts to improve the local infrastructure may well have a bearing on the success or failure of village promotional activites. Such improvements may be recommended as part of a development strategy to make a community more attractive for possible industrial or business development or to gain new residents who may work elsewhere. On the other hand, as Tweeten and Brinkman (1976) point out, the role of facilities in actually inducing economic development is unclear. They note that industrial managers, when rating importance of location factors, place community services below nearness to markets, availability of inputs (including labor), agglomeration economies, and adequate transportation. (See also the survey of Nebraska Manufacturers reported in Lonsdale et al. 1976.) Rural sociologists and others, moreover, often point out that rural development is not just economic development and that declining communities with little hope of attracting business should nevertheless consider actions to improve their social situation, including public infrastructure (Williams et al. 1975; Lassey 1977). Indeed, Copp (1972) argues that rural development is not infrastructure or factories but is about people, their well-being, and what they can become. Yet the mayors' responses above would suggest that a close connection is sometimes seen between facilities development and the potential for economic growth. Also, post hoc explanations of the nonmetropolitan turnaround often include the diminished differences in basic living facilities and available services between metropolitan and nonmetropolitan areas.

Obviously, the link between the expansion of community facilities and the growth process needs clarification. One view is that the development of community facilities is an important goal in and of itself; from another it is a possible means for additional economic activity. From yet another it may be simply a necessary consequence of population or economic growth. Though most facilities expansion should require some form of community mobilization, we are measuring here the outcome and must infer the prior social processes. Also, since our questions on promotion related directly to expanding and attracting new industry, it did not seem appropriate to make facilities development a dependent variable with promotion as an independent variable in this research. Further specification of these relationships is essential, but a step in that direction can be made in this work by showing something of the place of facilities development in the process of population and economic change for the sample of U.S. villages.

The items listed in Table 7–2 include the expansion of basic utilities such as sewer and water, fire and police protection, and recreation facilities, carried out by about one-half of the villages; less common activities such as the development of tourist attractions, reported in less than one village in nine; and second home developments, reported in only seven villages. Most of these items could be termed public services, but several (second home developments, elderly housing, tourist attractions) may well come from the private sector. Nevertheless, the latter items should require at least tacit public support and official sanction, and could be viewed as innovations

Table 7–2. Expansion of Facilities, 1975–80.

Activity	Percentage Expanded	Percentage with Government Funding[a]	Of Those Expanding, Percentage with Government Funding[a]
1 Fire and/or police	56	15	27
2 Recreational facilities	53	24	46
3 Public water service	53	31	60
4 Sewage treatment	46	36	80
5 Housing for elderly	37	35	95
6 Health services	17	10	59
7 Landfill disposal site	13	4	31
8 Tourist attractions	12	3	25
9 Second home developments	7	0	0

[a]Received county, state, or federal funding for the expansion.

Source: Survey of 100 Mayors. N = 99 because one village had disincorporated by 1980.

improving the community and/or making it more attractive for further development. We summed these nine elements to construct a facilities expansion scale. The distribution of villages on the scale shows that some expansion of facilities was almost universal, with at least one of these items reported by 90 percent of the mayors for the 1975–80 period. Cronbach's alpha was 0.61, with no indication that this would be improved by dropping items. Despite the marginal size of this coefficient, the scale was used for simplicity, although most of the analysis was duplicated with the individual items, with results reported where appropriate.

In addition to the expansion of these facilities and services, Table 7–2 provides the proportion of villages receiving county, state, or federal funding for these activities. Column 2 is the percentage of all villages, and column 3 the percentage among those expanding the service. The extent of reliance on public extralocal funding was high for major capital improvements such as sewer and water. One-third of the villages reported establishing housing for elderly, and 95 percent of these developments were based on extralocal funding. Government support for public housing has evidently led to an expansion of elderly housing in small villages across the country. Landfill disposal and tourist attractions, on the other hand, were low incidence items with limited public funding from outside the village. The availability of external funding from outside the village is undoubtedly an important incentive, if not a prerequisite for much of the facilities development in local communities. The dependence of these small places on external money is indicated by the fact that only twenty-nine village mayors reported receiving no outside funds and ten of these villages expanded no services or facilities.[4] The increased dependence of large and small municipalities on state and federal aid is a recent trend of considerable significance (Shannon and Ross 1977).

FACTORS ASSOCIATED WITH PROMOTION AND FACILITIES EXPANSION

What sorts of communities are likely to either engage in promotion efforts or expand facilities? We again must turn first to some basic variables utilized earlier: village size, accessibility to larger cities, and region of the country. There may well be a size threshold for promotional activities, just as there is for particular types of retail establishments or services. A community that is too small may lack the differentiation of roles necessary for effective collective action; extremely small places may have little basis for optimism concerning the likelihood that efforts may result in increased industry or business. Similarly, small populations may make problematic the cost-efficiency of expanding facilities.

Accessibility to larger places has been an important variable differentiating communities by population growth and characteristics and by change in economic activities. Its possible effect on mobilization is not easy to predict. One could speculate that accessible villages would have less autonomy, function more as residence centers and have, therefore, less incentive to promote growth through economic development. On the other hand, the residents of accessible places might have cause to be more optimistic about attaining new economic activities because of locational advantages, and they tend to have a younger, and hence presumably a more dynamic and forward-looking, population (Chapter 3). Also, accessible villages may be more likely to expand facilities in order to be closer to levels available in nearby larger cities.

Given the strong regional differences in village population growth, it is plausible that communities in the South and the West may be more aggressive in seeking to attract business and industry. Indeed, this is an assertion made by Angel (1980) in discussing urban entrepreneurship in the Sunbelt.

Population growth is seen by many people as being an important indicator of community well-being. Consequently, prior growth or decline could very well influence the extent to which a community will organize itself to attract industry or to seek to improve its facilities and services. For example, upon recognizing that their community is losing population, residents might seek to promote growth in economic activity. This is consistent with the findings of Humphrey and Krannich (1980). Similarly, development of infrastructure may be proposed in an effort to turn things around in declining communities or at least to improve community living conditions there. On the other hand, expansion of facilities might be hindered by a declining tax base. New residents in communities with a history of growth might demand improved services (see discussion later in this chapter), but they might be opposed to further growth or economic development, though survey evidence has not generally confirmed these commonly held assumptions. Research using counties as units has shown government expenditures to be positively associated with change in population and also to be associated with several population characteristics (Fox and Sullivan 1979; see also Stinson 1981). Again, although we can predict results in either direction, prior growth appears to be an important variable to consider, and we will include population change in the village over the 1960–70 period.

The above review illustrates the tentative nature of the present body of knowledge concerning these relationships. Unfortunately, other variables that have been used in previous comparative community analyses were not available to us (see research reviews in Bridgeland and Sofranko 1975 and Sofranko and Bridgeland 1972). Because our population units are so small, reliable estimates of socioeconomic status, occupational structure, or local governmental programs or expenditures, for example, cannot be obtained for individual villages from published or unpublished sources, and use of county variables as proxies could easily be misleading.

We regressed both the promotion and the facilities scale on log of village population size in 1970, log of the accessibility scale used throughout this work, a binary scale for region (South and West versus North), and population change 1960–70. Population change is measured as the residual from the regression of 1970 population on 1960 population, for consistency with subsequent analysis (see note 5). Bivariate correlations and multiple regression coefficients for both scales are given in Table 7–3.

None of the so-called community structure variables are important for the promotion scale except for population size as of 1970. Regardless of nearness to larger places, region, or history of population change, places larger in 1970 tend to be involved in more efforts to expand or attract business and industry than smaller places. The respective r and beta both are about 0.45, a high value for this research.

Similarly, initial size is most important, with r and beta greater than 0.5, in the correlations and regression with the facilities scale. But in this instance 1960–70 population change is also significant, being negatively associated with expansion of local services and facilities. Thus larger places and places with a history of population decline are more involved in expansion of services, net of the other variables included here. Location and region, though important variables in other contexts, are not associated with these two indices.

Table 7–3. Bivariate Correlations and Standardized Regression Coefficients (Betas) for the Association between the Promotion Scale and the Facilities Scale and the Independent Variables.

| Independent Variables | Dependent Variables | | | |
| | Promotion Scale | | Facilities Scale | |
	r	Beta	r	Beta
Village size, 1970 (log)	0.44[a]	0.45[a]	0.50[a]	0.58[a]
Accessibility (log)	0.04	−0.03	−0.07	−0.16
Population Change, 1960–70[b]	−0.04	−0.10	−0.20[a]	−0.23[a]
Region (South and West versus North) (Constant)	0.10	0.05	−0.09	−0.16
R		0.46		0.60
R²		0.21		0.36

[a]Significant at the 0.05 level.

[b]This measure of change is the residual from the regression of 1970 population on 1960 population. See text.

Source: Survey of 100 Mayors. N = 99 because one village had disincorporated by 1980.

Suggestive, though not significant, are the negative associations between expansion of facilities and both urban accessibility and region. Had these coefficients been larger we could have concluded that facility expansion is slightly more favored in the North and away from big cities, an area where population decline also was most common in the 1960–70 period.

In summary, these results underscore the importance of population size in influencing the extent to which community members can mobilize to carry out collective activities for the promotion of growth, or to expand or develop new facilities, a finding consistent with arguments found in Fischer (1975) on the nature of urbanism. In addition, a history of population decline appears to serve as an incentive for facility expansion, even controlling for size and the other variables, but that is not the case for efforts to attract industry.

In a similar study of approximately 100 Pennsylvania minor civil divisions ranging in size from 7,000 to 50,000 (evidently most are incorporated places), Humphrey and Krannich (1980) found no bivariate association between initial size and either growth promotion or efforts to expand services, but a negative association between both variables and urban accessibility. Also contrary to our work, they found 1960–70 population change to be inversely associated with growth promotion but not with efforts to expand community facilities. Perhaps the differences in location (Pennsylvania versus United States) are important, but our positive and strong size effect and their insignificant negative one also appear to indicate a threshold. Perhaps places over about 5,000 population have sufficient scale to be involved in the range of growth promotion and facilities expansion activities, with additional differences in size up to the 50,000 range making little difference in the degree of community mobilization as measured in the two research projects.

PROMOTION, FACILITIES EXPANSION, AND VILLAGE GROWTH

What about the consequences of these community activities? Does mobilization to attract or expand business yield results? Is the expansion of community facilities associated with aspects of economic growth? Much of the literature presents community development as a process by which people work together to set goals and strive to achieve them. Although not every little town can hope to industrialize or expand business activities, one can assume that those that organize and work to achieve such objectives are at a definite advantage. Yet there is widespread acceptance of the argument that small places are increasingly dependent upon larger units of society.

Despite the somewhat mixed views concerning the possible efficacy of development actions, there evidently has been little research associating local mobilization with presumed growth consequences. Adams (1969) in a comparative study of four Wisconsin and two Missouri small towns, concluded that the mobilization of key community leaders for action was necessary if communities were to achieve a stable or growing population. In a survey of industrial development projects involving the Cooperative Extension Service in twenty-six states, respondents reported 243 new firms expanding operations, with more than 20,000 new jobs created or saved (National Task Force Report 1980). With this approach, however, no information was available on comparable areas not having such programs. Smith, Deaton, and Kelch (1980) concluded from a survey of nonmetropolitan communities of Kentucky and Tennessee that many factors associated with industrial location can be influenced by local decisions and actions. Williams, Sofranko, and Root (1977), using a research design similar to this one, found that several measures of local mobilization to attract new industry were positively associated with acquiring new firms for 162 small communities in Illinois. Humphrey and Krannich (1980) and Krannich and Humphrey (1983) presented evidence that local mobilization is negatively associated with population growth.

In using population change as their basic dependent variable, Humphrey and Krannich followed a recent thrust in community research beginning with Molotch's (1976a) article on the city as a "growth machine" (see also Lyon et al. 1981). Without denying that population growth may follow economic development, we would hypothesize that a more immediate response to activities to expand or attract new industry should be the addition or expansion of industrial firms in the community. Particularly for villages, we submit that increase in firms may or may not result in much new employment leading to population increase and, further, that new employees may or may not live in the village itself. Indeed, Molotch's conception of growth was criticized by Logan (1976) for being unidimensional, combining both population and economic expansion. Molotch (1976b) replied that economic growth without population growth is relevant strategy only when dealing with a small unit locality—precisely our situation here.

To address these issues, the models that we examine include as dependent variables the reported 1975–80 change in the number of (1) industrial firms, (2) retail establishments, (3) professional services, (4) finance, insurance, and real estate firms, and (5) 1970–80 population change in the village from census sources. We were not able to measure expansion of already established firms but did obtain from the mayors their reports on the number of various types of firms in 1980 and losses and gains in number between 1975 and 1980. (For professional services the numbers of doctors, dentists, veterinarians, and lawyers were reported rather than the number of professional firms.) Accurate 1975 population figures are not available for villages, so it was necessary to measure 1970–80 population change instead of 1975–80 as would be preferred.

A set of regression models is shown in Table 7–4. For each of the five dependent variables considered in separate panels, we have introduced as controls the four variables included in the preceding analysis (Table 7–3)—initial size, urban accessibility, population change in the prior decade (1960–70), and region—along with the promotion and the facilities scales as independent variables. The first model in each panel (column 2) gives the regression of the dependent variable on the control variables, followed by the second (column 3), which includes in addition the promotion scale, the third (column 4), which includes the controls plus the facilities scale, and the fourth (column 5), which includes all independent and control variables. All of the change variables are residualized scores—that is, residuals of the regression of the 1980 value on the earlier value.[5]

Efforts to expand or attract business and industry are associated with 1975–80 change in the number of industrial establishments (see panel 1), net of all the control variables and the facilities scale. Although the bivariate correlation of the facilities scale and industrial change is close to significance, the beta is almost zero in the model that includes the promotion scale. Similarly the bivariate correlation with region is significant, showing more expansion of industry in the South and the West, and the beta coefficients remain relatively large, though only one is above significance in the regression models. There is also a suggestion (not significant) that industrial growth is more likely in less accessible locations, but the size effect disappears in models that include the promotion scale.[6]

Change in retail establishments is significantly associated (positively) with prior population change in these models, but neither scale is, though coefficients for both scales are in the expected direction (panel 2). One item in the promotion scale, "started or carried out a program to improve the downtown area," is an effort that appears to be directly related to the goal of increasing retail activity, and it was reported by more than one-third of the village mayors. This individual item was used in the models instead of the promotion scale (not shown), but it showed essentially no association with retail change either singly ($r = 0.04$) or with other variables in the model. In the analysis with individual elements of the facilities scale, however, the expansion of both tourist attractions and second homes was significantly associated with retail change.

The third panel concerns professional change—that is, changes in

Table 7–4. Bivariate Correlations and Standardized Regression Coefficients for Change Variables with Independent Variables.[a]

	r	Standardized Regression Coefficients			
		Without Promotion or Facilities	With Promotion	With Facilities	With Promotion and Facilities
		N = 99			
Dependent Variable: Industry Change, 1975–80					
Size, 1970 (log)	0.15	0.17	0.01	0.09	0.00
Accessibility (log)	−0.15	−0.15	−0.14	−0.12	−0.13
Population change, 1960–70	−0.06	−0.06	−0.02	−0.03	−0.02
Region (South, West versus North)	0.22[b]	0.19	0.17	0.21[b]	0.17
Promotion scale	0.37[b]		0.35[b]		0.34[b]
Facilities scale	0.18			0.14	0.03
R		0.30	0.44	0.32	0.44
R²		0.09	0.19	0.10	0.19
Dependent Variable: Retail Change, 1975–80					
Size, 1970 (log)	0.07	0.06	0.00	−0.03	−0.06
Accessibility (log)	−0.09	−0.14	−0.14	−0.12	−0.12
Population change, 1960–70	0.18	0.20	0.21[b]	0.24[b]	0.24[b]
Region (South, West versus North)	0.17	0.12	0.12	0.15	0.14
Promotion scale	0.13		0.13		0.10
Facilities scale				0.16	0.12
R		0.28	0.30	0.30	0.32
R²		0.08	0.09	0.09	0.10

(Continued on next page)

the number of medical doctors, dentists, lawyers, veterinarians, and hospitals. There are no significant coefficients in this panel, and indeed most associations are extremely low, with multiple correlations explaining only about 2 percent of the variance. Perhaps the results would have been different had we asked mobilization questions more directly related to activities aimed at attracting professional services. In looking at the individual elements of the facilities scale, a positive significant association was found between the improvement of health facilities and growth in professionals, as would be expected.

Table 7-4. continued

		Standardized Regression Coefficients			
	r	Without Promotion or Facilities	With Promotion	With Facilities	With Promotion and Facilities
		N = 99			
Dependent Variable: Professional Change, 1975–80					
Size, 1970 (log)	0.12	0.12	0.13	0.10	0.10
Accessibility (log)	0.05	0.01	0.01	0.01	0.01
Population change, 1960–70	0.11	0.03	0.03	0.04	0.04
Region (South, West versus North)	−0.07	−0.09	−0.09	−0.08	−0.08
Promotion Scale	0.03		−0.01		−0.02
Facilities scale	0.09			0.04	0.05
R			0.15	0.15	0.15	0.15
R^2			0.02	0.02	0.02	0.02
Dependent Variable: Finance, Insurance, and Real Estate Change, 1975–80					
Size, 1970 (log)	0.13	0.08	0.07	0.00	0.00
Accessibility (log)	0.17	0.12	0.12	0.15	0.15
Population change, 1960–70	0.18	0.13	0.13	0.16	0.16
Region (South, West versus North)	0.07	0.07	0.07	0.09	0.09
Promotion scale	0.06		0.02		−0.02
Facilities scale	0.09			0.14	0.15
R		0.24	0.27	0.27
R^2		0.06	0.07	0.07

(Continued on next page)

Results are rather similar for the next panel on changes in finance, insurance, and real estate firms. Only the standardized regression (beta) coefficients for accessibility, prior population change, and the facilities scale have any magnitude, and none in the regression models are significant.

Turning to population change, we find that neither the promotion nor the facilities scale was associated with 1970–80 population change for our sample, as seen in the next to last panel. An examination of

Table 7–4.   continued

		Standardized Regression Coefficients			
	r	Without Promotion or Facilities	With Promotion	With Facilities	With Promotion and Facilities
			N = 99		
		Dependent Variable: Population Change, 1970–80			
Accessibility (log)	0.17	0.10	0.10	0.10	0.10
Population change, 1960–70	0.33[b]	0.30[b]	0.30[b]	0.31[b]	0.31[b]
Region (South, West versus North)	0.07	0.05	0.06	0.05	0.07
Promotion scale	−0.05		−0.05		−0.08
Facilities scale	−0.05			0.03	0.06
R		0.34	0.35	0.35	0.35
R²		0.12	0.12	0.12	0.12
			N = 97		
		Dependent Variable: Population Change, 1970–80			
Accessibility (log)	0.17	0.13	0.14	0.13	0.15
Population change, 1960–70	0.32[b]	0.27[b]	0.25[b]	0.26[b]	0.27[b]
Region (South, West versus North)	0.19	0.18	0.21[b]	0.18	0.22[b]
Promotion scale	−0.21[b]		−0.22[b]		−0.25[b]
Facilities scale	−0.13			−0.04	0.07
R		0.38	0.43	0.38	0.44
R²		0.14	0.19	0.14	0.19

[a]Measures of change are the residuals from regression of the 1980 values (number of establishments or population) on the earlier values. See text.

[b]Significant at the 0.05 level.

Source: Survey of 100 Mayors. N = 99 because one village had disincorporated by 1980. In bottom panel N = 97 with deletion of village growing 423 percent and one growing 106 percent.

scatter diagrams, however, suggested that the results might be affected unduly by two places that grew very rapidly over the decade (106 and 432 percent). When these were eliminated, as the last panel shows, the promotion scale is negatively associated with 1970–80 population change, even controlling for all the other variables.

Population change for the previous decade is important and positively associated with 1970–80 change in both panels. Indeed, the correlation of population change between the two decades (+0.32) seems lower than might be expected, but this no doubt reflects the changes in growth patterns that are part of nonmetropolitan turnaround. Region also is associated with 1970–80 population change in the bottom panel (significant in the two models with the promotion scale) with higher levels of population change in the South and West. Accessibility, though not significant, shows a small association. These results parallel the findings of Chapter 2. (Population size is not included in these models because it is controlled in the dependent variable measure of population change.)

Thus, after removing two villages that grew very rapidly in the 1970–80 decade, we find that our results for population change parallel that of Humphrey and Krannich for Pennsylvania minor civil divisions. We went beyond their work, however, by examining actual changes in business and industry as reported by the mayors, which should logically be the more immediate result sought through most promotion efforts. The positive association found between the promotion score and the increase in the number of industrial firms supports the view that promotion activities may achieve some of their objectives.

DISCUSSION

In this chapter we extended analysis beyond the more detached perspective of the village as part of a regional or national hierarchy of places and moved to a consideration of social action at the community level. By means of a survey of 100 mayors, information was obtained on activities and relationships in their villages that might be associated with various aspects of community growth.

We found that three out of four villages were involved in some corporate activity seeking to expand or attract business and industry. These efforts are widespread among the villages and are not concentrated in regional locations or with respect to accessibility to cities. Nor does a history of population growth or decline (1960–70) influence the degree of these activities. For our villages, however, a larger initial population size increases the likelihood of economic promotion efforts.

In terms of possible consequences of these activities, we found that the promotion scale was associated with industrial growth, though not with growth in three other economic sectors. But promotion was not associated with population growth. Indeed, after dropping two cases that were extreme outliers in population growth, we found, as did Humphrey and Krannich, a negative association between 1970–80 population change and economic promotion, net of 1960–70 population change and the size and location variables.

With respect to variations in growth, are villages engulfed by forces they cannot control? Our limited findings must point to an answer of both yes and no. We would agree with the conclusions of Humphrey and Krannich (1980), Baldasarre and Protash (1982), and Krannich and Humphrey (1983), that the reasons for local population growth seem to have little to do with the mobilization of local resources. Nevertheless, local promotion of business and industry is associated in our sample with the expansion of industry, consistent with the findings of Williams, Sofranko, and Root (1977).

What appears to be problematic, at least for villages, is the assumption—stated by Molotch (1976a) in working with larger places and adopted by Humphrey and Krannich—that success at economic growth promotion activities should be measured by population increase. To be sure, many case studies of rural industrialization have shown that new industry leads to population growth (Summers et al. 1976) and we reported an association in Chapter six. But there is also concern about "leakage"—the situation where new jobs are taken by new people rather than local workers. This might mean migration into the community but also surely commuting by residents outside (Summers 1982).

For our sample, there is a great deal of commuting to other locations to work, and no doubt there is also commuting into the village. Only 15 percent of the mayors stated that most residents are employed in their village rather than elsewhere. Conversely, it is also the case that much of the population growth, particularly in the context of the turnaround, is not associated with the development of industry. A decline in the association of initial concentration in manufacturing and level of net migration for nonmetropolitan counties was documented by Heaton and Fuguitt (1979), and the association of new growth with retirement and recreation is well known. Of course it is also true that the timing of our population effect may have been incorrectly specified, since for accurate data we are limited to using census decades. Perhaps population growth would show up as a lagged effect later, assuming the new industries stay in place.

Despite the association between promotion and industrial growth, we would not want our study, though it is based on a national sample, to be construed as a general vindication of the force of local autonomy and effectiveness of community development efforts. This is, after all, a set of statistical associations based on 100 telephone interviews and should be followed by more intensive comparative work on the value of local development endeavors. Furthermore, whereas in the next chapter we will explore one of the possible consequences of population growth, the consequences of industrial or economic development have not been considered at all. That these may not all be positive has been discussed in a number of works (e.g., Whiting 1974a; Summers et al. 1976; Lonsdale and Seyler 1979).

We also looked at reported efforts to expand community facilities. Such efforts were almost universal among the entire spectrum of small, growing, and declining places, though the extent of these activities was strongly associated with initial size and negatively associated with 1960–70 growth. Reliance on county, state, and/or federal funding was reported for much of this work. Expansion of facilities was not positively associated with 1970–80 population change, contrary to what we might have expected, due to the need to provide services for an increasing population base (Fox and Sullivan 1979). Perhaps the greater expansion of facilities in places with a history of decline reflects a process of leveling inequalities, with external government funding leading to a "worst first" policy. But this assumes villages declining in population were deficient earlier in facilities expansion.

In any event, although it is possible that 1975–80 facilities development could encourage subsequent economic growth, the finding that expansion of facilities is not associated with industrial growth in 1975–80 (net of the other variables) supports the prescription by Tweeten and Brinkman (1976) that communities should provide services consistent with their needs and ability to pay, rather than in the hopes of inducing economic growth.

Without minimizing the usefulness of the findings reported here, they also point to the need for more elaborate designs, better measurement, and greater attention to possible lag effects in further work seeking to make appropriate causal inferences. From this line of comparative community research, firm generalizations may ultimately emerge concerning the significance of local social action and community development activities within our complex and changing settlement structure.

NOTES

1. With only one respondent for each village, there are concerns about the reliability of the data. Mayors should be most appropriate informants, however, for the questions covered in this chapter and in Chapter 8. Also, we are encouraged by the findings of Krannich and Humphrey (1983), who asked several respondents in each of their sample locations the same questions about their communities and found responses to be quite consistent.

2. Some of our questions are patterned after those of Humphrey and Krannich. Craig Humphrey kindly made their questionnaire available to us, and we acknowledge similar assistance from Al Sokolow and Bert Adams.

3. Of course, a village might encourage new business or industry but still be exclusionary in specific types of firms that they encourage, particularly at the negotiation stage. Such subtleties cannot be encompassed in a single index.

4. We saw no reason why a particular item, such as recreational facilities, should receive a higher weighting in the facilities scale if public funding were obtained. On the other hand, receiving public funding from sources outside the village certainly points to a degree of local mobilization that would otherwise be absent. Accordingly, we constructed a public funding scale by adding the number of facilities expanded through public funding for each village. The funding scale correlated 0.75 with the facilities scale, and results with the funding scale paralleled those to follow with the facilities scale, so the funding questions were not considered further.

5. Since in many cases the number of firms in a category and the number added or subtracted is quite small, this measure is preferable to others in minimizing the extreme effects that sometimes result from measuring change from a small base as was also the case in Chapter 6. Residualized scores also are not correlated with the initial score. Consequently population size in 1970 is not included in the models of population change (Bohrnstedt 1969).

6. The results of Tables 7-3 and 7-4 could have been organized into a path model, with the independent variables of 7-3 as antecedent and scales

intervening. By and large, this more formal approach would seem to add little to the understanding of these relationships.

8 NEWCOMERS AND OLDTIMERS

The new population trends of the 1970s have led researchers and those involved in policy planning and program activities at the local level to an increased interest in the problems and consequences of growth. The possible consequences of population decline have long been noted—the pessimism feeding on itself as decline continues, the debilitating effects of outmigration of the young adults who are presumably the most able, and the problems of providing services with a reduced tax base (Raup 1961; Klietsch et al. 1964; Whiting 1974b). Undoubtedly such problems continue to build in many areas—recall from Chapter 2 that one-third of the villages in our sample were declining in the 1970–80 period and 12 percent declined over all three decades. This leads to an estimate of about 1,200 incorporated villages in all that have declined for thirty years.

What are the social consequences of growth? The new trend in nonmetropolitan areas has generated considerable research so that we now have a good overview of the altered pattern of differential growth among various types of metropolitan and nonmetropolitan communities. We also know much about the characteristics of migrants and reasons for moving. Despite a growing number of studies, however, it is more difficult to make generalizations about the consequences of growth for smaller nonmetropolitan communities. These consequences may include higher land values, possible environmental degradation, need to expand public services due to an increased population or changing population composition, and changes in social relationships and community social structure.

A focal point of concern has been in the area of social relationships, particularly as newcomers and long-term residents accommodate one another and deal with a variety of issues, including those that are growth related. Coming from a different community setting, and with differing characteristics overall (i.e., higher education, higher occupational status, etc.), migrants to nonmetropolitan areas may become advocates of positions in opposition to oldtimers and not be reluctant to work for their goals through local governmental channels (Sokolow 1981a). Schwarzweller (1979) suggests that although the heavy outmigration of people from rural communities has been a significant economic drain with important social consequences, this may not be as disruptive to the prevailing social organization as the arrival of newcomers.

Nevertheless, in reviewing much of the previous research, Baldassare (1981a) concludes that findings do not provide convincing evidence that rapid nonmetropolitan growth results in severe personal and community disruptions. A similar position is argued by Gillard (1982) and Wilkinson et al. (1982) for research on boomtowns.

We can identify several somewhat overlapping research approaches. One is to infer consequences on the basis of differences between movers and nonmovers—in their social characteristics, attitudes toward public services, positions on policy issues, community satisfaction, and social participation (e.g., DeJong and Keppel 1979; Voss 1980; Sofranko et al. 1981; Bradshaw and Blakeley 1981; Lovejoy, Brown, and Ayers 1981; Rank and Voss 1982). Although differences are noted in some instances, among other things many of these studies report from a variety of settings that migrants tend to be better educated, typically do not express greater demands for services or more opposition to population or economic growth, and fairly quickly come to participate in community affairs.

Shading into the above are what might be termed case studies, either because they deal with smaller areas or a wider range of issues or tend to be more ethnographic in their research approach. Many of these focus on differences between oldtimers and newcomers in background, values, and goals, and how these may result in controversy or conflict, particularly in the local political arena (e.g., Graber

1974; Alanen and Smith 1977; Ploch 1978, 1980; Beegle and Rathge 1980; Daily and Campbell 1980; Stinner and Toney 1980, to name only a few). Results of this work are difficult to summarize briefly, and although there are accounts of growth-related problems and value clashes, there is little evidence of serious conflicts or disruption.

In another approach, communities with different levels of growth are compared. If growth has social consequences, one might well expect that measures of the consequences would be positively associated with rate of growth or inmigration in a single-time comparison of a set of communities. Studies include Baldassare and Pennie (1979) and Baldassare (1981b), who found essentially no difference in evaluations of place, social life, and well-being as reported in a national level attitude survey for respondents classed by the growth rates in their counties. Data from a study by Luloff (1978) on three Pennsylvania counties were reanalyzed by Baldassare (1981a), who compared these counties by level of net migration. The county with the most reported complaints regarding services and facilities, social conflict, and community spirit was the one that lost migrants between 1960 and 1975, and the county with the lowest percentage of complaints gained during the fifteen-year period.

In contrast, Price and Clay (1980), using the counties of Michigan, found a positive association between survey data on certain community problems and rate of net migration, controlling for urbanization, education, income, and age structure. Problems reported with this association were in municipal health care and local educational systems but not in the areas of recreational and cultural facilities, programs for elderly, or community solidarity. Further analysis showed the latter variable to have a curvilinear relation, with the respondents in both losing and rapidly gaining counties reporting problems with community solidarity.

The data from our telephone survey allows us to extend this line of comparative research, which up to now has been limited in amount and has given somewhat contradictory results. Using a few questions from the interview we can consider directly the reported presence of newcomer-oldtimer differences in the community. Mayors were asked several direct questions concerning possible newcomer-oldtimer differences in the community, which will be analyzed here. Although one must always be cautious in accepting the reports of individual informants, mayors should be aware of any community level differences and changes though, of course, not all the attitudes and feelings of old and new residents. (See note 1, Chapter 7). Our first objective is to determine the extent and nature of this phenomenon, as reported by the mayors for our sample of U.S. villages. Next, we will see whether such differences are associated with population, economic growth, and other village characteristics considered previously in this chapter. Instead of simply concentrating on rapidly growing places and their problems, this sort of comparative community analysis should move us closer to seeing what the possible effect of population and economic change might be, across a general cross-section of growing villages as the population units under inquiry.

The sequence of questions on this subject is found in Table 8–1. First, mayors were asked if they thought their towns had been growing or declining during the past ten years. Those sixty mayors who thought their towns had been growing were then asked the succeeding

Table 8–1. Questions on Newcomer-Oldtimer Relations in Growing Villages.

Questions	Yes	No	DK or NA[a]	Total
Has the population of your town been growing over the past ten years?	60	28	11	99
If answer is yes above, would you say this is good?	47	8	5	60
1. Are newcomers socially accepted?	51	5	4	60
. 2. Are there any cases where newcomers and oldtimers have been on different sides of the same issue?	11	45	4	60
3. Do newcomers want different things from local government than others?	15	41	4	60
Relations index (no on 1, and/or yes on 2, and/or yes on 3)	24	32	4	60

[a]Don't know or not ascertained.

Source: Survey of 100 Mayors. N = 99 because one village had disincorporated by 1980.

questions, although answers were not obtained for four cases. The remainder of this chapter is concerned with these fifty-six mayors and their villages. In five cases, communities whose mayors thought their towns were growing actually declined according to the census, from 2 to 9 percent. Since there can be newcomers even in declining settings, these cases were retained. (Indeed, four of these five mayors did report some newcomer-oldtimer differences.)

NEWCOMER-OLDTIMER DIFFERENCES

After general questions about where new people are coming from and why they are moving, the mayors of villages reported as growing were asked if they thought this was good or bad. Only eight of the mayors reported they thought the growth with its new migration was a bad thing (line 2 of Table 8-1). This is consistent with the growth machine hypothesis—that community leaders will most generally support economic and population growth. In a recent study of growth orientations among mayors of Kentucky cities, Maurer and Christenson (1982) similarly found only nine of seventy-five small-town nonmetropolitan mayors were opposed to growth in industry or business. In our study, among those eight saying growth was bad, there were concerns in two cases because newcomers were mostly retired people, in one because they were blacks, in one because the village was unable to annex new territory, and in one because of a limited resource:

> People are converting summer homes to year-round homes and retiring in the area. This is bad because the lake is about filled up.

Responses of two others indicated satisfaction with the status quo:

> We've tried to keep the village as it is. Most people don't want the town to grow.

The three questions following in the interview concerned relations between newcomers and oldtimers. For each question, the reported incidence of serious newcomer-oldtimer differences is low. Only five of the sixty respondents reported that newcomers are not socially accepted in their communities. This comes to 9 percent of the eligible fifty-six villages. Reasons why people are not socially accepted generally included social and ethnic considerations. The five responses are as follows:

Some are cheap. You wouldn't want them near you.

We don't mind Chicanos, but the "wetbacks" we do. They don't keep their property properly maintained.

Some oil workers are a little undesirable.

Ninety-five percent are (accepted). The other 5 percent, they're distant people (welfare cases).

We had a lot of trouble with the welfare cases. We built low-income housing, but the people who moved in let them get rundown. They steal too, you know.

The next question related to whether newcomers and oldtimers are on different sides of a community issue. Note that we asked whether there were any cases they could recall, and not whether that is a general problem. Nevertheless, only eleven mayors reported such instances, or 20 percent of the fifty-six responses. The specific issues reported are familiar from previous literature and journalistic accounts; most are related to the provision of services and growth policy:

Newcomers wanted a rock-fest in town at the fairgrounds but didn't get it because of the oldtimers.

Yes. Older people poorly managed funds. There was disagreement over cleaning up the community. Newcomers want people to listen when they talk. They want playgrounds, parks, and things.

Newcomers and oldtimers have been on different sides of issues concerning water and sewer rates, but they compromise very well.

Oh, definitely. Oldtimers defeated repaving of areas of town. Those who were able to afford it voted it down. Newcomers want snow removal and trash service and other services a small town can't provide.

Newcomers want more entertainment.

On opposite sides of water fluoridation. Newcomers for, oldtimers against. Newcomers are used to having more public services.

A couple of years ago we had a hell of a rhubarb. We had a great mayor a couple of years ago, but he fired the chief of police and created a real split in town. The newcomers didn't agree when he fired him. The mayor finally won out, but it was a long fight. There was a recall and everything.

Differences over how much growth will occur. Oldtimers are for development. Newcomers want to limit growth. Newcomers want more recreation activities. Many are retired and want different services.

Mainly environmental. Oldtimers want industry; newcomers want to preserve what is already here. Newcomers are used to more services and want these services, yet they don't want to pay for them.

Opposing views on both sides—progressive and attract business vs. stay the same.

Finally there was the specific question, "Do newcomers want different things from local government than others?" As mayors, our respondents should be uniquely qualified to answer this question. Again, however, Table 8-1 shows that this problem evidently is not widely prevalent, being reported by fifteen mayors, or 27 percent of the fifty-six responses. Many positive responses here referred to public services in general. Specific public services that they desire more than, or in contrast with, oldtimers included recreation activities or facilities (five villages), garbage pickup (three villages), snow removal, improved school systems, improved transportation (one village each). Several noted that newcomers are used to or expect more services than have been provided by the village. One negative response from a mayor was:

Newcomers are used to more services and want these services, yet they don't want to pay for them.

Because the number and proportion of newcomer-oldtimer differences in these responses were so low, we next set up a dichotomy of villages according to whether or not any such differences were reported. The last line of the table shows that this included twenty-four villages, with thirty-two of the fifty-six having no such differences. Because there is not much overlap between the questions, this proportion is considerably higher than any individual question, with 43 percent of the respondents (only five villages reported two of the three differences, and one reported all three).

DIFFERENCES AND LEVEL OF POPULATION GROWTH

Our next task was to determine whether there is an association between level of population growth and the reporting of newcomer-oldtimer differences. To do this, we carried out a regression analysis with the presence of any differences as a dichotomous dependent variable. Although there may be technical problems with this approach, it should be an appropriate way to present these results, particularly since the dependent variable proportion is close to 0.5. (A parallel bivariate procedure, using *t*-tests, led to identical conclusions.) Unfortunately, there is no reliable information for these individual small places on the number of inmigrants, but we would expect the proportion of population consisting of newcomers to be associated with population change.[1] Also, migrants to rapidly growing communities should be less similar to long-term residents in origins and characteristics than those moving into places experiencing continued decline.

Table 8–2 gives correlation coefficients and standardized regression coefficients for various regression models. We included our standard control variables—initial size, urban accessibility, and region—along with population change in each of the two decades.[2] Size in 1970, accessibility to large cities, or region of the country (South and West versus North) are not associated with the prevalence of newcomer-oldtimer differences, according to the first model. Similarly, there is not an association with either of the population change variables, either in the bivariate correlation coefficients or in the multivariate models controlling for the other variables (columns 3, 4, and 5). Indeed, no coefficient is near significance. In the table, for this part of the analysis, we have only an *n* of fifty-six cases. Nevertheless, the size of the correlation coefficients is so small, the largest being 0.12, that none of them would have been significant had they applied to the entire sample of ninety-nine. So we must conclude that the extent of population growth, either in 1960–70 or 1970–80, is not associated with the likelihood of newcomer-oldtimer differences. Nor are any of the common village characteristics—size, urban proximity, or regional location—of any use in predicting whether such differences (as reported by our key informants) will occur.

Finally, we examined the community activity closely associated with reported newcomer-oldtimer differences, i.e., the expansion of facilities. Greater demand for services by newcomers has been a prominent difference reported and speculated about in the literature and was an important component of our mayors' reports. Table 8–3 presents a multiple regression for our fifty-six cases that is identical to Table 7–3 with the addition of a binary variable for new-old differences. This variable includes villages with yes responses to either or both of the second and third questions of Table 8–1, since these appear to relate more directly to concerns about facilities than the first question on whether newcomers are socially accepted.

Table 8-2. Bivariate Correlations and Standardized Regression Coefficients for Newcomer-Oldtimer Differences with Selected Independent Variables.

| | | Standardized Regression Coefficients | | |
| | | Without Population Change | With Population Change, 1960–70 | With Population Change, 1970–80 |
	r			
Size, 1970 (log)	−0.03	−0.06	−0.07	−0.06
Accessibility (log)	0.11	0.13	0.10	0.13
Region (South and West versus North)	0.03	0.05	0.06	0.05
Population change, 1960–70[a]	0.12		0.11	
Population change, 1970–80[a]	0.03			0.00
R		0.13	0.17	0.13
R^2		0.02	0.03	0.02

[a]Measures of change are the residuals from regression of the later values on the earlier values.

Source: Survey of 100 mayors. N = 56, the subsample of mayors reporting population growth in their village in the previous ten years.

The results show that the difference measure is associated with facilities expansion with coefficients that approach significance. (Both r and the B or beta coefficients are significant at the 0.10 level.) As was true for all survey respondents, population size in 1970 is still the most important variable in association with facilities expansion. Population change over 1960–70 essentially has no association with facilities expansion among these (mostly) growing villages, and accessibility has a negative association that approaches significance as does region in the multiple regression. So there is at least tentative evidence that in villages where the mayor perceives differences between newcomers and oldtimers in positions taken on community issues, or in wanting different things from local government, there is

Table 8-3. Bivariate Correlations and Standardized Regression Coefficients (Betas) for the Association between the Facilities Scale and Old-New Differences with Other Independent Variables.

Independent Variables:	r	Beta
Village size, 1970 (log)	0.39[a]	0.50[a]
Accessibility (log)	−0.18	−0.28
Population change, 1960–70[b]	−0.04	−0.09
Region (North-other)	−0.12	−0.22
New-old difference[c]	0.19	0.22
(Constant)		
R		0.56
R²		0.32

[a]Significant at the 0.05 level.

[b]This measure of change is the residual from the regression of 1970 population on 1960 population. See text.

[c]Binary variable: 1 = report that newcomers on different sides of a community issue and/or want different things from local government; 0 = other villages.

Source: Survey of 100 mayors. N = 56, the subsample of mayors reporting population growth in their village in the previous ten years.

likely to be more facilities expansion reported, net of the other variables including 1960–70 population change. (The 1960–70 population change variable was used to parallel the model in Table 7–3. We found that population change for 1970–80 yields almost identical results.) So if this weak association is not spurious or due to sampling error, it seems to indicate that population size is important but increased need, as indexed by population growth, is not, whereas newcomer demand may make a difference in proceeding to expand community facilities.

DISCUSSION

In this chapter we have been concerned with some possible consequences of population growth and have given particular attention to
social relationships between established residents and newcomers.
Although mayors of four out of ten growing communities reported
some oldtimer-newcomer differences of the sort discussed in the
recent literature on growth impacts, we found nothing in their
responses to contradict Baldassare's (1981a) contention that such
differences should not generally lead to serious community problems.
We also found that newcomer-oldtimer differences were no more
prevalent in rapidly growing places than in those growing more
slowly, nor were there differences by size of place and location. There
is, however, tentative evidence that the presence of these differences
does go along with the expansion of facilities, even though expansion
is not associated with level of population change for these growing
communities.

Although citing possible dire consequences for communities in the
assimilation of new migrants is almost a cliché in the turnaround
literature, our modest findings are really not inconsistent with much
that we know about the new nonmetropolitan population trend. Research, for example, has emphasized the heterogeneity of this trend,
both in terms of types of communities and areas of the country and
also of different types of migrants (Brown and Beale 1981). Sokolow
(1981a) cites an Oregon study (Hennigh 1978) that reported newcomers in a rapidly growing county to range from "extreme right
wingers to communal hippies" who moved from different places for
quite different reasons. Sofranko, Williams, and Fliegel (1981) found
small differences by origin of newcomers, with migrants from nonmetropolitan areas generally more favorable to population growth,
development, and raising taxes for services, than metropolitan migrants or long-term residents. Ploch (1980) reported in one case study
that a coalition sometimes emerged between newcomers and older
long-time residents in supporting the status quo against younger
long-time residents who favor change. A conclusion of Sokolow
(1981a: 180) is apt:

> Thus the newcomer-oldtimer dichotomy may not be the central cleavage
> in growing rural communities that it was once thought to be. Instead of
> length of residence, the political divisions today seem to be based on class,

education, age, and how one views the world—all characteristics of politics in more urban places.

Given the differing characteristics of migrants and established residents in different community settings, it is perhaps not surprising that comparing a general cross-section of villages does not produce an association between population growth and newcomer-oldtimer differences. Indeed, from a demographic perspective, there is slippage here since growth is not due entirely to the addition of newcomers. In this era of generally low natural increase, however, population growth, the only variable we can use, should generally be highly associated with the number of new migrants.

In thinking about the dynamics of social relationships, moreover, one should not overlook the importance of the individual. Mayors who report newcomer-oldtimer differences may be responding to a few articulate and vociferous citizens whose presence need not be a function of the number of other migrants. Regardless of such individual idiosyncrasies, a longitudinal study might reveal that the differences between new and old here would be most visible early in the turnaround process before absolute and relative growth is very large.

A possible consequence of new-old differences, however, was suggested in the results associating this variable with facilities expansion. This tentative finding is consistent with expectations but must be corroborated with more intensive research on this specific issue by using additional data sources and by giving further attention to direction of causation. It may be that in some individual villages the process of expanding certain facilities increases the likelihood that new-old differences appear, rather than the other way around.

As is so often the case in social science research, then, this consideration of a problem with limited data from a broader study has underscored the need to disaggregate populations new and old and to move beyond simple stereotypes of social processes. Further work needs to include information from and about various groups involved in community interactions, along with a more elaborate specification of the nature of the demographic changes underway. Although it is easy to exaggerate the immediate problems in social relationships that will be faced by a community undergoing growth, work in this area may nevertheless have a long-term significance for understanding the future nature of village life. The social structure and culture of many rural communities will be determined by the relations that evolve through newcomer-oldtimer interactions, however varied they may be.

NOTES

1. We verified this association with the 1970 characteristics data set using villages in the complete sample grouped by 1960–70 population change in the five categories of Figure 2-1. The percentage of 1970 residents who lived in a different county in 1965 was a regular gradient, ranging from 15 for villages losing 10 percent or more to 25 for villages gaining 20 percent or more over the decade.
2. Other control variables that were considered are personal characteristics of the mayors, their length of residence in the village, and their length of time as mayor. One might expect respondents who were themselves oldtimers to be more likely to report differences. This, however was not the case; t-tests on these longevity variables between mayors reporting or not reporting differences were not significant. Further, the direction of difference was contrary to expectations. Mayors reporting differences had a mean length of residence of 29.5 years and a mean time in office of 4.2 years, whereas comparable figures for mayors not reporting a difference 32.5 and 5.7.

9 THE AMERICAN VILLAGE AND ITS FUTURE

We began this work with some questions about the place of the village in the American settlement system in the context of recent population distribution changes and about the often-stated prediction that villages will disappear as a population or functional unit. Decades of centralization have shifted population and business activities away from villages toward larger centers, suggesting that the village has become an obsolete settlement form in the modern urban-oriented society. Yet recent population trends have not conformed to the long-standing centralization patterns, raising the possibility of a different future for villages than was commonly predicted. Our purpose has been to document the actual process of change in population and economic activities in American villages during thirty years of significant transformations in rural society between 1950 and 1980. This work is an effort to understand how villages have responded not only to forces of centralization that encourage the migration of people and business activities to larger units in the urban system but also to the more recent countertrends that have been referred to as the nonmetropolitan turnaround.

Looking first at population trends, we observed in our data that villages (here defined as incorporated places of less than 2,500 population) have experienced increased incidence of growth during

197

the latter part of the 1950–80 period. This coincides with trends in the larger nonmetropolitan sector to which these villages belong and can be interpreted as part of a general decentralization process in the settlement system. Indeed, of considerable significance is the fact that the nonmetropolitan population outside any incorporated place in 1970 grew faster over 1970–80 than villages, followed by cities, in a complete reversal of the 1950–60 trend. Increased village population growth levels generally were found throughout the country in the most recent decade, although a notable minority of places continued to decline. Reasons given by village respondents for rapid population growth fall about evenly into two types, which might be termed consumptive and productive—the former referring to attractiveness due to amenities and recreation and the latter to industrial expansion.

Increased population growth results from changes in fertility, mortality, and migration, though in this circumstance migration appears to be the main cause of the change. Overall, village natural increase is low because of an advanced age structure in comparison with other population units, which is due largely to selective out-migration of the young and some inmigration of older people. Although recent growth through migration has probably included more young adults, a high number and proportion of elderly should continue to be the major demographic characteristic differentiating villages from other settlement types. Except for age, nonmetropolitan villages generally stand between cities and other rural areas in levels of demographic, socioeconomic, and occupational variables—closer to cities for some variables and closer to rural areas for others.

Village economic trends have clearly followed the centralization model in the case of retail and service activities—many have disappeared from individual villages, presumably absorbed by larger shopping centers in nearby cities. Decline in retail and service activities, while quite pronounced during the period of study, was not unique to those of higher order—that is, less common—although these activities were most severely affected. The survival of occasional high-order types of establishments might be interpreted as evidence of sharing among villages in a "dispersed city" arrangement.

While the village has become less important as a shopping center, it has increased in importance as an industrial center. The number of firms engaged in manufacturing, wholesaling, and construction increased during the period of the study, as did production-related firms that serve agriculture, such as irrigation suppliers and fertilizer dealers. Increase in manufacturing activity has been a general nonmetropolitan trend that may reflect advantages of these locations on the production cost side as for labor, along with greater availability and possibly lower costs of transportation and communication to offset locational disadvantages. Wholesaling and construction gains seem to be a response to growth, largely in agricultural production requiring storage and processing activities and the facilities to house and carry out these functions. Growth in rural housing may also have spurred the construction industry during this time.

These economic trends have changed the character of many villages, removing much of the activity from the main street and causing a visual impression of decline, yet less visible industrial activities remain viable as employment opportunities in some villages, as do opportunities in neighboring towns and cities through commuting. This retail decline is evidence that the village of today functions in a larger integrated system of places than it did previously. Further, we found for each time period a positive association between population change and retail change, so that even though there has been a structured shift of retail activities away from the village, those gaining population tend also to be gaining retail units or at least losing them at a slower rate than others. Undoubtedly, some villages have gained shopping facilities, especially where development has been strong, as in basic economic activities or in amenity-rich recreation areas. Continued growth in village population in a wider variety of settings may eventually bring activities back to many main streets if interest in small-town living continues to grow.

Evidence from our survey of activities during the late 1970s indicates that most villages have been actively promoting their cause, trying to stimulate development through infrastructure improvements and other more direct techniques. Local efforts to attract industry are at least statistically associated with increases in manufacturing and other industries, and the widespread prevalence of such activities speaks to the continued viability of villages as functioning communities. These mobilization efforts may be in part a response to the challenge of decline, since villages with population losses were apparently more active in promotional activities than growing villages.

Population growth seems to be generally perceived as good among village leaders and has therefore been a goal in development efforts. This is understandable, since village residents are concerned about the future of their community and the support of their revenue base and property values. Growth problems, as reported in the recent literature, have not affected the villages in this study to a great extent, as was reported by the respondents in our survey. Attitudes toward newcomers were generally favorable, and the differences between new and long-term residents were not viewed as a serious problem by most respondents from growing places.

In this macroscale analysis, we have compared characteristics for a representative set of U.S. villages. The strength of this approach has been the ability to make generalizations about villages in the nation or its regions; the limitation has been the inability to probe the economy and social structure of villages in depth or to allow for or detect local or subregional variability.

Our study has not addressed the very important but complex issue of village social and political processes and how these might have changed over time. For example, we recognize a need for continued work along the lines of Hatch's (1979) intensive study of social structure in a changing rural society. Villages and other rural segments of the population are becoming more integrated within a larger system that brings urbanites and villagers together in a two-way flow. Mobility of both urban and village residents allows frequent visits by each group for a change of scene, for a visit with friends or relations, or for business reasons. These contacts, along with media availability and use, have reduced villagers' reliance on the local social system for entertainment and other social needs.

Newcomers presumably do affect village social structure, though our data suggest it may not be in a totally unwelcome manner as other sources have suggested. Age, education, income, occupation, and other "objective" measures help to describe villagers, but needed also is information on attitudes, motivations, and actions in order to help reveal the direction of village developments.

VILLAGE TRENDS AND THE SETTLEMENT SYSTEM

In much of our analysis, we indexed the position of the village in the settlement system with three basic variables that were considered with other characteristics in order to help understand the pattern of village change. Two of these variables (region of the country and urban accessibility) describe village location, and the third (village initial size) describes the level of either population or economic magnitude at the beginning of each time period. The traditional view of the changing settlement system, consistent with overall national trends at the beginning of the thirty-year period, would lead to a prediction of more population and economic growth in the heartland region of the North and more population and industrial growth near large cities but less retail growth. From this perspective, one would also expect more population and economic growth in larger as contrasted with smaller villages and possible relative loss to nearby cities as part of a centralization process within the urban hierarchy.

Region

Looking back at the analysis by region of the country, we have seen a shift in the regional pattern of population change in villages. During the 1950s villages in the northern part of the country were experiencing the highest incidence and rate of growth. This changed in the 1960s to reduced growth among northern villages and the highest rate of growth in the South. Southern villages continued to grow at a relatively high rate during the 1970s but were surpassed by western villages, which showed the highest incidence and rates of growth among all regions. Western and southern communities dominated the recent growth patterns among villages as they have in other settlement situations.

Regional variation in the economic aspects of village communities was less pronounced. We discovered a variation in size as measured by the number of firms, with southern places being slightly larger, especially in the retail and service sector, but there was not a consistent regional pattern of change in business activities among villages. Patterns of growth and decline by general category of economic activity did not seem to vary among the regions.

Accessibility

We also found some regularities in the association of village population and economic characteristics with the degree of accessibility to larger members of the urban system. Villages with high levels of urban accessibility had higher rates of population growth than did more remote places during the 1950–80 period. This pattern was less pronounced and not statistically significant in the 1970–80 decade, however, when population change was more uniform among classes of our urban accessibility measure.

This same variable, however, showed the opposite direction of association with retail and service business activities. In this case, urban accessibility was inversely related to both the number of retail activities and the change in activities when population size and change were controlled respectively. In considering retail change here, population change needs to be controlled because of a conflicting effect. Villages closer to cities are more likely to grow in population (at least prior to 1970) and hence gain in retail business, which uncontrolled tends to balance the direct negative effect of accessibility on retail trade. On the other hand, level and growth in industrial activities were positively associated with accessibility in our models.

Size

Village size was another characteristic that helped describe patterns of change in both population and business. Traditionally this has been positively related to change in population. Our data support earlier findings for the 1950–60 and 1960–70 decades, with higher rates and incidence of growth for larger places, but this relationship changed in the 1970s. Annualized rates of change in population were actually highest among the smallest villages for 1970–80, even though the former pattern continued to prevail for incidence of growth.

Village population size was related to business activity as well in both static and dynamic comparisons. The association was positive in both instances, although the number of business establishments corresponding to population size decreased over time.

Size can also be measured by the number of business firms in a village, which in the case of retail and service activities we found to be related to the types of activities provided consistent with a central place hierarchy. In the process of functional change, larger villages gained at a higher rate and had lower rates of loss than did places of smaller functional size, yet the hierarchical order was retained throughout the 1950–70 period. For villages of a given size, loss of retail activities was not limited to those of higher order as might be predicted in a concentration process in which less common activities are shifted to larger places in the system. With this possible exception, however, we found no evidence of decay in the central place situation for villages, even though one might expect such decay as part of an increasingly diffuse distribution of people and activities in nonmetropolitan areas.

In sum, the most obvious deviations from the traditional expected results using these variables were found with population change, and these deviations occurred during the latest decade. The changing relationship between population size and change, and between urban accessibility and population change, signals a new direction in village settlement patterns that seems to conform to the general nonmetropolitan pattern. Regional shifts toward the South and West can also be viewed as part of a larger trend in national population distribution.

The reduced importance of urban accessibility in describing population trends raises some questions about the importance of urban proximity in a decentralizing settlement system. As discussed in Chapter 2, this has generally been found to be true for nonmetropolitan counties in association with population, industrial growth, and employment change. The meaning of accessibility may be changing along with the overall trend toward decentralization within the settlement system. Increased mobility and improved communications may have reduced the importance of physical proximity for residents and economic activities in recent years.

THE DYING VILLAGE

The issue of the dying village, with us since the nineteenth century, is difficult to put to rest. In terms of population, Brunner and associates (e.g., Brunner and Kolb 1933) noted relatively high overall growth in the early part of the century, with villages "holding their own" in the 1920s. Subsequent work indicated that the declining importance of the incorporated village could be attributed more to the growth of villages into small city status, with decreasing new incorporations following initial settlement, than to village disappearance (Chapter 2; Table A-1; Fuguitt 1965b). We have seen here a resurgence of village growth since 1970, though one-third of the sample places lost population over 1970–80 and 12 percent lost in all three decades since 1950.

Similarly, we have shown a growth in manufacturing and in service activities related to agriculture since 1950, with widespread decline found only in retail trade. Even here some new types of establishments have been entering the system. In contrast to more recent years, Brunner and associates noted an increase in retail activity in their agricultural villages between 1900 and 1930.

Though an exception to other trends, this overall decline in retail activity takes on considerable significance when one considers that a major reason for the establishment of many if not most villages has been to serve as retail trade centers for the surrounding area. Does this loss make the village a relic, regardless of other growth indicators? One is reminded of the headline that once appeared in a local newspaper: "Small Town Dies, but Life Goes On."

We would submit that such trends need to be understood as adaptations in the changing settlement system. The residential function is a legitimate, important function for most villages, seen dramatically in our finding that respondents for only 15 percent of the villages sampled reported that most people who lived in the village also worked there. Preference and community satisfaction surveys indicate that villages have qualities that many people find attractive for residential living. In part, this is because of the transformation in the structure of local trade, making a wider variety and choice of goods available to the consumer within a short distance. Villages simply would not be as attractive to many potential residents if larger centers were not accessible to provide more choice and variety in goods and services.

Nevertheless, there is another sense in which current trends might be viewed as evidence of decline, if not terminal illness. If trade is replaced by residence as a major reason for the existence of many villages, there may not be "defunctionalization." But there may be decline in differentiation between villages and other elements of the settlement system. If a village is simply a place to live, so is the open country (now growing faster than villages); and with the more and more diffuse location of businesses, work places, and residences, there appears to be little left of local autonomy.

In addressing this issue, we should point out first that this is not a village problem but a general issue in settlement and social organization today. There are similar long-standing concerns about functional and population change in metropolitan areas, currently accelerated by the spread of central city population decline (Bradbury et al. 1982). The notion of the self-centered city has been discarded amid arguments about whether the current situation is in the best interest of the nation (Elazar 1966; Woodruff 1980; Kasarda 1981). Yet we know cities were never independent units. Similarly, part of the dying village controversy has come from viewing current trends against an image of rural self-sufficiency that was never an accurate picture of the situation in rural America.

If we consider the community as a unit in which all ordinary sustenance needs are met, it is clear that virtually none of the places in our sample would qualify. Villages and rural areas must feel influence from the outside, including larger cities and non-place-oriented sources. Yet as Richards (1978) and Warren (1972) warn, further careful work needs to be done to specify the nature of these outside influences rather than to write off the village as absorbed by the "mass society"—whatever that might be.

At the macro level we showed in Chapter 3 that the village continues to be a distinct unit morphologically, with its residents as a whole differentiated in demographic, socioeconomic, and occupational terms from nonvillage rural nonfarm and nonmetropolitan urban categories. Given the scope of our study, information on local social relationships was necessarily limited, but other research has revealed strengthened or continued noneconomic community based activities in selected areas, even with a decline in retail trade (Richardson and Larson 1976; McGranahan 1980). We did find, however, that organized efforts to attract industry were widespread across the sample villages and further that these efforts appear to have some efficacy, which is hardly consistent with extreme loss of autonomy. As counter evidence, we saw that seven out of ten villages sought and obtained government money for improving facilities. Yet there may be a paradox here in that revenue sharing has increased the range and extent of activities that small local governments can undertake.

RURAL SETTLEMENT EFFICIENCY, PUBLIC POLICY, AND THE VILLAGE

A number of concerns have been expressed about the costs of serving a low-density population distribution (Anderson 1950; Real Estate Research Corporation 1974). Arguments have been centered on the costs of providing public services to households, especially in scattered low-density arrangements where consumers do not pay according to their actual cost. Examples of these services include mail delivery, school bus service, telephone, electricity, and other public utilities, all of which are more efficiently provided to high-density settlements. Density is a matter of scale, however, and villages lie between the "open country" population and larger, presumably more efficient cities, where scale economies occur. Since the most rapid growth in nonmetropolitan population has recently been outside of established population centers (see Chapter 2), the village may be a form of aggregation that should be encouraged as a more efficient arrangement of households.

Public policy regarding rural population distribution has not been explicit in the United States, but several areas of government policy have implicitly affected village communities. Facility and economic development grants and loans are a case in point, and we have seen that the use of government support for improving facilities was widespread in our village subsample. The consequences of the recent diminution of this support, along with the shift away from targeted programs toward block grants, need to be assessed. Many small rural communities may not have a sufficient tax base to expand needed public facilities without assistance. The strong association we found between population size and facilities expansion indicates that even with assistance available from state and federal sources, it is the larger places that have the organized ability to provide improved facilities. In general, there are questions about whether small governments can have the capacity or the willingness to carry out their varied and increasing responsibilities effectively (Sokolow 1981b).

More indirect consequences may come from state and federal regulatory control of such activities as intercity public transit, interstate trucking and rail service, and telephone and utility rate structures. Villages have been beneficiaries of some programs in which regulation has maintained services that market forces might have retracted. Arguments have been raised concerning justification for the current level of postal service in small communities, and deregulation has occurred in transportation services such as intercity bus lines. Further deregulation and/or reorganization of service administration could cause hardship for small communities.

There is a recognized need to spell out some of the positive and negative consequences of growth and development or stagnation and decline, in formulating government programs and policy (Deavers and Brown 1980: Bradshaw et al. 1983). Not everyone benefits from development. Rural areas, including villages, continue to have higher proportions of families with low incomes than other areas to an extent that cannot all be explained by cost-of-living differentials. We found that population turnaround villages as a whole had relatively high proportions of families with low income in 1970. The 1980 data, when it is available, may show that most of these places have undergone a considerable improvement in income level with population growth. But as suggested by Bradshaw et al. (1983), the expansion of a number of rural low-income ghettos might also be revealed by the new data, with poor people attracted to the very modest inexpensive housing found in some places. The consequences of demographic and economic decline, though a long-standing concern, also need to be better understood for villages, just as efforts are now underway to consider this trend in major central cities of the nation.

In considering rural settlement and public policy, it is important to seek to understand some of the advantages and disadvantages of the village as evidenced by recent trends and the views of residents and others. We will list some of these here:

Advantages of Villages

Housing and Property.   The process of centralization of population and business activities over several decades has resulted in residential and commercial property vacancies and consequent low property values in many villages when compared to areas in or near larger cities that have experienced growth. Village housing and other real property may therefore appear attractive to prospective residents or entrepreneurs. A related factor is the demographic structure of villages with their high proportion of elderly residents and single-person households. The potential for turnover in housing may therefore be relatively high in villages as mortality and moves to other residential settings create vacancies in existing houses. This condition, along with the addition of specific housing for elderly residents common in many villages, should continue to depress village housing values.

Residential Qualities.   Villages have many recognized advantages for residential living not found in larger cities or more remote rural settings. Compared to large cities, they are viewed by many as quiet, clean, safe, uncongested, friendly, less costly (for services, repairs, parking, taxes, and housing), slower paced, and offering good opportunities for children and adults to become involved in the community. They are also close to outdoor recreation opportunities in many areas.

Compared to other rural residential settings, they are more efficient to serve (i.e., with utilities and public services), which may lower costs to residents; more convenient to shops, schools, and other people; better served with police protection, sewage treatment, water, garbage collection, and social government; potentially more efficient for energy where community-scale projects are considered; and more accessible to the limited public transportation that does remain in some rural areas.

Economic Advantages. Many villages have proved to be good locations for industrial development, particularly in the handling or processing of primary products produced in their local area but increasingly in other forms of manufacturing where labor costs and land, building, and tax costs are more important than the advantages of an urban setting. Villages are accessible to labor-pool residents who live in the village or in nearby villages and who are generally available at lower cost than urban workers (Moser 1972). In addition, many villages have been willing to offer incentives to firms who choose to locate in their jurisdiction.

Village Liabilities

Villages have certain disadvantages that have inhibited their growth beyond the village level and may be responsible for decline as observed in this study. These liabilities stem from the following conditions:

Isolation. Compared to larger urban centers, villages are viewed by many as remote and isolated because of their typical settings and small size. Although these conditions vary with village location and indeed are seen as attractive qualities by some people, the small size is a disadvantage to those who prefer the offerings of the large city. Deficiencies usually expressed include the lack of cultural attractions, such as museums, theaters, major sporting events, and concerts, although many of these events are available via television as cable networks expand into rural areas. Villages also are limited in the number of potential social contacts within the community simply because of their small size. This is compounded by previous age-selective migration trends, which have reduced the number of younger people.

Lack of Freedom.   Related to remote location and small size is a concern about lack of anonymity, freedom from social controls, and tolerance of a wide range of views and life styles in villages and rural areas. Though one should be wary of accepting such stereotypes uncritically, there undoubtedly continues to be a basis for such concern in many areas, and this is still consistent with the way villages are viewed by many people.

Limited Goods and Services.   As low-order central places, villages lack the major stores, restaurants, and specialty shops common in larger cities. They also lack variety of selection among functions that are available. Our study has shown, however, that market forces seem to have reduced these options partly because local residents have chosen to travel to larger cities to do their shopping. Villages have also lagged behind larger places in the professional services, including medical, legal, and educational services such as music and dance, although some of these activities may be moving into villages, as was noted in our survey.

THE FUTURE OF THE VILLAGE

In looking to the future we are sympathetic with the problem faced by Brunner and Kolb in 1933 when they ended the first restudy of the 140 agricultural villages. Writing in the depths of the depression, they stated that they did not know whether their study of villages represented a basis for predicting the future or helped to describe the end of an era. Our recent economic downturn, though severe, does not approach the economic depression of the 1930s. Yet there is much concern today about basic structural shifts taking place in our society as we turn away from heavy industry to high technology and toward what some have termed the "information age" or the "postindustrial society." Many argue that the post-1970 shift in population settlement and economic location is a precursor of a fundamental change in our social organization—a transformation in what people do and where they do it—as distance constraints give way through computer-based communication and as service and information activities supersede the production of goods. (e.g., Bradshaw and Blakely 1979).

Needless to say, there are many unknown factors and elements only dimly seen in facing the possibility of such radical shifts, which is not unlike the situation felt by Brunner and Kolb. Yet we are somewhat encouraged in reviewing their work. While it is safe to say that America was never the same again after the depression of the 1930s, villages have prevailed; many of the patterns of change they traced have extended from that time to the present.

In their studies, Brunner and associates recognized the increasing interdependence between rural and urban people and communities. The trend in this direction can be illustrated by contrasting some of their findings and concerns with ours. For example, considerable attention was given in the 1924 study to relations between villages and people in their rural hinterlands, with restudies showing a trend toward greater cooperation. Today, this is not a salient issue; more attention is directed to relations between new residents—many of whom are from urban areas—and those who have lived in the community for an extended period. Similarly, the weakening importance of the retail trade function is indicated by comparing results of our survey with a mail questionnaire reported by Brunner and Kolb. They found more than two-thirds of respondents in villages reported buying most of their articles in their home town. We found, however, a much lower incidence of local purchase of even common goods among our villages in 1980.

It is clear that today we can no longer refer to villages as the "capitals" of rural America, as did Brunner and associates, for they appear to be much more closely integrated with the rest of society. Yet we believe they are, and should continue to be, differentiated units that are autonomous to a degree, although much more needs to be learned about the nature of this autonomy and how the influence of other units of society is felt at the local level.

Evidence suggests that adaptive skills, which may just be market forces rather than planned adaptation in most cases, have been important in the past in these communities. The shift from a retail trade center role to a more residential function during recent decades has been a common adjustment to market forces that has affected the retail/service sector. Further adaptation has come in the form of increased industrial activities in villages, some of which may have resulted from planned efforts to stimulate the local economy.

The number of new incorporations has declined each decade since 1920 and stabilized since 1950 at less than 5 percent of the total, indicating a slowed growth of villages as new settlement units. These additions are approximately matched by losses of villages that grew out of their size class along with disincorporations, so the total number of nonmetropolitan villages has remained relatively constant since 1920 (Table A-1). Renewed growth in rural areas could lead to some increased births of new villages, as has occurred in suburban areas of large cities, but probably also to losses of villages by growth to city status. The decline in the number of dropouts in the most recent decade is interesting and suggests a possible effect of revenue-sharing programs in promoting viability. If so, current program cutbacks may reverse this change in the next period. In sum, there is no basis to predict a greatly changed number of incorporated villages in the forseeable future.

Although we would expect a continuation of villages in about the same numbers and a retention of a certain degree of functional differentiation and autonomy, it seems safe to say that village trends are tied increasingly to those of other nearby units of settlement. This was illustrated in Chapter 2, which showed that growth of the county in which the place is located has become relatively more important in predicting village growth. Consequently, in thinking of the future of the village we must at least attempt to address the issues raised at the beginning of this section on possible societal transitions. This must be done with considerable skepticism, recognizing that only a decade ago virtually no one predicted the nonmetropolitan turnaround.

Even today we do not have a clear picture of the forces behind the turnaround, particularly as they might relate to broad societal changes. In terms of proximate causes, we know that rural industrialization is important and that in selected areas developments caused by increased energy needs played a role at least in the early part of the 1970s. Amenity and recreation areas showed a particularly strong shift to growth, in part due to retirement migration. Another factor in the turnaround is the cessation of serious migration losses related to the agricultural transformation. In terms of economic structure, certain changes have made it advantageous for firms to locate in less accessible settings. Attention also has been given to the increase in number of relatively "footloose" people who may seek rural amenities because they can afford them and enjoy them along with advantages formerly found only in urban areas but now available most everywhere. The turnaround also has spurred suppositions about the effects of increased transportation and communication availability on the location of firms and people, of implicit and explicit governmental programs and policies, of the shift toward services and market-oriented rather than resource-based industries, and of a general disillusionment with large complex organizations and bureaucracies in our society.

We will not attempt to untangle all this here; such an effort really requires another book. In looking to the future for nonmetropolitan villages in America, however, we want to go one step beyond simply invoking "postindustrial society" as the cause of, and reason to expect continuation of, the new trend by raising several questions that may have implications for the village:

1. What is the long-term future of rural industrialization?   Is it just a stage on the road to America's deindustrialization, so that future nonmetropolitan factories will be found instead (as many are now) in places like Korea, Taiwan, Brazil, and Mexico? Or will a stable structure, considerably more decentralized than before, evolve within our nation? If the latter is true, will necessary technical innovations lead to substantial labor displacement anyway? Overall, the new trends are resulting in a more varied occupational structure in nonmetropolitan areas, but at the local level places have become more vulnerable to individual plant closings than before the spread of industrial growth.

2. How will the information revolution affect our settlement pattern?   Speculations about overcoming the effects of distance through computer communication often relate to a small segment of the middle class—those who make their living by interpreting and transforming information. The movement of such people to villages and other rural areas could exacerbate social cleavages and bring little to benefit the residents already there. On the other hand, some of the needs of employers, such as data transfer operations, require only semiskilled labor because most decisions are made through computer programs. Such activities could well be carried out in many villages with an indigenous labor force. Although some high-technology establishments have come to selected nonmetropolitan areas in recent years (Bradshaw et al. 1983), most of the innovative components of the industry still seem to be located in clusters that reflect agglomerative advantages. At present, many university towns are hoping to attract such activities, but there does not seem to be much prospect here for nonmetropolitan villages.

3. How will an increasingly mobile population affect our settlement pattern?   Regardless of how much the information revolution frees us from specific locations for workplaces, an increased number of people will be in retirement and others will be sufficiently affluent to pay reasonable costs, as in foregone income, in order to live where they choose. The question then becomes, Can we assume that given such a choice many people will still choose to live in nonmetropolitan villages?

Our love affair with small places definitely has blown hot and cold through the years. In the 1920s many popular authors emphasized the sterility and repressive nature of the village. Today, weary of the sterility and repressive nature of large-scale bureaucracies (public and private) and the social and economic problems of big cities, many appear to be attracted to villages and rural areas as a place to maximize personal satisfaction. Will there be a countercurrent of disillusion as residents face increased problems in growing small towns? Will we perhaps see a trend (for a small minority) away from leaving the mainstream to find oneself and back to achieving where the action is? The positive qualities of cities may make them increasingly attractive for some and good candidates for revitalization after decades of decline.

To be sure, residential preference surveys have shown a continuing and even increasing preference for living in rural areas. But it is well to keep in mind that allowing everyone to live where they choose need not necessarily lead to a more rural distribution of people and activities any more than the introduction of practices leading to fertility control will necessarily lead to zero population growth.

4. Will decreases in the availability or increases in the price of energy attenuate or reverse the deconcentrating settlement pattern? Lack of gasoline availability may have retarded nonmetropolitan growth temporarily during the 1973-74 oil embargo, and severe shortages may have a similar effect in the future. But at this time the possible effect of rising fuel prices is unclear. Indeed, real gasoline costs may have increased little overall during the past decade, if one allows for inflation and the expanded use of more fuel-efficient automobiles. A recent study has shown commuting time is actually less in nonmetropolitan than in metropolitan areas and furthermore that there is relatively little commuting between the two types of areas, even for recent migrants (Bowles and Beale 1980). Energy costs other than for transportation could be less in rural settings, for example, with using available wood for fuel. If energy concerns become salient, villages as cluster settlements may be favored over the open country. In short, despite speculation that the population turnaround must be temporary because of our energy problems, we lack a firm basis to predict either what the energy situation may be in the near future or how it will affect metropolitan or nonmetropolitan population change.

These questions are not intended to paint a bleak picture of the future of rural America but rather to underscore our lack of knowledge for making confident predictions. Recent research has indicated that the nonmetropolitan turnaround was continuing at a slower rate by the end of the 1970–80 decade, particularly in remote rural areas (Richter 1983). Such a diminution may well be reversed again with economic recovery. It is also possible however, that future growth patterns for rural areas will again become more urban oriented and not inconceivable that the turnaround as a whole will be reversed, possibly due to factors related to some of the questions raised above. But we would not expect a renewed growth pattern that is strongly concentrating everywhere but in the immediate vicinity of large cities and generally favoring larger places and larger SMSAs, as was true in the 1950–60 period. Regardless of the specific course of various societal changes in the near future, too many factors are in place supporting a generally deconcentrating pattern of population and economic activities to make such a drastic return to concentration at all likely, in our view. Indeed, a decline and even mild reversal of the nonmetropolitan turnaround is not inconsistent with equilibrium-based theoretical explanations of the phenomenon (Wardwell 1977) in which, for example, a decline of rural-urban differences may lead to almost undifferentiated migration streams in either direction with increasingly diffuse location across metropolitan-nonmetropolitan boundaries. In this context there will continue to be a place for the village as an element in the settlement structure—increasingly inter-dependent with other units but nevertheless autonomous in some respects, including, for incorporated places, the degree of independence given by having a separate local government. Perhaps the latter fact will become more significant in the future if the current impetus for increasing governmental decentralization prevails (Brown 1983).

In this work we have sought to provide a systematic assessment of the American village by looking at its place in the settlement system during a period of major societal change. We have examined demographic and economic characteristics that appear to have been affected by changes in both the rural and urban space-economy. Rural areas, including the thousands of villages scattered across the nation, are very diverse, and little of this diversity can be revealed here in our quest for generalizations.

Despite evidence of recent revival of population growth and economic development, many villages undoubtedly have remained much the same. The turnaround is indeed a revolutionary change from previous patterns, but it has not been a universal phenomenon and has not stood the test of time as a truly established change in direction from previous settlement trends.

The village has proven to be a resilient form of settlement in the United States and may be experiencing a renewed opportunity to participate in a reviving but geographically less orderly population settlement process. The new pattern of settlement has not been directed toward existing places or modes of settlement to the extent that earlier patterns were, but it does carry with it an influence on village growth. Many small remote villages, formerly declining and with characteristics associated with decline, have experienced growth recently. This leads to some renewed optimism concerning prospects for villages in America, whether or not the net balance of population change continues to favor nonmetropolitan areas.

It is difficult to see similar prospects for the village service role, however, as centralizing trends seem to be continuing, causing decline at the village level. All villages are unlikely to survive as trade centers without significant changes in personal habits and expectations among area residents. The future of the trade center function in villages will likely depend on population growth patterns, including the structural and behavioral characteristics of the future population, and indirectly on the developments in other more basic economic activities that support resident nearby populations.

APPENDIXES

SAMPLE DESIGN

A 5 percent random sample was drawn from the universe of incorporated places with less than 2,500 population as of 1960 located outside 1960 SMSA counties in the conterminous United States. The sample was stratified according to:

1. Census division (nine groups of states);
2. Size (more or less than 500 in 1960);
3. Location (whether or not in a county within fifty miles of an SMSA central city); and
4. Growth (increased or decreased in size between 1950 and 1960 or incorporated since 1950).

In selecting the sample, places were simultaneously cross-classified according to these attributes, and random selections were made with the number selected proportional to the size of each stratum.

The use of a national sample is necessary because of the large number of villages in this size class and the extensive time involved in collecting the economic and locational data. The sample is stratified according to region, size and change in size, and proximity to urban places, with the major variations on each of these variables represented in accordance with the total population. These variables were chosen for stratification because they are basic to the analysis anticipated with the sample, including the present work.

Table A-1. Balance Sheet of Number of Nonmetropolitan Incorporated Places under 2,500 Population, United States, 1900–80.[a]

	Beginning of Period	Add[b]		Subtract[c]		End of Period
		New	Decline In	Grow Out	Drop-out	
1900–10	7,496	2,647	44	−315	− 80	9,792
1910–20	9,792	1,473	51	−284	−167	10,865
1920–30	10,865	898	69	−246	−204	11,382
1930–40	11,382	336	29	−239	−300	11,208
1940–50	11,208	399	22	−336	−119	11,174
1950–60	11,174	545	46	−320	−111	11,334
1960–70	11,334	511	51	−264	−399	11,233
1970–80	11,233	535	51	−340	− 51	11,428

[a]Located in counties nonmetropolitan as of 1960.

[b]New places are those reported in the census at end of period but not beginning; places declining are those greater than 2,500 population at beginning but less than 2,500 at end of period.

[c]Places growing out are those less than 2,500 population at beginning but greater than 2,500 at end; dropouts are those reported in census at beginning but not in census at end of period.

Source: Compiled by authors.

The initial sample was drawn from the universe of villages as of 1960, but for some of the demographic analysis we wished to consider places qualifying as villages at the beginning of each of the three decades. Consequently, the sample was modified by adding a proportional number of cases drawn systematically across all divisions to include: (1) fifteen places that were less than 2,500 in 1950 but greater than 2,500 in 1960; (2) twenty-three places that were less than 2,500 in 1970 but not listed in 1950 or 1960; and (3) two places that were greater than 2,500 in 1960 but less in 1970. These additions made it possible to utilize in Chapter 2 separate probability samples of the universes of incorporated places under 2,500 population as of 1950, 1960, and 1970. Though perhaps more appropriate analytically, this modification had virtually no effect on the results. The number of cases used may vary slightly among the chapters as a result of missing data.

ACCESSIBILITY MEASURE

Previous research on population and business trends in villages has demonstrated the importance of village location relative to larger cities in determining the pattern of change. To test this influence, an index of urban accessibility was developed for each village in the sample. The structure of the accessibility index was:

$$A_i = \sum_{j=1}^{n} \frac{P_j}{d_{ij}^2}$$

where A_i is the accessibility score for village i; P is the population of a city within fifty miles with a population of at least 10,000; and d is the airline distance from the village to the edge of city j. Where major obstacles were found between i and j, highway distance was used instead of airline distance. The value of A increases with the population in surrounding urban centers and is reduced by the distance to these nodes. The exponent of 2 for distance in the denominator was selected as a medium-range estimate for the friction of distance. This exponent has been shown to vary with regional location and mode of travel in previous studies using potential and gravity models (see Ikle 1954; Olsson 1965).

EVALUATION OF DUN AND BRADSTREET REFERENCE BOOK LISTINGS AS A SOURCE OF ECONOMIC DATA FOR SMALL COMMUNITIES

The lack of published census data for business activities in small communities (under 10,000 population) has led researchers concerned with economic activities in rural areas to search for other sources. Dun and Bradstreet Reference Book listings have been the alternative source for a number of studies in the past (e.g., Landis 1932; Lively 1932a, 1932b; Trewartha 1943; Chittick 1955; Hodge 1965; Folse and Riffe 1969). Most of these studies have accepted it as the best available source for small towns, although Trewartha, in his study of unincorporated hamlets (1943), included a comparison of Dun and Bradstreet data with other sources in an attempt to evaluate the source. His work, however, was not concerned with actual business listings but instead used Dun and Bradstreet as a source of data on population for hamlets, which he compared with other sources of population data. Verway (1980) has critically evaluated Dun and Bradstreet listings for one village in Michigan, concluding that it underrepresented business activities in this case. Birch (1979), on the other hand, gives Dun and Bradstreet computer files a favorable review in a comparison with census data sources on business activities.

Because the analysis of business activities in this study covers a larger area than previous research and three observations in time, it was deemed necessary to consider the accuracy and consistency of the data source for village communities. Particular questions relevant to our study were:

1. What are listing procedures used by Dun and Bradstreet?
2. How complete is the coverage nationally—that is, do listing procedures vary by location?
3. How complete is the coverage within a given community?
4. How consistent have listing procedures been over the 1950–70 time period?
5. How are multiple function firms handled?
6. How are branch stores, franchise, and chain stores listed?

To answer these questions, we first contacted Dun and Bradstreet's main office and various regional offices to obtain information on listing procedures. We then designed a comparison survey of Dun and Bradstreet listings with Yellow Page directories in telephone books (another commonly used source) for a sample of communities selected from various parts of the country. Finally, a field check was made in two communities familiar and nearby for a check with contemporary listings.

DUN AND BRADSTREET LISTING PROCEDURE

According to Dun and Bradstreet personnel, listing of a firm in the Reference Book is made in response to a request by the firm or by another firm, bank, credit agency, or insurance company that is concerned about a credit transaction or the relative size or credit rating of a business. When a new business orders goods, equipment, insurance, or applies for a loan, the suppliers often check for credit ratings with Dun and Bradstreet. If the business is not listed, an inquiry request may be made with a Dun and Bradstreet office. A field representative then contacts the business and completes the listing procedure. Few businesses refuse to be listed in Dun and Bradstreet because it provides a form of advertising without charge and makes credit transactions easier to obtain. If credit or other financial data is not provided, the representative may attempt to get it from a bank or will list the business only as to its Standard Industrial Classification (SIC) category and abbreviated firm description. The SIC system is used to categorize all listed firms. In the case of multiple-line firms, the dominant line of business is listed first, followed by other activities. Each major line of business performed by the firm will be listed along with its SIC description.

As to the current accuracy of published listings, Dun and Bradstreet personnel stated that the time lag in entry is short since most inquiries are made as a firm sets up business and applies for credit, either for capital stock or some other credit need. The time lag for deletion if a firm closes or leaves a community may extend to a maximum of one year. A questionnaire is sent to each listed firm each year and, if not returned, is followed by a phone or field check. If a business has closed, a deletion is made from the listing; if it has changed hands, a new listing will usually be made. Dun and Bradstreet is responsible to its clients for keeping current listings for both credit and market information services.

Dun and Bradstreet claims that its listing is nearly 100 percent complete for retail, wholesale, and manufacturing activities and slightly less complete for service activities, but consistent within the service categories. They do not list barber and beauty services.

Listing procedures for branch stores, branch plants, and franchise operations are less consistent than for locally based firms. Large supermarket chains such as Safeway and Kroger are listed for certain large cities as "branch of Cincinnati" and so forth but are not consistently listed for all outlets in one city or all cities. Branch plants for manufacturing firms are listed more consistently in their local directory as "branch of . . ." and so forth. Franchise outlets—especially common in the restaurant category—are listed where the headquarters of the particular franchise operator are located (e.g., if a franchise owner is located in the same city as the unit, the outlet will be listed under the local directory), but if the franchise holder is in another city, the outlet is listed there along with any other outlet held under the same franchise owner.

From the standpoint of data consistency, large chain stores and franchise operations are the least consistent. These may be under-represented or misrepresented, depending on whether the store outlet is located in the franchise location or another place. However, a store that carries a national branch such as IGA, Coast to Coast, or Gambles will be listed by the store address just as would a Texaco, Firestone, or Ford dealer.

COMPARISON WITH YELLOW PAGE DIRECTORIES

To check the completeness of Dun and Bradstreet at the community level we selected twenty-five villages at random from the sample to compare with Yellow Page telephone directories for the years 1950, 1960, and 1970. It was necessary to do this comparison at the Library of Congress because that was the only collection of telephone directories for small communities that we could find. Even local telephone companies and libraries in the sampled villages did not have back copies of these directories.

Our procedure was simply to compare each listing with the other, noting discrepancies between the two. Several problems arose in this attempt due largely to the different listing procedures used by the two directories. The major problems in comparison resulted from the following conditions:

1. Dun and Bradstreet tends to list a firm by the proprietor name while Yellow Pages list commonly by the trade name, so that a Dun and Bradstreet listing of "John H. Calhoun . . . rst" might be the same firm as "The Big Steer" or "The Pancake House," a trade name that reveals nothing about John H. Calhoun, its proprietor.

2. Dun and Bradstreet lists a firm with the nearest post office community so that some outlying firms are listed as in a particular village. Yellow Page listings did not always compare in area coverage. It seemed that telephone service areas did not always comply with those used by Dun and Bradstreet, a problem of multilevel service areas that made data comparison difficult.

3. Yellow Pages do not use the SIC system and therefore use different categories for business activities. Their breakdown is much finer in some areas and lists the same store under several product headings. Listing of the same store may therefore occur under several categories.

4. Yellow Pages do not include nonsubscribing firms. Just as Dun and Bradstreet may not be a total listing at any one time, Yellow Pages include only firms who choose to advertise in this manner. In several cases, Yellow Pages did not list firms known to be located in the community. A check of white-page listings substantiated this occasionally. The additional charge for listing seems to inhibit some firms from subscribing.

5. Finally, Yellow Pages are mainly a listing of retail and service activities designed primarily as an advertising medium. It is less complete for production firms such as manufacturing and other basic activities.

The validity of either source, therefore, cannot be ascertained using a list-by-list comparison. However, of the two sources, Dun and Bradstreet had consistently more entries than Yellow Pages and was more complete in manufacturing and other basic activities. Major advantages of the Dun and Bradstreet source are its use of the SIC as a consistent classification scheme and its listing of firms only for those activities that provide a significant share of their business activity.

FIELD CHECK OF CURRENT LISTING

As a final evaluation of Dun and Bradstreet, a field check was carried out in two communities comparing the current listing with actual business locations. A familiarity with the community helped in this approach, along with advice from local people who knew the proprietors of local business establishments.

In the first village a total of sixty-nine establishments were counted using both telephone listings and field observation. Seven (10 percent) of the sixty-nine establishments were not listed in the Dun and Bradstreet Reference Book current at that time. Of the seven unlisted firms, two were small businesses operated out of the owner's home (i.e., an interior decorator and an electrician). The five others were a Montgomery Ward catalog store, a bottle gas fuel dealer, a service station, a tavern, and a mortuary. Of the seven firms, all but the tavern and the mortuary were less than two years old. The mortuary had recently changed ownership and had been listed in Dun and Bradstreet for the prior year. Presumably it will be relisted in the future.

In the second village, a total of fourteen establishments were counted, of which two (14 percent) were not listed. These were a service station and a tavern. Each had been in business for several years under the present owner but was not listed in the present directory. No explanation could be found except that no inquiry had been made to generate a listing.

SUMMARY

Attempts to verify Dun and Bradstreet as a data source for rural communities have not appeared in most studies using the data for measurement of business activities. This has been an effort to clarify the nature of the data and to reveal its possible shortcomings and strengths as a data source.

Since no official census exists for places within the size group of interest to our study, the most consistent and complete nonofficial source is sought as the best alternative. In looking at the Dun and Bradstreet policy of listing business activities, we can see some shortcomings—namely, the problem of large chain stores and franchise outlets in terms of their actual business location and the criteria for inclusion being a request from another source. Since the data are not intended to be a census, the shortcomings must be interpreted in light of our own needs. Considering the listing procedures, one can expect an undercount at any time of business establishments listed in the Reference Book. The amount of underrepresentation may vary but probably would average about 10 to 15 percent based on our own admittedly limited observations.

Assuming that the undercount is reasonably consistent across the sample of places and is not biased toward a particular line of business, the data should be valid for demonstrating relationships between business activities and other village characteristics. Similarly, relationships within the data set should be valid if the undercount is random across business and village lines.

Dun and Bradstreet personnel claim that the representation is unbiased in terms of place size except for extremely small centers, which are less apt to be in the directory. Places with less than 100 population are apt to be merged with nearby communities, although their business firms are just as likely to be listed as those in larger towns.

The only significant bias along business lines, as stated earlier, is in the underlisting of service activities. Barber and beauty shops are not counted, and perhaps other small service activities that are run from a person's home are less apt to be listed.

The problem of franchise firms and large chain stores is more difficult to dismiss as these types of business become more common. However, in villages of less than 2,500 population, large stores and "franchise malls" are just beginning to appear. The spread of these activities, as with many other innovations, has begun at or near the top of the urban hierarchy and probably reaches the village community much later (Cohen 1972). Therefore, in using Dun and Bradstreet data for the time span 1950-70 we probably are not as affected by the problem as we would be in the decade 1970 to 1980 in small communities.

The Dun and Bradstreet data are therefore considered our best alternative to study economic activities in rural villages. As with all data of this sort, some error exists. If the likelihood of error and the kinds of problems are understood, however, the results of the analysis can be interpreted in light of the data reliability. The problems with Dun and Bradstreet must thus be recognized throughout the analysis presented in this study.

REFERENCES

Adams, Bert. 1969. "The Small Trade Center: Processes and Perceptions of Growth or Decline." In *The Community*, edited by Robert French, pp. 471–84. Itaska, Ill.: Peacock Press.

Alanen, A.R., and K.E. Smith. 1977. "Growth Versus No-Growth Issues, with an American Appalachian Perspective." *Tijdschrift Voor Economische en Sociale Geografie* 68:32–42.

Alexander, John W. 1954. "The Basic-Nonbasic Concept of Urban Economic Functions." *Economic Geography* 30:246–61.

Alonso, William. 1973. "Urban Zero Population Growth." *Dedalus* 102:191–206.

Anderson, A.H. 1950. "Space as a Social Cost." *Journal of Farm Economics* 32:411–31.

———. 1961. *The Expanding Rural Community*. Lincoln: Nebraska Agricultural Experiment Station Bulletin 464.

Angel, William D., Jr. 1980. "Zenith Revisited: Urban Entrepreneurship and the Sunbelt Frontier." *Social Science Quarterly* 61:434–45.

Appelbaum, Richard P. 1978. *Size, Growth and U.S. Cities*. New York: Praeger Publishers.

Baldassare, Mark. 1981a. "The Social Impacts of the Population Turnaround in Nonmetropolitan Areas." In *Nonmetropolitan America in Transition*, edited by Amos H. Hawley and Sarah Mills Mazie, pp. 116–43. Chapel Hill: University of North Carolina Press.

———. 1981b. *The Growth Dilemma: Resident's Views and Local Population Change in the United States*. Berkeley: University of California Press.

Baldassare, Mark, and Robert C. Pennie. 1979. "The Effects of Nonmetropolitan Growth on the Community and the Individual." Paper given at the annual meeting of the Population Association of America, Philadelphia, Pennsylvania.

Baldassare, Mark, and William Protash. 1982. "Population Growth and Community Satisfaction." *American Sociological Review* 47:339–46.

Banks, Vera J., and Calvin L. Beale. 1973. *Farm Population Estimates, 1910–1970.* Washington, D.C.: Rural Development Service, U.S. Department of Agriculture, Statistical Bulletin 523.

Barkley, Paul. 1962. *The Changing Role of Small Communities in South-Central Kansas.* Manhattan: Kansas State University Cooperative Extension Service.

Beale, Calvin L. 1974. "Quantitative Dimensions of Decline and Stability Among Rural Communities." In *Communities Left Behind,* edited by L.D. Whiting, pp. 3–21. Ames: Iowa State University Press.

———. 1975. *The Revival of Population Growth in Nonmetropolitan America.* Washington, D.C.: Economic Research Service, U.S. Department of Agriculture, ERS–605.

Beale, Calvin L., and Glenn V. Fuguitt. 1978. "The New Pattern of Nonmetropolitan Population Change." In *Social Demography,* edited by Karl Taeuber, Larry Bumpass, and James Sweet, pp. 157–77. New York: Academic Press.

Beegle, Allan J., and Richard Rathge. 1980. "Consequences of Population Growth for the Nonmetropolitan Community: Osceola County, Michigan." Paper given at the Fifth World Congress for Rural Sociology, Mexico City.

Bell, Thomas, S. Lieber, and G. Rushton. 1974. "Clustering of Services in Central Places." *Annals of the Association of American Geographers* 64:214–15.

Berry, Brian J.L. 1967. *Geography of Market Centers and Retail Distribution.* Englewood Cliffs, N.J.: Prentice-Hall.

———. 1972. "Hierarchical Diffusion: The Basis of Developmental Filtering and Spread in a System of Growth Centers." In *Growth Centers in Regional Economic Development,* edited by Niles M. Hansen, pp. 108–38. New York: Free Press.

———. 1973. *Growth Centers in the American Urban System.* Vol. I. Cambridge, Mass.: Ballinger Publishing Co.

———. 1978. "The Counter-Urbanization Processes: How General?" In *Human Settlement Systems,* edited by Niles M. Hansen, pp. 25–49. Cambridge, Mass.: Ballinger Publishing Co.

Berry, Brian J.L., and Donald C. Dahmann. 1980. "Population Redistribution in the United States in the 1970s." In *Population Redistribution and Public Policy,* edited by Brian J.L. Berry and Lester P. Silverman, pp. 8–49. Washington, D.C.: National Academy of Sciences.

Berry, Brian J.L., and W.L. Garrison. 1958. "The Functional Basis of the Central Place Hierarchy." *Economic Geography* 34:145–54.

Berry, Brian J.L., and John D. Kasarda. 1977. *Contemporary Urban Ecology.* New York: Macmillan Publishing Co.

Berry, Brian J.L., and Allan Pred. 1965. *Central Place Studies: A Bibliography of Theory and Applications.* Philadelphia: Regional Science Research Institute Bibliography Series 1.

Birch, David L. 1979. *Using Dun and Bradstreet Data for Micro Analysis of Regional and Local Economies.* Cambridge, Mass.: Massachusetts Institute of Technology Program on Neighborhood and Regional Change.

Bogue, Donald J. 1949. *The Structure of the Metropolitan Community: A Study of Dominance and Subdominance.* Ann Arbor: Horace H. Rackham School of Graduate Studies, University of Michigan.

Bohrnstedt, George W. 1969. "Observations on the Measurement Change." In *Sociological Methodology,* edited by E.F. Borgotta and George W. Bohrnstedt, pp. 113–34. San Francisco: Jossey-Bass.

———. 1970. "Reliability and Validity Assessment in Attitude Measurement." In *Attitude Measurement,* edited by Gene Summers, pp. 80–99. Chicago: Rand McNally.

Borchert, John R. 1967. "American Metropolitan Evolution." *Geographical Review* 57:301–32.

Borts, George H. 1968. "Patterns of Regional Economic Development in the United States and Their Relation to Rural Poverty." In *Rural Poverty in the United States,* edited by George L. Wilbur and C.E. Bishop, pp. 130–40. Washington, D.C.: U.S. Government Printing Office.

Bourne, Larry S., and J.W. Simmons, eds. 1978. *Systems of Cities: Readings on Structure, Growth, and Policy.* New York: Oxford University Press.

Bowles, Gladys K., and Calvin L. Beale. 1980. *Commuting Patterns of Nonmetro Household Heads, 1975.* Athens: U.S. Department of Agriculture and University of Georgia.

Bradbury, Katherine L., Anthony Downs, and Kenneth A. Small. 1982. *Urban Decline and the Future of American Cities.* Washington, D.C.: The Brookings Institution.

Bradshaw, Ted K., and Edward J. Blakely. 1979. *Rural Communities in Advanced Industrial Society Development and Developers.* New York: Praeger.

———. 1981. *Resources of Recent Migrants to Rural Areas for Economic Development: Policy Implications.* Berkeley: University of California Cooperative Extension Service.

Bradshaw, Ted K., Edward J. Blakely, Philip Shapira, and Nancey Leigh-Preston. 1983. "Formulating Rural Economic Development Policy: A Strategy for the U.S. in the 1980's." Unpublished paper, Institute of Governmental Studies, University of California at Berkeley.

Bridgeland, William M., and Andrew J. Sofranko. 1975. "Community Structure and Issue-Specific Influences: Community Mobilization over Environmental Quality." *Urban Affairs Quarterly* 11:186–214.

Briggs, Ronald, and J. Rees. 1982. "Control Factors in the Economic Development of Nonmetropolitan America." *Environment and Planning* 14:1645–66.

Brinkman, George L. 1973. "Effects of Industrializing Small Communities." *Journal of the Community Development Society* 4:69–80.

Brown, David L. 1976. *Social and Economic Characteristics of Growing and Declining Counties.* Washington, D.C.: Economic Development Division, Economic Research Service, U.S. Department of Agriculture.

———. 1983. "Sociodemographic Trends and Their Implications for Economic Development." Unpublished paper, Economic Development Division, U.S. Department of Agriculture.

Brown, David L., and Calvin L. Beale. 1981. "Diversity of Post–1970 Population Trends." In *Nonmetropolitan America in Transition*, edited by Amos H. Hawley and Sarah Mills Mazie, pp. 27–71. Chapel Hill: University of North Carolina Press.

Brown, David L., and John M. Wardwell, eds. 1980. *New Directions in Urban-Rural Migration: The Population Turnaround in Rural America.* New York: Academic Press.

Brown, Lawrence A. 1981. *Innovation Diffusion.* New York: Methuen.

Brunner, Edmund deS. 1928. *Village Communities.* New York: George H. Doran Co.

Brunner, Edmund deS., G.S. Hughes, and M. Patten. 1927. *American Agricultural Villages.* New York: George H. Doran Co.

Brunner, Edmond deS., and John H. Kolb. 1933. *Rural Social Trends.* New York: McGraw-Hill.

Brunner, Edmund deS., and Irving Lorge. 1937. *Rural Trends in the Depression Years.* New York: Columbia University Press.

Brunner, Edmund deS., and T. Lynn Smith. 1944. "Village Growth and Decline, 1930–40." *Rural Sociology* 9:103–15.

Brush, John E. 1953. "The Hierarchy of Central Places in Southwestern Wisconsin." *Geographical Review* 43:380–402.

Burton, Ian. 1963. "A Restatement of the Dispersed City Hypothesis." *Annals of the Association of American Geographers* 53:285–89.

Carlyle, John. 1931. "Villages Are Dying and Who Cares?" *Nations Business* 19:23–6.

Chisholm, Michael. 1962. *Rural Settlement and Land Use.* London: Hutchinson University Library.

Chittick, Douglas. 1955. *Growth and Decline of South Dakota Trade Centers, 1901–1951.* Brookings: South Dakota Agricultural Experiment Station Bulletin 448.

Christaller, Walter. 1966. *The Central Places of Southern Germany*, translated by C.W. Baskin. Englewood Cliffs, N.J.: Prentice-Hall.

Cohen, Richard A. 1977. "Small Town Revitalization Planning: Case Studies and a Critique." *Journal of the American Institute of Planners,* 43:3–12.

Cohen, Y.S. 1972. *Diffusion of an Innovation in an Urban System: The Spread of Planned Regional Shopping Centers in the United States.* Chicago: University of Chicago, Department of Geography Research Paper 140.

Colladay, Morrison. 1952. "The Passing of the American Village." *Commonwealth* 56:363–64.

Commission on Population Growth and the American Future. 1972. *Population and the American Future.* Washington, D.C.: U.S. Government Printing Office.

Converse, Paul D. 1928. *The Auto and the Village Merchant.* Urbana: University of Illinois Bureau of Business Research Bulletin No. 19.

Copp, James H. 1972. "Rural Sociology and Rural Development." *Rural Sociology* 37:515–33.

Dahms, Fred A. 1980. "The Evolving Spatial Organization of Small Settlements in the Countryside—An Ontario Example." *Tijdschrift Voor Economisch en Sociale Geografie* 71:295–306.

Daily, George H., Jr., and Rex R. Campbell. 1980. "The Ozark-Ouachita Uplands: Growth and Consequences." In *New Directions in Urban-Rural Migration,* edited by David L. Brown and John M. Wardwell, pp. 233–65. New York: Academic Press.

Davis, Charles M. 1938. "The Cities and Towns of the High Plains of Michigan." *Geographical Review* 28:644–73.

Deavers, Kenneth L., and David L. Brown. 1980. "The Rural Population Turnaround: Research and National Public Policy." In *New Directions in Urban-Rural Migration,* edited by David L. Brown and John M. Wardwell, pp. 51–70. New York: Academic Press.

De Jong, Gordon F., and Kenneth G. Keppel. 1979. *Urban Migrants to the Countryside.* University Park: Pennsylvania State University, College of Agriculture Bulletin 825.

Dillman, Don A. 1979. "Residential Preference, Quality of Life, and the Population Turnaround." *American Journal of Agricultural Economics* 61:960–66.

Doxiadis, Constantinos A. 1968. *Ekistics.* New York: Oxford University Press.

Dun and Bradstreet Inc. 1950, 1960, 1970. *Reference Book of Dun and Bradstreet.* New York: Dun and Bradstreet Inc.

Duncan, Otis Dudley, and Albert J. Reiss. 1956. *Social Characteristics of Urban and Rural Communities, 1950.* New York: John Wiley & Sons.

Duncan, Otis Dudley, William Richard Scott, Stanley Lieberson, Beverly Davis Duncan, and Hal H. Winsborough. 1960. *Metropolis and Region.* Baltimore: The Johns Hopkins Press.

Eberle, Nancy. 1982. *Return to Main Street*. New York: W.W. Norton and Co.

Elazar, Daniel. 1966. "Are We a Nation of Cities?" *Public Interest* 4:42–58.

Fischer, Claude. 1975. "Toward a Subcultural Theory of Urbanism." *American Journal of Sociology* 80:1319–41.

Fisher, James, and Ronald L. Mitchelson. 1981. "Forces of Change in the American Settlement Pattern." *Geographical Review* 7:298–310.

Fletcher, Henry J. 1895. "The Doom of the Small Town." *Forum* 19:214–23.

Folse, Clinton L., and W.W. Riffe. 1969. "Changing Patterns of Business Services and Population Change in Illinois Rural Villages." *Illinois Agricultural Economics* 9:26–32.

Ford, Thomas R., and Willis A. Sutton, Jr. 1964. "The Impact of Change on Rural Communities and Fringe Areas: A Review of a Decade's Research." In *Our Changing Rural Society: Perspectives and Trends*, edited by James H. Copp, pp. 198–229. Ames: Iowa State University Press.

Foust, J.B., and A.R. DeSouza. 1975. *The Economic Landscape: A Theoretical Introduction*. Columbus, Ohio: Charles E. Merrill.

Fox, William F., and Patrick J. Sullivan. 1979. "Revenue Needs in Growing and Declining Areas." In *Revenue Administration*, proceedings of the forty-seventh annual meeting of the National Association of Tax Administrators, Madison, Wisconsin, pp. 212–21. Washington, D.C.: Federation of Tax Administrators.

Frankena, Fredrick. 1980. *Community Impacts of Rapid Growth in Nonmetropolitan Areas: A Literature Survey*. East Lansing: Michigan State University Agricultural Experiment Station, Rural Sociology Studies 9.

Friedmann, John, and John Miller. 1965. "The Urban Field." *Journal of the American Institute of Planners* 31:312–19.

Frisbie, W. Parker, and Dudley L. Poston, Jr. 1975. "Components of Sustenance Organization and Nonmetropolitan Population Change: A Human Ecological Investigation." *American Sociological Review* 40:773–84.

———. 1976. "The Structure of Sustenance Organization and Population Change in Nonmetropolitan America." *Rural Sociology* 41:354–70.

Fry, C. Luther. 1926. *American Villagers*. New York: George H. Doran Co.

Fuguitt, Glenn V. 1965a. "Trends in Unincorporated Places, 1950–60." *Demography* 2:363–71.

———. 1965b. "The Growth and Decline of Small Towns as a Probability Process." *American Sociological Review* 30:403–11.

———. 1968. "Some Characteristics of Villages in Rural America." In *Rural Poverty in the United States*, edited by George L. Wilbur and C.E. Bishop, pp. 51–73. Washington, D.C.: U.S. Government Printing Office.

———. 1972. "Some Demographic Aspects of the Small Town in the United States." *Sociologia Ruralis* 7:147–61.

———. 1977. "Recent Trends in Nonmetropolitan Net Migration." Paper given at the annual meeting of the American Association for the Advancement of Sciences, Denver, Colorado.

Fuguitt, Glenn V., and Calvin L. Beale. 1976. *"Population Change in Nonmetropolitan Cities and Towns."* Washington, D.C.: U.S. Department of Agriculture, Agricultural Economic Report 323.

―――. 1978. "Population Trends of Nonmetropolitan Cities and Villages in Subregions of the United States." *Demography* 15:605-20.

Fuguitt, Glenn V., and Nora A. Deeley. 1966. "Retail Service Patterns and Small Town Population Change: A Replication of Hassinger's Study." *Rural Sociology* 31:53-63.

Fuguitt, Glenn V., and Donald R. Field. 1972. "Some Population Characteristics of Villages Differentiated by Size, Location, and Growth." *Demography* 9:295-308.

Fuguitt, Glenn V., and John Kasarda. 1981. "Community Structure in Response to Population Growth and Decline: A Study in Ecological Organization." *American Sociological Review* 46:600-15.

Fuguitt, Glenn V., Daniel T. Lichter, and Calvin L. Beale. 1981. *Population Deconcentration in Metropolitan and Nonmetropolitan Areas of the United States, 1950-1975.* Madison: University of Wisconsin, Department of Rural Sociology, Applied Population Laboratory, Population Series 70-15.

Gallagher, Art. 1961. *Plainville Fifteen Years Later.* New York: Columbia University Press.

Galpin, Charles J. 1915. *The Social Anatomy of an Agricultural Community.* Madison: Wisconsin Agricultural Experiment Station Bulletin 34.

Gillard, Quentin. 1982. "What Do We Know about Boomtowns?" Paper given at the annual meeting of the Association of American Geographers, San Antonio, Texas.

Gillette, John M. 1923. "Declining Villages of America and the Function of Communication in Their Improvement." In *Town and Country Relations,* proceedings of the Fourth National Conference of the American Country Life Association, pp. 28-35. Chicago: University of Chicago Press.

Golledge, R.G., G. Rushton, and W.A.V. Clark. 1966. "Some Spatial Characteristics of Iowa's Dispersed Farm Population and Their Implications for the Grouping of Central Place Functions." *Economic Geography* 42:261-72.

Gordon, P. 1979. "Deconcentration without a 'Clean Break.' " *Environment and Planning* 11:281-90.

Goudy, Willis J., and Vernon T. Ryan. 1982. "Changing Communities." In *Rural Society in the U.S. Issues for the 1980s,* edited by Don A. Dillman and Darryl J. Hobbs, pp. 256-63. Boulder, Colo.: Westview Press.

Graber, Edith E. 1974. "Newcomers and Oldtimers: Growth and Change in a Mountain Town." *Rural Sociology* 39:504-13.

Hage, Jerald. 1979. "A Theory of Nonmetropolitan Growth." In *Nonmetropolitan Industrial Growth and Community Change,* edited by Gene F. Summers and Arne Selvik, pp. 93-104. Lexington, Mass.: Lexington Books.

Hamilton, Joel, D.V. Patterson, and R. Reid. 1976. *Small Towns in a Rural Area: A Study of the Problems of Small Towns in Idaho.* Moscow: University of Idaho Agricultural Experiment Station Research Bulletin 91.

Hansen, Niles M. 1970. *Rural Poverty and the Urban Crisis: A Strategy for Regional Development.* Bloomington: University of Indiana Press.

———, ed. 1972. *Growth Centers in Regional Economic Development.* New York: The Free Press.

———. 1978. "Preliminary Overview." In *Human Settlement Systems,* edited by Niles M. Hansen, pp. 1–21. Cambridge, Mass.: Ballinger Publishing Co.

Hart, John F., and N.E. Salisbury. 1965. "Population Change in Middle Western Villages: A Statistical Approach." *Annals of the Association of American Geographers* 55:140–60.

Hart, John F., N.E. Salisbury, and E.G. Smith. 1968. "The Dying Village and Some Notions about Urban Growth." *Economic Geography* 44: 343–49.

Hassinger, Edward. 1957. "The Relationship of Retail/Service Patterns to Trade Center Population Change." *Rural Sociology* 22:235–40.

Hatch, Elvin. 1979. *Biography of a Small Town.* New York: Columbia University Press.

Hathaway, Dale E., J. Allan Beegle, and W. Keith Bryant. 1968. *People of Rural America: A 1960 Census Monograph.* Washington, D.C.: U.S. Government Printing Office.

Hawley, Amos H. 1950. *Human Ecology.* New York: Ronald Press.

———. 1978. "Urbanization as Process." In *Handbook of Contemporary Urban Life,* edited by David Street, pp. 3–26. San Francisco: Jossey-Bass.

Hawthorn, Horace B. 1926. *The Sociology of Rural Life.* New York: The Century Co.

Heaton, Tim B., and Glenn V. Fuguitt. 1979. "Nonmetropolitan Industrial Growth and Net Migration." In *Nonmetropolitan Industrialization,* edited by Richard E. Lonsdale and H.L. Seyler, pp. 19–35. Washington, D.C.: V.H. Winston and Sons.

Heaton, Tim B., William B. Clifford, and Glenn V. Fuguitt. 1981. "Temporal Shifts in the Determinants of Young and Elderly Migration in Nonmetropolitan Areas." *Social Forces* 60:41–60.

Hennigh, Lawrence. 1978. "The Good Life and the Taxpayers Revolt." *Rural Sociology* 43:178–90.

Hines, Fred K., David L. Brown, and J.M. Zimmer. 1975. *Social and Economic Characteristics of the Population in Metropolitan and Nonmetropolitan Counties, 1970.* Washington: Economic Research Service, U.S. Department of Agriculture, Agricultural Economic Report 272.

Hoch, Irving. 1976. "City Size Effects, Trends and Policies." *Science* 193:856–63.

Hodge, Gerald. 1965. "The Prediction of Trade Center Viability in the Great Plains." *Papers of the Regional Science Association* 15:87–115.

Hodgson, M.J. 1972. "Variability in the Growth of Small Urban Areas." In *Urban Systems Development in Central Canada*, edited by L.S. Bourne and R.D. Mackinnon, pp. 132–46. Toronto: University of Toronto, Department of Geography.

Holmes, John H. 1971. "External Commuting as a Prelude to Suburbanization." *Annals of the Association of American Geographers* 61:774–90.

Hudson, John C. 1969a. "Location Theory for Rural Settlement." *Annals of the Association of American Geographers* 59:365–81.

———. 1969b. "Diffusion in a Central Place System." *Geographical Analysis* 1:45–58.

———. 1977. "The Plains Country Town." In *The Great Plains—Environment and Culture*, edited by Brian Blouet and Frederick Luebke, pp. 99–118. Lincoln: University of Nebraska Press.

Humphrey, Craig R., and Richard S. Krannich. 1980. "The Promotion of Growth in Small Urban Places and Its Impact on Population Change, 1975–1980." *Social Science Quarterly* 61:581–94.

Ikle, Fred C. 1954. "Sociological Relationship of Traffic to Population and Distance." *Traffic Quarterly* 8:123–36.

Jackson, J.B. 1952. "The Almost Perfect Town." *Landscape* 2:116–31.

Jenkins, David B. 1940. *Growth and Decline of Agricultural Villages*. New York: Bureau of Publications, Teachers College, Columbia University.

Johansen, Harley E. 1979. "Agricultural Adjustments to Urban Sprawl in Midwestern Counties." Paper given at the annual meeting of the Association of American Geographers, Philadelphia, Pennsylvania.

Johansen, Harley E., and Glenn V. Fuguitt. 1973. "Changing Retail Activity in Wisconsin Villages: 1939–1954–1970." *Rural Sociology* 38:207–18.

———. 1979. "Population Growth and Retail Decline: Conflicting Effects of Urban Accessibility in American Villages." *Rural Sociology* 44:24–38.

———. 1981. "Changing Functions of Villages in Sparsely Populated Areas: The American West." In *Settlement Systems in Sparsely Populated Regions*, edited by R.E. Lonsdale and J.H. Holmes, pp. 148–68. New York: Pergamon Press.

Johnson, Kenneth M. 1982. "Organizational Adjustment to Population Change in Nonmetropolitan America: A Longitudinal Analysis of Retail Trade." *Social Forces* 60:1123–39.

Kasarda, John D. 1981. "The Implications of Contemporary Distribution Trends for National Urban Policy." *Social Science Quarterly* 61: 373–400.

Kendall, Diana. 1963. "Portraits of a Disappearing Village." *Sociologia Ruralis* 3:157–65.

Kenyon, James B. 1967. "The Relation between Central Function and Size of Places." *Annals of the Association of American Geographers* 57: 736–50.

Klaff, Vivian, and Glenn V. Fuguitt. 1978. "Annexation as a Factor in the Growth of U.S. Cities, 1950–60 and 1960–70." *Demography* 15:1–11.

Klietsch, Ronald G., W.H. Andrews, W.W. Bauder, J.A. Beegle, J.A. Doerflinger, D.G. Marshall, M.J. Taves, and M.P. Riley. 1964. *Social Response to Population Change and Migration.* Ames: Iowa State University Agricultural Experiment Station Special Report 40.

Kolb, John H. 1923. *Service Relations of Town and Country.* Madison: University of Wisconsin Agricultural Experiment Station Research Bulletin 58.

Krannich, Richard S., and Craig R. Humphrey. 1983. "Local Mobilization and Community Growth: Toward an Assessment of the 'Growth Machine' Hypothesis." *Rural Sociology* 48:60–81.

Landis, Paul H. 1932. *The Growth and Decline of South Dakota Trade Centers: 1901–1933.* Brookings: South Dakota Agricultural Experiment Station Bulletin 274.

Lassey, William R. 1977. *Planning in Rural Environments.* New York: McGraw-Hill.

Lentz, Peggy A., and Harley E. Johansen. 1975. "Simulating Spatial Decay in a Regional Retail System." *Modeling and Simulation* 6:1213–17.

Lewis, G.J. 1979. *Rural Communities.* North Pomfret, Vt.: David and Charles.

Little, J.D. 1972. "Employers' Needs for Labor Market Information in Order to Locate and Operate in Rural Areas." In *Labor Market Information in Rural Areas,* edited by Collette Moser, pp. 47–50. East Lansing: Michigan State University, Center for Rural Manpower and Public Affairs.

Lively, Charles E. 1932a. "The Decline of Small Trade Centers." *Rural America* 10:5–7.

———. 1932 b. *Growth and Decline of Farm Trade Centers in Minnesota, 1905–1932.* St. Paul: Minnesota Agricultural Experiment Station Bulletin 287.

Logan, John. 1976. "Notes on the Growth Machine: Toward a Comparative Political Economy of Place." *American Journal of Sociology* 32:349–52.

Long, John. 1978. "The Deconcentration of Nonmetropolitan Population." Paper given at the annual meeting of the Population Association of America, Atlanta, Georgia.

———. 1981. *Population Deconcentration in the United States.* Washington, D.C.: U.S. Bureau of the Census, Special Demographic Analyses, CDS-81-S.

Long, Larry H., and Diana DeAre. 1980. *Migration to Nonmetropolitan Areas: Appraising the Trends and Reasons for Moving.* Washington, D.C.: U.S. Bureau of the Census, Special Demographic Analyses, CDS-80-2.

———. 1982. "The Economic Base of Recent Population Growth in Nonmetropolitan Settings." Paper given at the annual meeting of the Association of American Geographers, San Antonio, Texas.

Long, Larry H., and William H. Frey. 1982. *Migration and Settlement: 14. United States.* Laxenburg, Austria: International Institute for Applied Systems Analysis, RR-82-15.

Lonsdale, Richard E., and Clyde E. Browning. 1971. "Rural-Urban Locational Preferences of Southern Manufacturers." *Annals of the Association of American Geographers* 61:255-68.

Lonsdale, Richard E., John C. Kinworthy, and Thomas R. Doering. 1976. *Attitudes of Manufacturers in Small Cities and Towns of Nebraska.* Lincoln: Nebraska Department of Economic Development.

Lonsdale, Richard E., and H.L. Seyler. 1979. *Nonmetropolitan Industrialization.* Washington, D.C.: V.H. Winston and Sons.

Losch, August. 1954. *The Economics of Location,* translated by William Wogland with W.F. Stolper. New Haven: Yale University Press.

Lovejoy, Stephen B., Deborah J. Brown, and Janet S. Ayres. 1981. "Satisfaction with Public Services in Nonmetropolitan Communities: Newcomers vs. Oldtimers." Unpublished paper, Department of Agricultural Economics, Purdue University.

Luloff, Albert. 1978. "Identifying the Focus for Action: What Local Residents Have to Say." *Small Towns* 9:11-14.

Lyon, Larry, Lawrence G. Felice, M. Ray Perryman, and E. Stephen Parker. 1981. "Community Power and Population Increase: An Empirical Test of the Growth Machine Model." *American Journal of Sociology* 32:309-32.

Maki, Wilbur R. 1968. "Infrastructure in Rural Areas." In *Rural Poverty in the United States,* edited by George L. Wilbur and C.E. Bishop, pp. 86-109. Washington, D.C.: U.S. Government Printing Office.

Marshall, John U. 1969. *The Location of Service Towns.* Toronto: University of Toronto Press.

Martin, Walter T. 1957. "Ecological Change in Satellite Rural Areas." *American Sociological Review* 22:173-83.

Maurer, Richard C., and James A. Christenson. 1982. "Growth and Nongrowth Orientations of Urban, Suburban and Rural Mayors: Reflections of the City as a Growth Machine." *Social Science Quarterly* 63:350-58.

McCarthy, Kevin F. 1980. "Recent Patterns of Population Change in America's Urban Places." Santa Monica, Calif.: Rand Corporation, Paper P-6528.

McCarthy, Kevin F., and Peter Morrison. 1979. *The Changing Demographic and Economic Structure of Nonmetropolitan Areas in the United States.* Santa Monica, Calif.: The Rand Corporation, R-2399-EDA.

McGranahan, David A. 1980. "Changing Central Place Activities in Northwestern Wisconsin." *Rural Sociology* 45:91-109.

Menchik, Mark David. 1981. "The Service Sector." In *Nonmetropolitan America in Transition,* edited by Amos H. Hawley and Sara Mills Mazie, pp. 231-54. Chapel Hill: University of North Carolina Press.

Mess, Henry A. 1938. "The Growth and Decay of Towns." *The Political Quarterly* 9:389–407.

Molotch, Harvey, 1976a. "The City as a Growth Machine: Toward a Political Economy of Place." *American Journal of Sociology* 82:309–32.

———. 1976b. "Varieties of Growth Strategy: Comments on Logan." *American Journal of Sociology* 82:352–56.

Morganthau, Tom, Frank Maier, Jacob Young, Susan Argrest, Dan Shapiro, Martin Kasindorf, Holly Morris, and Jerry Buckley. 1981. "America's Small Town Boom." *Newsweek* 48:26–37.

Morrill, Richard L. 1979. "Stages in Patterns of Population Concentration and Dispersion." *Professional Geographer* 31:55–65.

Morrison, Peter. 1973. "A Demographic Assessment of New Cities and Growth Centers as Population Distribution Strategies." *Public Policy* 21:367–82.

Morrison, Peter, and Judith Wheeler. 1976. *Rural Renaissance in America?* New York: Population Reference Bureau, Population Bulletin 31-3.

Moser, Collette, ed. 1972. *Labor Market Information in Rural Areas.* East Lansing: Michigan State University, Center for Rural Manpower and Public Affairs.

National Task Force Report. 1980. *An Impact Study of Selected Extension Programs That Assist People to Recognize and Pursue Economic Opportunities.* State College: Mississippi State University Cooperative Extension Service.

Nelson, Lowry. 1961. "Farm Retirement in the United States." *Geriatrics* 16:465–70.

Nesmith, Dwight A. 1963. "The Small Rural Town." In *A Place to Live— The Yearbook of Agriculture,* edited by Alfred Stefferud, pp. 178–84. Washington, D.C.: U.S. Government Printing Office.

Northam, Ray M. 1963. "Declining Urban Centers in the United States: 1940–1960." *Annals of the Association of American Geographers* 53:50–59.

Ogburn, William F. 1937. *Social Characteristics of Cities.* Chicago: International City Managers Association.

Olson, R.E. 1952. "The Functional Decline of Oklahoma Villages: A Case Study." *Oklahoma Academy of Sciences Proceedings* 321:132–36.

Olsson, Gunnar. 1965. *Distance and Human Interaction: Review and Bibliography.* Philadelphia: Regional Science Institute.

Pappenfort, Donnell M. 1959. "The Ecological Field and the Metropolitan Community: Manufacturing and Management." *American Journal of Sociology* 64:380–85.

Parr, John B., and Kenneth G. Denike. 1970. "Theoretical Problems in Central Place Analysis." *Economic Geography* 46:568–86.

Paulsen, Arnold, and J. Carlson. 1961. "Is Rural Main Street Disappearing?" *Better Farming Methods* 33:12–13, 19.

Petrulis, M.F. 1979. *Growth Patterns in Metro-Nonmetro Manufacturing Employment.* Washington, D.C.: U.S. Department of Agriculture, Economic Development Division, Rural Development Research Report 7.

Ploch, Louis A. 1978. "The Reversal in Migration Patterns—Some Rural Development Consequences." *Rural Sociology* 43:293–303.

———. 1980. "Effects of Turnaround Migration on Community Structure in Maine." In *New Directions in Urban-Rural Migration,* edited by David L. Brown and John M. Wardwell, pp. 291–312. New York: Academic Press.

Powers, Ronald C. 1969. "Multicounty Units as a Basis for Domestic Change Programs." In *Selected Perspectives for Community Resource Development,* edited by Luther T. Wallace, Daryl Hobbs, and Raymond D. Vlasin, pp. 211–26. Raleigh: North Carolina State University, Agricultural Policy Institute.

Pred, Allan R. 1966. *The Spatial Dynamics of U.S. Urban-Industrial Growth, 1800–1914.* Cambridge, Mass.: M.I.T. Press.

———. 1977. *City Systems in Advanced Economies.* London: Hutchinson.

Price, Michael L., and Daniel C. Clay. 1980. "Structural Disturbances in Rural Communities: Some Repercussions of the Migration Turnaround in Michigan." *Rural Sociology* 45:591–607.

Puryear, David. 1977. "The Relevance of City Size." In *Small Cities in Transition: The Dynamics of Growth and Decline,* edited by Herrington J. Bryce, pp. 155–66. Cambridge, Mass.: Ballinger Publishing Co.

Rank, Mark R., and Paul R. Voss. 1982. "Patterns of Rural Community Involvement: A Comparison of Residents and Recent Immigrants." *Rural Sociology* 47:197–219.

Ratcliff, S.C. 1942. "Size as a Factor in Population Changes of Incorporated Hamlets and Villages, 1930–1940." *Rural Sociology* 7:318–28.

Raup, Philip M. 1961. "Economic Aspects of Population Decline in Rural Communities." In *Labor Mobility and Population in Agriculture,* pp. 95–106. Ames: Iowa State Center for Agricultural and Economic Adjustment.

Real Estate Research Corporation. 1974. *The Costs of Sprawl.* Washington, D.C.: Council on Environmental Quality, the Department of Housing and Urban Development, and the Environmental Protection Agency.

Rice, Rodger R., and J. Allan Beegle. 1972. *Differential Fertility in a Metropolitan Society.* Morgantown: West Virginia University, Rural Sociological Monograph Series 1.

Richards, Robert O. 1978. "Urbanization of Rural Areas." In *Handbook of Contemporary Urban Life,* edited by David Street, pp. 551–91. San Francisco: Jossey-Bass.

Richardson, Joseph L., and Olaf F. Larson. 1976. "Small Community Trends: A 50-Year Perspective on Socio-Economic Change in 13 New York Communities." *Rural Sociology* 41:45–59.

Richter, Kerry. 1983. "Nonmetropolitan Growth in the Late 1970's: The End of the Turnaround?" Working Paper 83-20, Center for Demography and Ecology, University of Wisconsin at Madison.

Roseman, Curtis C. 1977. *Changing Migration Patterns within the U.S.* Washington, D.C.: Association of American Geographers, Resource Papers for College Geography 77-2.

Rowles, Graham D. 1983. "Geographical Dimensions of Social Support in Rural Appalachia." In *Aging and Milieu: Environmental Perspectives on Growing Old*, edited by Graham D. Rowles and Russell J. Ohta, pp. 111–30. New York: Academic Press.

Saunders, Irwin T., and Gordon F. Lewis. 1976. "Rural Community Studies in the United States: A Decade in Review." *Annual Review of Sociology* 2:35–53.

Schwarzweller, Harry. 1979. "Migration and the Changing Rural Scene." *Rural Sociology* 44:7–23.

Shaffer, Ronald E., and Luther G. Tweeten. 1974. *Economic Changes from Industrial Development in Eastern Oklahoma.* Stillwater: Oklahoma Agricultural Experiment Station Bulletin B-715.

Shannon, John, and John Ross. 1977. "Cities: Their Increasing Dependence on State and Federal Aid." In *Small Cities in Transition: The Dynamics of Growth and Decline*, edited by Herrington J. Bryce, pp. 189–211. Cambridge, Mass.: Ballinger Publishing Co.

Shryock, Henry S., and Jacob S. Siegel. 1975. *The Methods and Materials of Demography.* Washington: U.S. Government Printing Office.

Slesinger, Doris P. 1974. "The Relationship of Fertility to Measures of Metropolitan Dominance: A New Look." *Rural Sociology* 39:350–61 (addendum in 40:85–86).

Sly, David F., Thomas R. Dye, William Serow, and Wilbur Zelinsky, eds. 1980. "Metropolitan and Regional Change in the United States." Special issue of *Social Science Quarterly* 61:369–675.

Smith, Eldon D., Brady Deaton, and David Kelch. 1980. "Cost-Effective Programs of Rural Community Industrialization." *Journal of the Community Development Society* 11:113–23.

Smith, Suzanne M. 1970. *An Annotated Bibliography of Small Town Research.* Madison: University of Wisconsin, Department of Rural Sociology.

Smith, T. Lynn. 1933. *Farm Trade Centers in Louisiana.* Baton Rouge: Louisiana Agricultural Experiment Station Bulletin 234.

———. 1942. "The Role of the Village in American Rural Society." *Rural Sociology* 7:10–21.

———. 1974. "Sociocultural Changes in Twelve Midwestern Communities, 1930–70." *Social Science* 49:195–207.

Sofranko, Andrew J., and William M. Bridgeland. 1972. "A Community Structure Approach to Data Collection and Recommendations for More Effective Use of Data Banks." *Journal of the Community Development Society* 3:110–28.

Sofranko, Andrew J., James D. Williams, and Fredrick C. Fliegel. 1981. "Urban Migrants to the Rural Midwest: Some Understandings and Misunderstandings." In *Population Redistribution in the Midwest,* edited by Curtis C. Roseman, Andrew J. Sofranko, and James D. Williams, pp. 97-128. Ames: Iowa State University, North Central Regional Center for Rural Development.

Sokolow, Alvin D. 1981a. "Local Politics and the Turnaround Migration: Newcomer-Oldtimer Relations in Small Communities. In *Population Redistribution in the Midwest,* edited by Curtis C. Roseman, Andrew J. Sofranko, and James D. Williams, pp. 169-90. Ames: Iowa State University, North Central Regional Center for Rural Development.

———. 1981b. "Local Governments: Capacity and Will." In *Nonmetropolitan America in Transition,* edited by Amos H. Hawley and Sara Mills Mazie, pp. 704-35. Chapel Hill: University of North Carolina Press.

Stafford, Howard A. 1963. "The Functional Bases of Small Towns." *Economic Geography* 39:165-75.

Star, Alvin D., and M.Z. Massel. 1981. "Survival Rates for Retailers." *Journal of Retailing* 57:87-99.

Stephenson, John B. 1968. *Shiloh: A Mountain Community.* Lexington: University of Kentucky Press.

Stinner, William F., and Michael B. Toney. 1980. "Migrant-Native Differences in Social Background and Community Satisfaction in Nonmetropolitan Utah Communities." In *New Directions in Urban-Rural Migration,* edited by David L. Brown and John M. Wardwell, pp. 313-31. New York: Academic Press.

Stinson, Thomas F. 1981. "Overcoming Impacts of Growth on Local Government Finance." *Rural Development Perspectives.* Washington, D.C.: U.S. Department of Agriculture, Economic Development Division, RDP-4.

Summers, Gene F. 1982. "Industrialization." In *Rural Society in the U.S.: Issues for the 1980's,* edited by Don A Dillman and Daryl J. Hobbs, pp. 164-74. Boulder, Colo.: Westview Press.

Summers, Gene, Sharon Evans, Frank Clemente, E.M. Beck, and Jon Minkoff. 1976. *Industrial Invasion of Nonmetropolitan America.* New York: Praeger.

Thomas, Donald. 1970. "The Regional Effect as a Factor in Small Town Growth and Decline in the United States." Ph.D. dissertation, University of Wisconsin.

Thompson, Wilbur R. 1969. "The Economic Base of Urban Problems." In *Contemporary Economic Issues,* edited by Neil W. Chamberlain, pp. 1-50. Homewood, Ill.: Irwin.

———. 1975. "Economic Processes and Employment Problems in Declining Metropolitan Areas." In *Post Industrial America: Metropolitan Decline and Inter-Regional Job Shifts,* edited by George Sternlieb and James W. Hughes, pp. 187-96. New Brunswick, N.J.: Rutgers-The State University of New Jersey, Center for Urban Policy Research.

Till, Thomas E. 1981. "Manufacturing Industry: Trends and Impacts." In *Nonmetropolitan America in Transition,* edited by Amos H. Hawley and Sara Mills Mazie, pp. 194–230. Chapel Hill: University of North Carolina Press.

Trewartha, Glenn T. 1943. "The Unincorporated Hamlet: One Element in the American Settlement Fabric." *Annals of the Association of American Geographers* 33:32–81.

Tweeten, Luther. 1974. "Enhancing Economic Opportunity." In *Communities Left Behind,* edited by L.R. Whiting, Chapter 8. Ames: Iowa State University Press.

Tweeten, Luther, and George L. Brinkman. 1976. *Micropolitan Development Theory and Practice of Greater-Rural Economic Development.* Ames: Iowa State University Press.

Ullman, Edward L. 1954. "Amenities as a Factor in Regional Growth." *Geographical Review* 44:119–32.

U.S. Bureau of the Census. 1972. "Employment and Population Changes— Standard Metropolitan Statistical Areas and Central Cities." *Special Economic Reports,* Series ES20(72)-1. Washington, D.C.: U.S. Government Printing Office.

———. 1981. *Statistical Abstract of the United States, 1981.* Washington, D.C.: U.S. Government Printing Office.

Verway, David I. 1980. "A Critical Examination of the Dun and Bradstreet Data Files." *Review of Public Data Use* 8:369–74.

Vidich, Arthur J., and Joseph Bensman. 1968. *Small Town in Mass Society,* revised edition. Princeton, N.J.: Princeton University Press.

Vining, Daniel R., and Thomas Kontuly. 1978. "Population Dispersal from Major Metropolitan Regions: An International Comparison." *International Regional Science Review* 3:49–73.

Vining, Daniel R., and Anne Strauss. 1976. "A Demonstration that Current Deconcentration Trends Are a Clean Break with Past Trends." Discussion Paper 90, Regional Science Research Institute, University of Pennsylvania.

Vogt, P.L. 1917. *Introduction to Rural Sociology.* New York: D. Appleton.

Voss, Paul R. 1980. "A Test of the 'Gangplank Syndrome' among Recent Migrants to the Upper Great Lakes Region." *Journal of the Community Development Society* 11:95–111.

Wadsworth, H.A., and J.M. Conrad. 1966. *Impact of New Industry on a Rural Community.* Lafayette: Purdue University Agricultural Experiment Station Research Bulletin 811.

Wagner, Fredrick W., R.D. Minvielle, and R.E. Thayer. 1979. "Averting Economic Disaster in a Single Industry Town: The Value of Political Leadership." *Municipal Management,* 1:108–10.

Wakeley, Ray E. 1961. *Types of Rural and Urban Community Centers in Upstate New York.* Ithaca: Cornell University Agricultural Experiment Station Bulletin 59.

Wardwell, John M. 1977. "Equilibrium and Change in Nonmetropolitan Growth." *Rural Sociology*, 42:156–79.

———. 1980. "Toward a Theory of Urban-Rural Migration in the Developed World." In *New Directions in Urban-Rural Migration,* edited by David L. Brown and John M. Wardwell, pp. 71–114. New York: Academic Press.

Warren, Roland L. 1956. "Toward a Reformulation of Community Theory." *Human Organization* 15:8–11.

———. 1972. *The Community in America,* revised edition. Chicago: Rand McNally.

Wheat, Leonard F. 1976. *Urban Growth in the Non-Metropolitan South.* Lexington, Mass.: Lexington Books.

White, A.G. 1978. *Urban Anti-Growth: A Growing Movement.* Monticello, Ill.: Council of Planning Librarians, Exchange Bibliography 1468.

Whiting, Larry R., ed. 1974a. *Rural Industrialization: Problems and Potentials.* Ames: Iowa State University Press.

———, ed. 1974b. *Communities Left Behind: Alternatives for Development.* Ames: Iowa State University Press.

Wightman, Ralph. 1954. "The Village Is Still Alive." *British Agricultural Bulletin,* 6:337–48.

Wilkinson, Kenneth P. 1978. "Rural Community Change." In *Rural USA Persistence and Change,* edited by Thomas R. Ford, pp. 115–25. Ames: Iowa State University Press.

Wilkinson, Kenneth P., James Thompson, Robert R. Reynolds, Jr., and Lawrence M. Ostrech. 1982. "Local Social Disruption and Western Energy Development: A Critical Review." *Pacific Sociological Review* 25:275–376.

Williams, Ann S., Russell C. Youmans, and Donald M. Sorensen. 1975. *Providing Rural Public Service: Leadership and Organizational Considerations.* Corvallis: Oregon State University, Western Rural Development Center Special Report 1.

Williams, James D. 1981. "The Nonchanging Determinants of Nonmetropolitan Migration." *Rural Sociology* 46:183–202.

Williams, James D., Andrew J. Sofranko, and Brenda Root. 1977. "Will Social Action Have Any Impact? Change Agents and Industrial Development in Small Towns." *Journal of the Community Development Society* 8:19–29.

Woodruff, Archibald M. 1980. *The Farm and the City: Rivals or Allies?* Englewood Cliffs, N.J.: Prentice-Hall.

Wu, Pek Si. 1945. "The Social Characteristics of Increasing, Stable and Decreasing Cities." Ph.D. dissertation, University of Chicago.

Yeates, Maurice H. 1968. *An Introduction to Quantitative Analysis in Economic Geography.* New York: McGraw-Hill.

Zelinsky, Wilbur. 1978. "A Bibliography of the Recent Turnaround in Metropolitan-Nonmetropolitan Population Change in the Advanced Countries." Working Paper 1978-11, Population Issues Research Center, Pennsylvania State University.

Ziegler, Arthur P., and W. Kidney. 1980. *Historic Preservation in Small Towns: A Manual of Practice*. Nashville, Tenn.: American Association for State and Local History.

Zimmerman, Carle C., and G.V. Moneo. 1971. *The Prairie Community System*. Ottawa: Agricultural Research Council of Canada.

Zuiches, James J. 1981. "Residential Preferences in the United States." In *Nonmetropolitan America in Transition*, edited by Amos H. Hawley and Sara Mills Mazie, pp. 72–115. Chapel Hill: University of North Carolina Press.

Zuiches, James J., and Jon R. Reiger. 1978. "Size of Place Preferences and Life Cycle Migration: A Cohort Comparison." *Rural Sociology* 43: 618–33.

INDEX

Accessibility score: for village sample, 221; change due to highway improvement, 34

Accessibility: 145–148, 170, 174, 178, 190; and growth or decline, 33–35, 36, 43–44, 45, 48–49, 71–77, 169, 201–202; effect on turnaround, 211; measure of sample 221

Adams, Bert, 109, 172, 181

Adaptation, 210

Advantages of villages, 207–208

Age structure: and urban hierarchy, 63–66; 198–207; accessibility and growth, 72–73

Agriculture: effect on growth, 22, 46–49, 52; and economics, 86, 93, 98, 147, 153; changes in, 102, 198

Alanen, A.R., 185

Alexander, John W., 148

Alonso, William, 8, 60

Amenities: as reason for population growth, 23, 80, 198; effect on non-metropolitan activity, 46, 198, 211; hotels as a measure of, 46

Anderson, A.H., 15, 108, 145, 205

Andrews, W.H., 183

Angel, William D., Jr., 169

Annexation: relation to growth and decline, 25, 56

Appelbaum, Richard P., 60

Argrest, Susan, 7

Autonomy, 179, 204, 211; of small communities, 13–14, 163, 180, 210; loss by villages, 205

Ayres, Janet S., 184

Baldassare, Mark, 162–163, 179, 184–185, 193

Banks, Vera J., 89

Barkley, Paul, 15

Basic industries and villages, 86–87; effect on village growth, 152–158; relation to multiplier effect; 148

Bauder, W.W., 183

Beale, Calvin, 3, 8, 15, 21–23, 25–26, 33–34, 37, 54, 77, 89, 149, 193, 213

Beck, E.M., 16, 46, 73, 179–180

Beegle, J. Allan, 14, 60, 66, 183, 185

Bell, Thomas, 109, 111, 126–127

Bensman, Joseph, 13, 163

Berry, Brian J.L., 4–6, 17, 44, 87, 109–110, 125, 138, 142–143, 146–147

Birch, David L., 223

Blakely, Edward J., 184, 206–207, 209, 212

Bogue, Donald, J., 61, 149

Bohrnstedt, George W., 150, 165, 181

Borchert, John R., 6

Borts, George H., 161

Bourne, Larry S., 4

Bowles, Gladys K., 213

Bradbury, Katherine L., 24, 204

Bradshaw, Ted K., 184, 206–207, 209, 212

Branch stores (Dun and Bradstreet listing), 225, 228

Bridgeland, William M., 170

Briggs, Ronald, 21

Brinkman, George L., 153, 166, 180

Brown, David L., 21, 61, 77, 193, 206, 214

Brown, Deborah J., 184

Brown, Lawrence A., 110

Browning, Clyde E., 16

Brunner, Edmund deS, xviii, 17, 19–20, 36, 61, 85–87, 89, 93, 137, 203, 206, 209

Brush, John E., 111

Bryant, W. Keith, 14, 60

Buckley, Jerry, 7

Building construction and trade, 95, 101

Burton, Ian, 7, 110

Business activity: distribution of, 96–98; by establishments and functions, 112–116; individual, 116–120; since 1950, 88–102; since 1970, 102–105, 130–134; relation to village population change and accessibility, 150–159; relation to village population size, 139–145

Business district, main street, 111–112, 199

Campbell, Rex R., 185

Carlson, J., 2, 15, 87, 120

Carlyle, John, 2, 15

Central Place Theory, 8, 16–17, 87, 111; association with nonmetropolitan growth, 55

Change measures: population and business activities, 150; definition of annualized change, 57–58

Characteristics: of village population, 14, 63–71

Chisolm, Michael, 2

Chittick, Douglas, 15, 108, 148, 223

Christaller, Walter, 4, 16–17, 108–109, 142

Christenson, James A., 187

Cities (SMSAs) and growth. See Accessibility and growth or decline

Clark, W.A.V., 15

Clay, Daniel C., 185

Clemente, Frank, 16, 46, 73, 179, 180

Clifford, William B., 34, 44, 46, 56

Cohen, Richard A., 15

Cohen, Y.S., 92, 228

Colladay, Morrison, 2

Commission on Population Growth and the American Future, 161

Communication, 209; effect of lowered cost, 199; effect on turnaround, 211

Community: human ecological perspective, 4, 13; study of social organization, 13; case studies on, 13, 184–185, 200; facilities expansion of, 162, 166, 180; mobilization, 163, 172–173; and relating to village decline, 199; development, 180; definition of development, 172

Commuting, 199; effect on population, 152, 179; effect on village retail sector, 155

Competition, 109; decline in village activity due to, 148; effect on villages, 92, 158; increase due to consumer decrease, 92; relation to urban proximity, 150

Conrad, J.M., 153

Consequences of growth, 183–185; 206

Construction, 93–95; 101, 147; as indicator of industrial activity, 153; increase in number of establishments, 198

Consumer goods and services, villages as centers for, 87

Converse, Paul D., 89

Copp, James H., 166

Counterurbanization, 5–6

Counties and growth, 24, 31–35, 44–50, 54

Cronbach's Alpha: scale reliability, 165, 168

Dahmann, Donald C., 4

Dahms, Fred A., 88, 91, 103, 110

Daily Urban Systems, 5, 44

Daily, George, H., Jr., 185

Data sources, for samples, 12

Davis, Charles M., 16

DeAre, Diana, 6, 56, 57

DeJong, Gordon F., 184

DeSouza, A.R., 142, 143, 148

Deaton, Brady, 173

Deavers, Kenneth L., 206

Decline: in business, 2, 86–96, 116; of village, 114, 161

Deeley, Nora A., 108, 111

Demographic characteristics. See Characteristics, demographic

Denike, Kenneth G., 17–18, 109, 125, 148

Dependency: of small communities. See Autonomy

Diffusion: of retail and service functions, 110

Dillman, Don A., 23

Dispersed city market sharing, 7, 110–111, 132

Doerflinger, J.A., 183

Doering, Thomas R., 166

Downs, Anthony, 24, 204

Doxiadis, Constantinos, 5

Dun and Bradstreet reference book listings, 12, 20, 24, 52, 85, 88, 91, 103, 106, 112, 126, 130, 152, 159, 223–229; as souce of economic data, 223ff; comparison with Yellow Page directories, 224–226; field check of, 227; listing procedure, 224–225

Duncan, Beverly Davis, 4, 61

Duncan, Otis Dudley, 4, 12, 14, 60–61, 82

Dye, Thomas R., 4

Dying Village, 203–205

Eberle, Nancy, 7

Economic activity, 8, 69–71, 85ff, 223; inventory of, 90–91; distribution of, by year, 96–98, 113

Economic advantages, 208

Economic change: patterns of, 98–102; by region, 201

Economic growth, promotion, facilities expansion and, 162, 172–178

Economic opportunities, 77

Economic trends, 15–16, 198, 201, 207, 209

Economies of scale, 22, 161

Educational attainment, 67–68, 72–73, 82

Elazar, Daniel, 204

Elderly, 83, 198, 207; village characteristics, 81–82

Employment characteristics, 69–70, 73–77, 80–83

Energy availability/costs and settlement patterns, 16, 34, 208, 211, 213–214

Establishments. *See* Economic activity

Evans, Sharon, 16, 46, 73, 179, 180

Facilities expansion, 166–168, 190, 192; scale, 168, 174, 176; associated factors 168–172, 193–194

Federal aid. *See* Government funding

Felice, Lawrence G., 173

Field, Donald R., 61, 73, 75, 77

Fischer, Claude, 171

Fisher, James, 6–7

Fletcher, Henry J., 2

Fliegel, Frederick C., 184, 193

Folse, Clinton L., 15, 149, 223

Ford, Thomas R., 13

Forestry, 95

Foust, J.B., 142–143

Fox, William F., 170, 180

Franchise firms: Dun and Bradstreet listing, 225–228

Frankena, Fredrick, 14–16

Freedom, lack of, in villages, 209

Frey, William H., 4

Friedman, John, 5, 44

Frisbie, W. Parker, 61

Fry, C. Luther, 20

Fuguitt, Glenn V., 4, 8–9, 12, 14–15, 18, 22–23, 25–26, 33–34, 44, 46, 54–56, 60–61, 73, 75–76, 77, 83, 179, 203

Function, 110–111, 209; definition, 112, retention of higher order, 132; growth and decline, 127–131, 134; relation to threshold population, 158; classification, 107; complexity, 108; size, 134

Future of the village, 209–215

Gallagher, Art, 13

Galpin, Charles J., 15–16

Garrison, W.L., 109, 142–143

Gillard, Quentin, 16, 184

Gillette, John M., 2

Golledge, R.G., 15

Gordon, P., 6

Goudy, Willis J., 13

Government funds: reliance on county, state and/or federal, 168, 180, 205

Graber, Edith E., 184

Growth Machine concept, 165, 187

Growth center strategy of regional planning, 5, 161–162

Growth patterns of villages 37–41, 71ff

Guttman scale for central place hierarchy, 108, 111, 120–127, 149

Hage, Jerald, 7

Hamilton, Joel, 108, 142–143

Hansen, Niles M., 4–5

Hart, John F., 15, 18, 32, 36, 110, 132, 149

Hassinger, Edward, 108, 111, 127, 149

Hatch, Elvin, 13, 200

Hathaway, Dale E., 14, 61

Hawley, Amos H., 4, 6

Hawthorn, Horace B., 89

Heaton, Tim B., 34, 44, 46, 56, 76, 179

Hennigh, Lawrence, 193

Hierarchy. *See* Settlement

Hines, Fred K., 61

Hoch, Irving, 60

Hodge, Gerald, 15, 108, 145, 165

Hodgson, M.J., 33, 149

Holmes, John H., 16

Horizontal linkages, 7

Housing and property, 207

Hudson, John C., 17, 110, 112

Hughes, G.S., 17, 20, 85, 93, 137

Humphrey, Craig R., 163, 169, 172–173, 178–179, 181

Ikle, Fred C., 221

Income, family, 68, 73–75, 78, 80, 82–83

Incorporation: as criterion for sample, 12; trends in, 210–211

Index of Retention, 117

Industrial composition: by urban hierarchy, 70; by accessibility and growth, 75–77, 80, 83; by population growth, 46, 50, 53

Industrial development: change 101–103, 172–173, 198–199, 208; consequences of, 180; associated with change in trade, population, accessibility, 153ff; associated with promotion, 163ff, 173–179; future of, 209, 212; and economics 93–94, 96, 98; impact on nonmetropolitan communities 16, 211; role in retail change, 159, 199

Industries, primary and village. *See* Basic industries and villages

Information revolution. *See* Communication

Infrastructure: as development stimulator, 199

Inmigrants, 195, 198; information on numbers of, 190; consequences of, 185, 193

Institutions of higher learning: effects on growth, 45, 47–49

Interdependence and integration, 210, 214

Isolation of villages, 208

Jackson, J.B., v

Jenkins, David B., 61

Johansen, Harley E., 15, 18, 119, 137–138, 148

Johnson, Kenneth M., 55

Kasarda, John D., 5, 55, 73, 204

Kasindorf, Martin, 7

Kelch, David, 173

Kendall, Diana, 2

Kenyon, James B., 138, 143

Keppel, Kenneth G., 184

Kidney, W., 15

Kinworthy, John C., 166

Klaff, Vivian, 25

Klietsch, Ronald G., 183

Kolb, John H., 20, 89, 108, 203, 209–210

Kontuly, Thomas, 6

Krannich, Richard S., 163, 169, 172–173, 178–179, 181

Labor force participation, 69–70, 73, 82–83

Landis, Paul H., 15, 108, 148, 223

Larson, Olaf F., 13, 20, 205

Lassey, William R., 166

Leigh-Preston, Nancey, 206–207, 212

Lentz, Peggy A., 148

Lewis, G.J., 13

Liabilities of villages, 208–209

Lichter, Daniel T., 22–23, 34

Lieber, S., 109, 111, 126–127

Lieberson, Stanley, 4, 60

Little, J.D., 95

Lively, Charles E., 2, 223

Local government: capacity, 206; newcomer-oldtimer differences, 189

Local mobilization. *See* Community mobilization

Location, 166; association with village growth, 61; definition in sample, 219; effect on village life, 208; importance to village, 158, 221; population patterns, 15; relative to larger centers, 8, 60, 137; relation between population and establishments, 138; relating to newcomer-oldtimer differences, 193. *See* accessibility

Logan, John, 173

Long, John, 4, 22–23

Long, Larry H., 4, 6, 56–57

Lonsdale, Richard E., 16, 73, 106, 180

Lorge, Irving, 20, 87, 89
Losch, August, 16
Lovejoy, Stephen B., 184
Luloff, Albert, 185
Lyon, Larry, 163, 173
Maier, Frank, 7
Main street. *See* Business district, main street
Maki, Wilbur R., 77
Manufacturing, 83, 93, 101–102, 103–105, 147, 153, 198; effect on village economy, 16; turnaround villages, 80; association with village growth, 49; impact on decentralization, 46; relation to retail change, 159; relation to primary industry, 86
Market area, 18; population of, 138; 143; population mobility of, 133. *See also* Transportation
Marketing and distribution centers, villages as, 87
Marshall, D.G., 183
Marshall, John U., 108, 138
Martin, Walter T., 5
Mass society: concept, 14; effect on villages, 205
Massel, M.Z., 131
Maurer, Richard C., 187
Mayor's survey, 12, 52–56, 85, 103–105, 131–133, 186–195
Mayor's views: on population change, 50–53, 186–187; on promotion of growth, 162–165; on newcomers-oldtimers, 185–189, 207
McCarthy, Kevin F., 4, 7, 22, 117
McGranahan, David A., 205
Menchik, Mark David, 6
Mess, Henry A., 2
Migration: age-selective, 208; as cause of change, 198; effect of agricultural loss on, 211
Military activity: as rural growth industry, 45, 47–50

Miller, John, 5, 44
Mining, 95, 103, 147
Minkoff, Jon, 16, 46, 73, 179–180
Minvielle, R.D., 16
Mitchelson, Ronald L., 6–7
Mobilization. *See* Community mobilization
Molotch, Harvey, 163, 165, 173, 179
Moneo, G.V., 108, 114, 116
Morganthau, Tom, 7
Morrill, Richard L., 6
Morris, Holly, 7
Morrison, Peter, 4, 7, 117, 161
Moser, Collette, 208
Multiplier effect, 148; projection from regional economic models, 153
Multivariate analysis of growth, 45, 47–50
National Task Force Report, 173
Nelson, Lowry, 64
Nesmith, Dwight A., 64, 161
Newcomer-Oldtimer differences and social relationships, 184, 187–189, 191, 193, 200, 210; and population change, 189–192
Nonmetropolitan: definition of, 25; turnaround, 4, 21, 60, 77–81, 83, 135, 158, 162, 178–179, 197, 211, 214–215; role of village in turnaround, 53–54
Nonvillage nonfarm segment: identification, 62
Northam, Ray M., 33
Occupational distribution, 70, 73–76, 80, 82, 198
Ogburn, William F., 61, 77
Olson, R.E., 2
Olsson, Gunnar, 221
Ostrech, Lawrence M., 184
Outmigration, effects of village, 183, 198
Outsized Functions, 18, 110; village specialization in, 132, 133

Pappenfort, Donnell M., 7
Parker, E. Stephen, 173
Parr, John B., 17–18, 109, 125, 148
Patten, M., 17, 20, 85, 93, 137
Patterson, D.V., 142–143
Paulsen, Arnold, 2, 15, 87, 120
Pennie, Robert C., 185
Perryman, M. Ray, 173
Petrulis, M.F., 76
Ploch, Louis A., 185, 193
Population change: characteristics, 74–75; conclusions, 54–57; trends since 1900, 3; decline factors, 52–53, 71–77, 161; growth factors, 22ff, 53, 71–77, 80–81, 149, 169, 198; and newcomer-oldtimer relations, 189–192; patterns, 22, 37–41; by region, 27–31, 201; and promotion, 162, 176–178, 199; percentages, 25–27; trends, 14–15, 21ff, 183ff, 197–198; social consequences of, 183, 184–185; 193; variables, 27ff
Population mobility and settlement patterns, 212
Population size of villages, 8, 202–203; relation to population change, 24, 35–39; 43–44, 55; relation to trade, 139–140; relation to promotion, 170–171, 179; relation to facilities expansion, 170–171, 206; relation to newcomer-oldtimer differences, 193
Population threshold requirements. See Threshold population
Population turnaround. See Non-metropolitan turnaround
Population-trade relationships: models, 148–158; ratios by accessibility and industry, 145–148; by region, 140–142; trends in, 139–148, 199. See also Population change

Population: decline in villages, 110, 183; outside incorporated places, 50; per village establishment, 139–140; services in low density area, 205, related to retail change, 199
Postindustrial society, 6, 209
Poston, Dudley L., 60
Poverty, 68–69, 73, 81–82
Powers, Ronald C., 161
Pred, Allan R., 7, 87, 148
Price, Michael L., 185
Primary individual: percentage as village characteristic, 65, 81–82
Professional services: change in, 173–176
Promotion activities, 163–165, 199; associated factors, 168–172; scale, 164, 170, 174, 178
Protash, William, 162–163, 179
Public Services: proportional cost to villages, 205. See also Facilities expansion
Public policy and rural settlements, 206–209
Puryear, David, 60, 68
Range of good or service: definition, 109; in central place system, 17; changes in, 111
Rank, Mark R., 184
Ratcliff, S.C., 36
Rathge, Richard, 185
Raup, Philip M., 183
Real Estate Research Corporation, 205
Recreation and retirement, effects on population change, 34, 46, 48–49, 52–53, 152, 179, 198
Rees, J., 21
Region, 8, 27–31, 54, 140, 178, 190, 200–203; delineations, 9, 88; effect on villages, 24, 41, 168–169; as dependent variable, 174
Reid, R., 142–143

Reiger, Jon R., 4
Reiss, Albert J., 12, 14, 60–61, 82
Research themes, 12–18
Residential centers: village as, 137ff, 179, 204
Residential preference: for rural areas, 4, 213
Residential qualities, 207–208
Retail/Service activity, 71, 76, 88–89, 92, 96, 107ff; change in, 98–100, 116–120, 134, 198–199, 203, 210, 215; models of, 148–158; by size, 126–130; distribution of villages by, 114–116; hierarchy, 108, 120–126; limitations of, 209; structure of, 120–130; trends since 1970, 103–104, 130–134; and growth promotion, 173–175. *See also* Population-trade relationships
Retail/Service establishments and functions, 112–120
Retirement. *See* Recreation and retirement
Reynolds, Robert R., Jr., 184
Rice, Rodger R., 66
Richards, Robert O., 14, 205
Richardson, Joseph L., 13, 20, 205
Richter, Kerry, 214
Riffe, W.W., 15, 149, 223
Riley, M.P., 183
Root, Brenda, 173, 179
Roseman, Curtis C., 33, 149
Ross, John, 168
Rowles, Graham D., 13
Rural development: relation to economic development, 166
Rural industrialization: long-term future, 212. *See also* Industrial development
Rural population distribution: public policy regarding, 206. *See also* Growth centers
Rushton, G., 15, 109, 111, 126–127

Ryan, Vernon T., 13
Salisbury, N.E., 14, 18, 32, 36, 110, 132, 149
Sample: description of, 9–12; design of, 219ff; map of, 10; distribution of, 11
Saunders, Irwin T., 13
School dropouts, 83
Schwarzweller, Harry, 184
Scott, William Richard, 4, 60
Serow, William, 4
Service center, village as. *See* Trade center
Services and nonmetropolitan turn-around, 80; occupations, 71, 76–77; and population change, 176; problems of providing, 183; Dun and Bradstreet listing of, 225, 228
Settlement: efficiency and public policy, 205–209; hierarchy, 4–5, 7, 16–17, 22, 55, 62–71, 82, 108, 111, 120, 134; system, 4–6, 9, 200–203; patterns and information revolution, 212, process, 18
Seyler, H.L., 73, 180
Shaffer, Ronald E., 153
Shannon, John, 168
Shapira, Philip, 206–207, 212
Shapiro, Dan, 7
Shopping center: importance of village as, 134
Shryock, Henry S., 58
Siegel, Jacob S., 58
Simmons, J.W., 4
Size of place. *See* Population size
Slesinger, Doris P., 66
Sly, David F., 4
Small, Kenneth A., 24, 204
Smith, E.G., 18, 110, 132
Smith, Eldon D., 173
Smith, K.E., 185
Smith, Suzanne M., 14
Smith, T. Lynn, 13, 20, 36, 64

Social characteristics, 59ff; data and procedures, 61–62; summary and discussion 81–83

Social process, in the community, 9, 13–14, 162, 183ff, 199, 200

Socioeconomic variables 67–69, 198

Sofranko, Andrew J., 170, 173, 179, 184, 193

Sokolow, Alvin D., 181, 184, 193, 206

Sorenson, Donald M., 166

Stafford, Howard A., 138

Standard Industrial Classification (SIC), 95, 224, 226

Standard Metropolitan Statistical Area (SMSA), 5, 9, 45, 50; growth and change in, 23

Star, Alvin D., 131

Stephenson, John B., 13

Stinner, William F., 185

Stinson, Thomas F., 170

Strauss, Anne, 6

Subsample, of mayors. See Mayor's survey

Sullivan, Patrick J., 170, 180

Summers, Gene F., 16, 46, 73, 179–180

Sustained growth or decline, 37–41

Sutton, Willis A., 13

Taves, M.J., 183

Thayer, R.E., 16

Thomas, Donald, 31

Thompson, James, 184

Thompson, Wilbur R., 4, 76

Threshold population, 17, 142–145, 158, 172; concept of, 109–110; changes, 111; effect on economy, 150

Till, Thomas E., 6, 56, 70, 76

Toney, Michael B., 185

Trade center, village as, 86, 87–88, 106, 137ff; village survival as, 215

Trade employment: village characteristic, 81–82

Transportation, 5, 166; effect on range of function, 109; effect on population change 15, 211; effect of lowered cost, 199; effect on amenity areas, 47; village advantage, 208; effect on retail trade, 89, 92, 135

Trewartha, Glenn T., 14, 223

Turnaround growth and decline, of villages, 37–41, 80–81. See also Nonmetropolitan turnaround

Tweeten, Luther, 16, 153, 166, 180

U.S. Bureau of the Census, 52, 68–69

Ullman, Edward L., 46

Unincorporated places, 12

Urban Field, 5, 8, 44

Urban accessibility. See Accessibility

Urban proximity. See Accessibility

Verway, David I., 223

Vidich, Arthur J., 13, 163

Village economy: relation of retail/service sector to population, 15

Village: definition of, 7; population change factors, 23–24, 47, 54; population growth patterns, 37–41; population growth 3, 50–51, 98; social and economic characteristics, 59; prediction for decline, disappearance, 2, 197; importance as shopping center, 198; community satisfaction, 204; preference for, 204; quality of life, 59, 207; change in functions, 56

Vining, Daniel R., 6

Vogt, P.L., 89

Voss, Paul R., 184

Wadsworth, H.A., 153

Wagner, Fredrick W., 16

Wakely, Ray E., 15

Wardwell, John M., 6, 21, 214

Warren, Roland L., 13–14, 163, 205

Wheat, Leonard F., 24
Wheeler, Judith, 7
White, A.G., 162
Whiting, Larry R., 73, 180, 183
Wholesale activities: establishments, 93, 96, 103, 147, 153; increase in number, 101, 198
Wightman, Ralph, 2
Wilkinson, Kenneth P., 13, 184
Williams, Ann S., 166, 184
Williams, James D., 46, 173, 179, 184, 193

Winsborough, Hal H., 4, 60
Woodruff, Archibald M., 204
Wu, Pek Si, 61
Yeates, Maurice H., 142
Yellow Page directories, 224–226
Youmans, Russell C., 166
Young, Jacob, 7
Zelinsky, Wilbur, 4, 21
Ziegler, Arthur P., 15
Zimmer, J.M., 61
Zimmerman, Carle C., 108, 114, 116
Zuiches, James J., 4, 23

ABOUT THE AUTHORS

Harley E. Johansen is a professor of Geography and head of the Department of Geography at the University of Idaho. After early work on innovation diffusion, his research has focused on processes of change in rural society with an emphasis on small town business and population trends. He received his doctorate in geography at the University of Wisconsin in 1974 and served on the faculty at West Virginia University from 1973 to 1981.

Glenn V. Fuguitt is a professor of Rural Sociology, University of Wisconsin–Madison. His work has dealt with rural-urban relations and population redistribution, with special attention to part-time farming, population characteristics and trends in villages and small towns, and population growth and migration in nonmetropolitan and metropolitan areas. He has served as editor of the journal, *Rural Sociology*, and is past president of the Rural Sociological Society and the International Rural Sociology Association.